D. ...
no...
c ...

... these issues ...

... N

...ARY AND ...OUR

Mile End ...

...N daytime loan 10am - 4pm

overnight loan 6pm - 10am

Due for return

...un ... in the process also looking
ws ... on demand. Plea... ondon Underground and
computer-aided design ... ...ice. Social interaction
forms a particular focus of ... ... the way individuals use various tools and tech... ...actions and
activities with each other. The au... ...eo based field
studies of work and interaction can in... ...evelopment and
deployment of new ...chnology in this va... ...ource for acade-
mics, researchers a... ...ctitioners.

Technology in Action

Learning in Doing: Social, cognitive and computational perspectives

General editors: Roy Pea
John Seely Brown
Christian Heath

Technology in Action

Christian Heath

King's College, London

Paul Luff

King's College, London

CAMBRIDGE
UNIVERSITY PRESS

PUBLISHED BY THE PRESS SYNDICATE OF THE UNIVERSITY OF CAMBRIDGE
The Pitt Building, Trumpington Street, Cambridge, United Kingdom

CAMBRIDGE UNIVERSITY PRESS
The Edinburgh Building, Cambridge CB2 2RU, UK   www.cup.cam.ac.uk
40 West 20th Street, New York, NY 10011-4211, USA   www.cup.org
10 Stamford Road, Oakleigh, Melbourne 3166, Australia
Ruiz de Alarcón 13, 28014 Madrid, Spain

First published 2000

Printed in the United Kingdom at the University Press, Cambridge

Typeset in Plantin 10/12 pt in QuarkXPress™   [SE]

A catalogue record for this book is available from the British Library

Library of Congress Cataloguing in Publication data

Heath, Christian, 1952–
    Technology in action / Christian Heath, Paul Luff
        p.   cm. – (Learning in Doing)
    Includes bibliographical references and index.
    ISBN 0 521 56033 0 (hardback) – ISBN 0 521 56869 2 (paperback)
        1. Technology – Social aspects.   2. Information technology – Social
    aspects.   I. Luff, Paul.   II. Title.   III. Series.
    T14.5.H45   2000
    303.48′3 – dc21   99-29372   CIP

ISBN 0 521 56033 0 hardback
ISBN 0 521 56869 2 paperback

Contents

Preface

[The future of the telephone will mean] . . . nothing less than a reorganisation of society – a state of things in which every individual, however secluded, will have at call every other individual in the community, to the saving of no end of social and business complications, of needless goings to and fro, of disappointments, delays, and a countless host of great and little evils and annoyances which go so far under present conditions to make life laborious and unsatisfactory.

Scientific American (1880: 16)

That's a funny kind of thing, in which each new object becomes the occasion for seeing again what we see anywhere; seeing people's nastinesses or goodnesses and all the rest, when they do this initially technical job of talking over the phone. The technical apparatus is, then, being made at home with the rest of our world. And that's a thing that's routinely being done, and it's the source for the failures of technocratic dreams that if only we introduced some fantastic new communication machine the world will be transformed. Where what happens is that the object is made at home in the world that has whatever organisation it already has.

Sacks (1972 (1992): 548)

Though each generation is startled by some innovation which they fear will change a familiar world, for many of us the digital revolution has indeed transformed our working lives. Over the past couple of decades our offices have become littered with equipment; technologies which it was believed would supersede our paper world and its accompanying paraphernalia. Whilst few of us have achieved, or would want to achieve, the inhuman order of the futuristic office, the computer has had a profound impact on the ways in which we work and how we work with others. Despite our reluctance, these technologies have been made at home in our world and have come to play an inevitable part in almost all the activities in which we engage. We are told that this is just the beginning. These bits and pieces of equipment are the crude precursors to a golden age of digital technology which will transform how we work, where we work and who we work with. Technology will lead some into a glorious future with the rest shuffling in the shadows behind.

The emergence of new technologies has been accompanied by a wealth of academic research in both the social and cognitive sciences. Despite the enormous contribution of this research to our understanding of such issues as the information society, human–computer interaction and the social construction of objects and artefacts, there remain relatively few studies concerned with how new technologies feature in our day-to-day working lives and our interaction with each other. This book is a small attempt to redress the balance. It forms part of a growing corpus of ethnographies concerned with technology and social action; research which is proving of relevance to not only contemporary debates within the social and cognitive sciences, but also more practical interests in the design and deployment of advanced systems.

This book consists of studies of different types of technology in a variety of organisational domains. It begins by discussing the introduction of a basic information system into general medical practice, and towards the end explores interpersonal communication in an advanced media space designed to support collaborative working. Between these two, seeming extremes, we examine news production at Reuters, command and control in London Underground and the Docklands Light Railway, and Computer-Aided Design (CAD) in an architectural practice. Each of these studies is based on extensive field work and video-recording of the day-to-day activities of the participants themselves. The studies draw on ethnomethodology and conversation analysis to examine the practices and reasoning on which participants rely to accomplish their actions and activities in the workplace and how technologies feature in the production and co-ordination of their everyday conduct. Social interaction – talk, visual and material conduct – forms a particular focus of many of these studies, as they address the ways in which participants collaborate in and through the tools and artefacts which are readily available to hand. The studies therefore are concerned with the seemingly 'fine details' of work and interaction, details that we hope to show are critical to a sociological understanding of both technology and organisational behaviour.

In the first chapter, we explore the rather curious provenance of these and related ethnographic studies of technology and work. We begin by pointing to the ways in which sociology has tended to disregard how these new tools and artefacts feature in social action and interaction and has left the field inadvertently dominated by cognitive psychology and, in particular, Human–Computer Interaction more commonly known as HCI. The conceptual and methodological basis to much of this research has been subject to sustained criticism in recent years, and in consequence there is a growing interest, both within cognitive science and in other disciplines, in the social and situated character of technology, thought and action. These debates converge with developments in other fields such as Computer Supported Cooperative Work (CSCW) and requirements engineering, and together they have provided a springboard for the emergence of a body of naturalistic research from various disciplines concerned with how technologies feature in everyday organisational conduct and communication. These contemporary academic debates and developments have been enhanced by the growing recognition that technologies not only can fail, sometimes with tragic consequences, but in many cases, despite the good intentions of both designers and management, do not uphold their promise. For those who are less familiar with the sort of research discussed in the book, we have also included a brief note on our own approach, and in particular how we use video-recordings, augmented by field work, to examine the socially organised character of practical action and interaction in the workplace.

Chapter two is concerned with the introduction of information technology into medicine and in particular general practice. The original aims of the system were to provide a treatment database and to assist with the issuing of prescriptions. It was also expected that it would largely replace the traditional paper record that general practitioners had used since the foundation of the health service. Some years following the introduction of the system however, many general practitioners still rely upon the original paper medical record cards and use the two technologies alongside each other. We consider why this might be so. In particular, we examine the ways in which doctors assemble and use the medical record within the consultation, and how their seemingly idiosyncratic jottings and notes are designed with regard to the practicalities of their work, especially their everyday dealings with patients. Unfortunately the original system, despite the best of intentions, made small but significant changes to the ways in which data are stored and retrieved in the record, and in consequence undermined the doctor's ability to use the information within the day-to-day practicalities of consultative work.

Chapter three adopts a rather different standpoint; it considers how the use of a particular technology is co-ordinated with the concurrent actions and activities of others within the immediate domain. The setting is the editorial section of an international news agency which provides on-line news to financial institutions, newspapers, and radio and television stations. The journalists receive the stories, on-line, from agencies throughout the world. They have to check the stories, rewrite and edit them, and, where necessary, make sure the relevant customers receive the right news in the appropriate form. In some cases, the turn-around time for a story should be less than a minute. When working on stories, journalists remain sensitive to whether particular stories are relevant to other editorial desks, and, if they believe they are, they have to pass the stories to colleagues, with dispatch. It is important, however, that journalists do not overwhelm their colleagues with information or interrupt the activities in which they are engaged. In the chapter, we discuss the ways in which they make stories visible to others within the domain, and invite, but not demand, that others pick up on particular items. In this way, the chapter is concerned with the collaborative production of news stories and how journalists shape their activities with regard to the interests and conduct of colleagues.

Parallel issues arise in the control rooms of London Underground. The control rooms include various staff who are responsible for dealing with the day-to-day problems and difficulties which inevitably arise in the operation of a major urban transport system. Within the rooms there is a relatively strict division of labour, with some staff responsible for signalling, others for delivering information to passengers and line controllers who have overall responsibility for dealing with problems. To help their work, the control rooms include an array of multimedia technologies, including closed-circuit television (CCTV), electromechanical diagrams, digital displays of traffic locations and service operation, and communication devices such as radios, touch-screen telephones and public address systems. In dealing with problems and crises, it is critical that staff maintain some compatible sense of what is happening and how it is being dealt with. Indeed, without this intelligence, the various information displays are almost useless. The difficulty is that in times of stress staff rarely have the time nor the inclination to tell each other what they are doing or what is happening. The chapter explores how individuals coordinate the actions and activities with each other in the line control rooms, and how various tools and technologies are used in managing problems, and in making sense of each other's conduct including the conduct of others outside the control room like station staff and drivers. Of particular importance are the ways in which personnel participate in each other's activities and how they remain sensitive to the conduct of others, even though they themselves are engaged in seemingly distinct and unrelated tasks.

Chapter five is also concerned with a control room of an urban transportation system, that of the Docklands Light Railway in the East of London. Although the personnel in the London Underground control room considered in chapter four and those in the Docklands Light Railway in this chapter have broadly similar responsibilities for command and control, a different configuration of technology has been deployed. This is principally because an automatic train supervision system (or ATS) allows trains to be operated without drivers. Despite the original objectives behind the deployment of the technology, the system requires frequent intervention from the controllers. Chapter five focuses on the 'uses' of the ATS system, a fairly conventional command-and-control system, in the control room, and explores how the technology is immersed within the action and interaction of the participants. In particular, we explore how the entry of commands into the system by one controller is co-ordinated with the conduct of colleagues, and how their conduct is inextricably related to their colleague's use of the system.

The collaborative nature of activities surrounding the use of computer technologies is also the focus of chapter six. Here, we examine a domain that has been of interest to researchers and developers within both HCI and CSCW – design, or, more particularly, architectural design. In particular, we look at the uses within an architecture practice of a CAD system. We explore in detail not only how screen-based activities are accomplished, but how these seemingly individual actions on personal workstations can be related to those of other colleagues within the setting, particularly to accomplish collaborative activities. We examine, therefore, both the use of a graphical user interface, a concern for those in HCI, and an aspect of shared drawing, an area of interest for those in CSCW. Like previous chapters, the analysis points to the ways in which it becomes empirically difficult and conceptually problematic to clearly distinguish between the 'individual' and 'collaborative' use of the technologies.

Chapter seven considers the use of technologies rather distinct from those considered in the earlier chapters. We examine the use and development of innovative and prototype systems designed to support collaborative work amongst individuals who are located in distinct physical spaces. These systems, commonly known as 'media spaces', consist of audio-visual and computing infrastructures, which allow individuals in different locations to see and talk to each other, and in some cases to share documents and even see each other's local environment. The chapter discusses the introduction of these technologies and the ways in which individuals act and interact with and through the system. The analysis reveals how the technologies transform the very ways in which individuals are able to communicate with each other, and how resources and assumptions on which we ordinarily rely are rendered problematic by the technology. We then discuss how the findings of the research have been used to inform the development of further prototype systems, systems which attempted to address some of the difficulties with the technology, in particular, to provide more flexible and variable access between participants. We briefly discuss some of the results of these experiments and their consequences for the development of media spaces and other collaborative technologies.

In the final chapter, we briefly address an issue which has become of increasing importance to workplace studies over the past few years, namely, to what extent can they provide a foundation to the design and deployment of new technologies. For our own part, though many of the studies discussed in the book have been part of 'design projects', we believe that the importance of these and related ethnographic studies of work and technology, does not principally lie in their short-term contributions to particular systems. So, whilst the chapter illustrates how specific studies can inform design, and thereby perhaps form exemplars for future projects, we are more concerned with demonstrating how these and other workplace studies can provide a body of distinctive findings concerning the use of technologies in organisational environments. Aside from their empirical contributions, these observations and findings are forming the foundation to a reconsideration and respecification of many of the key concepts and findings which have hitherto underpinned both research and design in areas such as HCI and CSCW. The empirical and conceptual implications of these naturalistic studies of work, interaction and technology are also, we believe, of relevance to contemporary research in various other fields including the sociology of work, organisational behaviour and studies of language use and interaction. In a small way, therefore, we hope to demonstrate that, by placing technology in action at the heart of the analytic agenda, we have the opportunity to further develop an understanding of social interaction and work which is of both academic and practical relevance.

The research discussed here was originally begun at the Xerox Research Centre in Cambridge (formerly known as EuroPARC). Bob Anderson and Tom Moran, Lucy Suchman, Austin Henderson, Gitty Jordan and John Seeley-Brown provided us with the opportunity of developing a series of projects to readdress the 'interaction' between people and computers in the workplace. These projects would not have been possible without the kindness and generosity of the members of various organisations including London Underground, and in particular the Bakerloo Line, the Elms Medical Practice Liverpool (and its patients), Reuters London and Zurich, the Docklands Light Railway, and the architectural practice. John Gardner, Peter Campion, Fay Luckhurst (née Fisher), Chris Milner, Chris Pocock, Eddie Goddard, Barry Hodges, Stephen Yakeley and Phil Wardle deserve special mention for their efforts in helping to secure access to such rich and rewarding domains.

Since beginning the projects at EuroPARC we have undertaken the research at a number of universities including Surrey, Konstanz, Nottingham and King's College London. We have received much support and encouragement from academic colleagues and friends both in Britain and abroad. They have helped us with observations, commented on presentations, scrutinised papers and provided well-deserved criticism. It would be difficult to list all those who have given such invaluable support, but it is important to name at least a few: Jon Hindmarsh, Hubert Knoblauch, Isaac Joseph, Kjeld Schmidt, Bernard Conein, Abi Sellen, Bill Gaver, Paul Dourish, Victoria Bellotti, David Greatbatch, John Gumperz, Graham Button, Wes Sharrock, William Newman, Mik Lamming, Richard Harper, Mike Robinson, Liam Bannon, Nigel Gilbert, Matthew Chalmers, Mike Molloy, Ian Daniel, Mike Flynn, Bill Buxton, Jack and Marilyn Whalen, David Middleton, Yrjö Engeström, Lauren Resnick, Mike Smyth, Elizabeth Pollitzer, Peter Campion, Charles Goodwin, Rod Watson and Steve Benford. It should be added that we have been most fortunate over the last decade to participate in the emergence of CSCW; an 'academic community' which has provided an extraordinary opportunity for sociologists and computer scientists to meet and to discuss how technologies feature, and might feature, in organisational conduct.

The studies discussed here have been facilitated by funding from both the European Commission and the UK research councils. These projects include Metaphors for Telecommunication Services (MITS) (EC RACE Programme), Multimedia Environments for Mobiles (MEMO) (EC ACTS Programme), 'The social organisation of human–computer interaction' (Joint Council Initiative on Cognitive Science and Human–Computer Interaction) and, more recently, 'Objects in social interaction in co-present and virtual environments' (ESRC) and PORTRAIT (ESRC/DTI Link Prograamme).

A version of section 2.9 in chapter two was prepared and published with David Greatbatch. An earlier version of chapter three was written and published with G. N. Nicholls. A previous version of chapter seven was written and published with Abi Sellen.

Without the support, patience and affection of Gillian Heath, Marina Jirotka and our families this book would not have been possible.

During the preparation of this book we both suffered the sad loss of members of our families. This book is dedicated to their memory: Morris and Mary Manley, and Norman Luff.

CHRISTIAN HEATH
PAUL LUFF

1 Technology and social action

The full introduction of the computer system effectively did away with the radio and telephone calls to stations, with the computer dispatching crews to answer calls. But within hours, during the morning rush, it became obvious to crews and control room staff that calls were going missing in the system; ambulances were arriving late or doubling up on calls. Distraught emergency callers were also held in a queuing system which failed to put them through for up to 30 minutes.

> Ian MacKinnon and Stephen Goodwin (*Independent* 29 October 92)

The medium-term future [1983–90], therefore, will see the first shift towards a decentralisation of commercial and business life. The importance of the city office, with its *mêlée* of agitated human beings passing each other redundant messages of paper and the printed word, will be rapidly eroded. More and more often, office and home will be combined, the public transport system will give way to giant data communication networks, the business motorcar will be traded in for the latest videoconference system. For the first time since Man began to behave as a social animal and gather his kind together into ever larger working and communicating units, a significant trend will emerge. The cities will empty and expensive office blocks will gather dust. For centuries Man has been accustomed to the notion that he must travel to find his work; from the 1980s into the 1990s the work – such as is to do – will travel to meet Man.

> Evans (1979: 142)

In the early autumn of 1992, the London Ambulance Service, at the time the largest ambulance service in the world, introduced a system for Computer-Aided Dispatch into the control room. The principal aim of the system was to replace the outmoded and inefficient practice of documenting the details of emergency calls on paper slips. It was recognised that the system would necessitate some change in working practices, not only amongst control room staff but also for the ambulance drivers. Details from the emergency calls entered into the computer system could be matched with the location of ambulances sent from the vehicles, in order to schedule and allocate crews automatically. This would mean that, amongst other things, call takers and dispatchers would not have to

1

rely on the current paper-based system, and that ambulance stations would no longer have any responsibility for which crew dealt with which call. The day it went 'live', 26 October, problems began to emerge. On not a particularly busy day, response times to arrive at an incident were longer than usual: less than 20% were arriving within the target time of 15 minutes. More importantly, the time taken to answer the calls began to rise alarmingly; the average time a call to the control room was left ringing peaked at 10 minutes. Together, these delays also meant that the number of calls also started to increase, with patients ringing in to find out whether an ambulance was on its way. For the ambulance crews, the automated system was causing some frustration. The system needed near-perfect information about the location of the ambulances which it was not possible to produce. Without this, the system began to allocate crews incorrectly. More than one ambulance would arrive at the scene of an emergency, or the closest ambulance would not be allocated. These problems led to crews transmitting more requests to the control centre and the control centre sending more messages. Unfortunately, as the volume of the messages increased, so did difficulties with the system: messages were lost and the 'awaiting attention' and 'exception message' lists on the computer became so long that items scrolled off the top of the screen and were forgotten. Distraught citizens called saying that they had been waiting for more than half an hour for an ambulance. In the control room personnel began to lose track of which cases had been successfully allocated and dealt with, and in all the confusion crews began to receive incorrect information concerning the location and 'status' of particular cases. Following a second day of problems, the service reverted to a semi-manual system and on the 4th of November the system crashed completely. Personnel returned to the original paper-based system and reinstated some semblance of order.

The difficulties which arose following the introduction of the Computer-Aided Dispatch into the London Ambulance Service are not the most costly disaster to occur when new technology is introduced into a working environment. For example, it has been estimated that the TAURUS project, designed to replace paper certification in the London Stock Exchange with a computerised system, cost the Exchange alone about £75 million and with other firms building interrelated systems the total spent might have been as much as £400 million (Collins and Bicknell, 1997). Despite more than three years work on the project, the system was never introduced, and it has taken more than five years for an alternative and less ambitious technology to be deployed. TAURUS is one of many computer disasters reported in popular publications and the press, where systems either fail to work when they are introduced, or even never reach a stage where they do get introduced (Collins and Bicknell, 1997; Neumann, 1995; Wiener, 1993) . Putting to one side such dramatic failures, there are numerous examples where seemingly innovative and reliable systems have failed when introduced into organisational environments. In many of these cases, the system in question does not cause severe problems; it simply sits there underused. Indeed, it is hard to find a modern organisation which has not had its problems in attempting to exploit the apparent benefits of new technology.

The official inquiry into the London Ambulance Service fiasco (Page et al., 1993) identified a number of key issues which led to the problems which arose. Perhaps the most important of these is that the project team assumed that the computer system would naturally bring about changes in the working practices of personnel; practices which in part were seen as outmoded and inefficient. The report of the inquiry suggests:

Management were misguided or naive in believing that computer systems in themselves could bring about [such] changes in human practices. Experience in many different environments proves that computer systems cannot influence change in this way. They can only assist in the process and any attempt to force change through the introduction of a system with the characteristics of an operational 'strait-jacket' would be potentially doomed to failure. (London Ambulance Service Inquiry Report (Page et al., 1993: 40))

This disregard for the ways in which people organise their work, coupled with a disdain for the ordinary resources on which they rely, is a common feature of many projects involving new technology. Management can seem dazzled by the splendours of computers, and terms such as multimedia, the internet and digital age are used to suggest that technology will soon transform our mundane workaday world. The idea of the paperless office might bring a wry smile to the face, but many contemporary organisations still believe that technology alone is the solution. Even the world of fine art is haunted by the banal prediction that 'painting is dead', unable to survive the splendours of the digital age.

Technological failures have led to a growing interest amongst those in both industry and academia in developing new and more reliable ways of identifying the requirements for complex systems. There is a growing recognition that what are unfortunately classified as 'non-functional requirements' need to be taken seriously, and that 'human factors' consist of more than a concern with the interface between an individual and a workstation, but may involve the social and the organisational. Methods from the outer reaches of the social and cognitive sciences are being unearthed, and viewed with regard to whether they alone, or in some curious combination, might provide the key to designing technology which seamlessly supports and transforms what people do. There is even a growing recognition that more traditional ways of working, and seemingly mundane tools such as pens and paper, may be worth taking seriously in design as resources for thinking about innovative solutions to organisational problems.

More strangely, notwithstanding the growing body of research concerned with the relationship between the 'social and the technical', is how little we know about the ways in which individuals, both alone and in concert with each other, use tools and technologies in the practical accomplishment of their daily work. There is little to which engineers and designers can turn to find out about how technology is used in the workplace. For example, if we consider the problems which arose with the introduction of Computer-Aided Dispatch into the London Ambulance Service, it is curious to realise that we have little idea as to how paper documents are used by personnel to co-ordinate organisational activities, or, for example, how individuals, in the course of talking to others either face-to-face or over the telephone, document relevant details of an event and the encounter. We know even less about the advantages of paper as opposed to computers, and why, despite the onslaught of new technology, our offices remain littered with documents. Our relative ignorance of the use of paper in organisations is complemented by our understanding of the use of complex systems. Despite a substantial body of research, we still have little understanding of the ways in which new technologies feature in practical organisational conduct. Individuals glance at screens, they refer to documents, they discuss plans, they send messages to each other, they turn talk into data, they discover facts and findings; that is, they use these technologies within the practicalities and constraints of their everyday activities. The ways in which these tools and technologies, even basic information systems, are embedded in and depend upon practical activities within the workplace and the practices, procedures and reasoning of personnel, remain largely unknown. Tragedies such as the introduction of Computer-Aided Dispatch into the London Ambulance Service, throw into relief how little we know of the ways in which tools and technologies, ranging from pen and paper through to complex multimedia workstations, feature in day-to-day organisational activities. It is hardly surprising, therefore, that designers turn to the methods of the social sciences to enrich their understanding of the workplace, since we have so little to say about the operation and organisation of even the most mundane objects and artefacts which inhabit our workplace.

There is, however, a growing body of research concerned with the ways in which tools and technologies feature in work and interaction in organisational environments. This body of research, commonly known as 'workplace studies', has emerged within both the social and cognitive sciences over the past decade, and largely consists of naturalistic studies, 'ethnographies', of a broad range of organisational domains. There are, for example, studies of work and technology in air traffic control, emergency dispatch centres, newsrooms, architectural practices, consulting rooms, banks, trading rooms and construction sites. These studies remain relatively unknown in the social sciences, and yet have an increasing influence on research in such areas as Computer Supported Cooperative Work (CSCW), Cognitive Science, and Human–Computer Interaction (HCI). In this chapter we wish to discuss the curious provenance of workplace studies, including our own studies, and show how they have emerged in the light of convergent debates and developments in research on HCI, CSCW, requirements engineering and organisational behaviour. Before doing so, however, it is perhaps worthwhile saying one or two words concerning how technology has formed a topic in social science and in particular sociology.

Over the past decade or so, a substantial body of literature has emerged concerned with the social aspects of technology. Perhaps the most important and wide-ranging contributions are concerned with the ways in which new computer and communication technologies are changing the character of contemporary society and in particular the organisation of work. It is argued that new technology has penetrated almost every sphere of contemporary life, computer networks, digital communications and the like permeating the private, public and market sectors and transforming the activities of individuals and more generally society. These massive changes are characterised in various ways. Bell's (1976) 'post-industrial society' has been replaced with a host of different terms, ranging from Böhme and Stehr's (1986) 'knowledge society', Kreibich's (1986) 'science society' and Münch's (1991) 'communication society'. As Knoblauch (1996, 1997) points out, the most widely accepted scientific and lay characterisation of these changes is the 'information society'. It is argued by Castells (1996) and Webster (1995) however, that the term 'information society' and its counterparts such as the 'information economy' lead to more confusion than clarification, and there continues to be wide-ranging debate as to what changes are taking place and how they should be conceptualised. Attempts to operationalise the concept of the information society and related characterisations have met with some difficulty. It is unclear how a reliable and sensitive measure of 'information' can be identified and transformed into a satisfactory empirical object. As Aldridge suggests, little attention has been paid to the semantic content or the quality of information, rather 'theorists have leapt from quantitative measurements of the volume of information and the velocity of its circulation to sweeping conclusions about the qualitative changes in culture and society' (Aldridge, 1997: 389). More recent attempts to define the information society in terms of work and occupational structure have not added much light to the concept. As Hensel (1980), Webster (1995) and Knoblauch (1997) suggest, the idea of 'information work' has generated an array of seemingly *ad hoc* distinctions concerning the character of particular occupations, and said little about the ways in which 'information' features in the performance of organisational activities.

From a rather different standpoint, there is a growing body of research concerned with the impact of new technology on the workplace, and in particular the ways in which information and communication systems lend support to, and engender, new forms of organisation. So, for example, it is argued that the movement from more bureaucratic and, more recently, matrix forms of organisation towards 'disaggregation' and 'dynamic networks of firms' is increasingly facilitated by the widespread availability and access to digital technologies (e.g. Barnatt 1995, 1997). The argument, and in particular the idea that new forms of organisation are supported, if not engendered, by technological change, has a long-standing tradition in the social sciences. From the early writings of Marx onwards, it has been argued that technologies have a profound impact on organisational arrangements, and successive 'schools' from socio-technical systems onwards have delineated ways in which tools and technologies shape work and organisations. Whatever reservations are voiced with respect to particular approaches, at least they place the technical and social at the heart of the analytic agenda, even if, as Grint and Woolgar (1997) argue, a technological determinism underpins much of the work. Unfortunately however, despite the important contribution of studies of technology and organisations, research is principally concerned with the ways in which communication and information systems influence, and are influenced by, such aspects as the division of labour, work-force skilling and de-skilling, occupational structure and associated features such as power, job opportunity and unionisation. This is hardly surprising. Such topics and issues are undoubtedly critical to a sociological understanding of new technology and the characteristics of organisational and occupational structure, but unfortunately draw attention away from how technology features in the production and co-ordination of workplace activities.

In a very different vein, we have seen the emergence of a growing body of research concerned with the social shaping and construction of technology. For example, in a series of essays, Mackenzie (1996) and Mackenzie and Wajcman (1985) have powerfully demonstrated how the meanings of technology shift not only between different socio-historical contexts, but also in the light of the positioned influence of particular social groups. They speak of 'natural trajectories' in technological change and how they are constituted in and through the activities of particular individuals and organisations, and contrast their own approach with the technological determinism which haunts much of the social science literature. At times the argument can appear to reproduce the sorts of arguments we find in certain organisational studies: class relations, gender and the like, shaping people's responses to and sense of particular technologies. However, the underlying theoretical argument takes a more radical standpoint on the relationship between the social and the technical, in which, for example, the technical is constituted by human activity (see in particular, Mackenzie, 1996). As Mackenzie notes, a parallel body of research with related analytic concerns has emerged over the past decade; a body of research which has begun to reconsider many of the key concepts and issues which inform our understanding of technology and social organisation. Whilst this research embodies an array of analytic standpoints, ranging from actor–network theory through to more socio-historical models, in various ways all reflect a concern with reconfiguring the social and the technical, destroying the spurious boundaries between each, and pursuing an 'empirical programme of relativism' (Bijker et al., 1990). Such research has led to a rich and rewarding body of 'thick description', 'looking into what has been seen as the black box of technology', and has powerfully demonstrated how particular groups ascribe, dispute, exclude and cohere the sense and meaning(s) of technologies. Despite the important contribution of such studies, and their powerful demonstration of the shortcomings of technological determinism, their substantive concerns and commitment have directed attention away from how technology features in mundane activities in ordinary working environments (see Button, 1993).

In purely substantive terms therefore, it is interesting to note how the use of technology in practical organisational conduct has escaped the sociological eye. It is acknowledged that new technology is having a profound impact on work and human interaction, and yet the ways in which computers and other tools and artefacts feature in the accomplishment of organisational activities have disappeared from view. Contemporary sociological research concerned with technology seems in various ways to separate systems, both technical and human, from social action, so that we are unable to recover just how tools and artefacts and the 'rest of the furniture' of the modern organisation is constituted in and through the activities of the participants themselves. Even if we ignore debates concerning agency, context and meaning, it would seem unfortunate to rest with a sociology which treats as epiphenomenal the socially organised competencies and reasoning on which personnel rely in using technologies, whatever they might be, as part of their daily work. Indeed, for the naive, it might appear somewhat peculiar that we know so much about the social organisation of technology in one sense, yet so little about the part it plays in everyday organisational activities and interaction.

1.1   Computers and situated conduct

Despite prevailing trends within sociological studies of technology, we have begun to witness a growing interest in the ways in which complex tools and artefacts feature within practical organisational conduct. Workplace studies are concerned with the work, interaction and technology in complex organisational environments. They are ethnographies, naturalistic studies of domains such as air traffic control rooms, architectural practices, newsrooms, construction sites, banks, dealing rooms and emergency centres. In various ways, they are concerned with how technologies, ranging from complex systems through to mundane tools, feature in the practical accomplishment of organisational activities. These ethnographies are informed by various analytic standpoints ranging from symbolic interactionism through to distributed cognition, but, for reasons which will become increasingly apparent, it is perhaps ethnomethodology and conversation analysis which have had the most profound influence on the emergence the workplace studies.

Workplace studies have emerged in the light of at least three developments which have driven analytic attention towards the *in situ* organisation of technologically informed practical activities. In the first place, we have witnessed a wide-ranging critique of the more conventional models which inform our understanding of human–computer interaction, models which have permeated HCI, Artificial Intelligence (AI), and cognitive science. Secondly, there has been a growing interest in developing technologies to support collaborative activities amongst personnel who may be co-present or located in distinct physical domains. Thirdly, a series of well-publicised technological failures has led to a growing interest amongst computer scientists and engineers in finding new and more reliable methods for the identification of requirements for complex systems. These developments have been accompanied by a growing recognition that technological deployment is more complex than hitherto assumed; work practices do not necessarily change to make systems work. The provenance of workplace studies, therefore, involves a curious mix of academic debate with more practical problems.

As far back as the 1970s, Dreyfus (1972) and others, including Coulter

(1979) and Searle (1980), developed a wide-ranging critique of artificial intelligence and cognitive science; in particular the idea that computers reflected, or provided a model for, the cognitive and social competencies of human beings. The criticisms were not concerned with debunking the technical ambitions of developers of new technologies and systems, despite some initiatives, such as the understanding of natural language, proving highly intractable. Rather, these critiques were concerned with the idea that human intelligence was akin to, and could be modelled by, the operation of a computer. In particular, Dreyfus and others set out to counter the idea that human conduct could be adequately explained in terms of an individual's ability to process information through the manipulation of symbols and by developing appropriate representations, and that intelligible action and interaction is accomplished following predefined goals, plans or scripts. One consequence of these assumptions for HCI has been the idea that, by looking at how individuals use or 'interact' with technology, one might be able to discover the 'grammar of the head' (Payne and Green, 1986) or the 'structure and process of a person's mind' (Carroll, 1984). It has even been argued that, by studying the use of technology in terms of the mental models of the user, themselves based on an analogy with computers, it would be possible to design a system which mirrors the cognitive processes of its users (Norman, 1983).

Assumptions concerning the nature of human conduct drawn from cognitive science have not only permeated the theoretical work undertaken within HCI, but have had a profound influence on the methods which have been adopted. Both specific evaluations of particular technologies and general analyses of the nature of computer use tend to adopt an experimental paradigm focusing on the individual user at the workstation. Analyses of the users' activities on the computer may draw upon such measures as the time to react to happenings on the screen or how long it takes to achieve a predefined task, but these are frequently also considered against some model of the activity, concerning, for example, the 'information processing' required by the user: how the user's conceptions, plans and interpretations are processed to solve problems and execute actions through the interface.

It is not the first time, nor will it be the last, that the operation of technology has provided a model for the scientific characterisation of the workings of the human mind. Earlier this century, for example, the newly invented telephone exchange served as a metaphor for mental processes, with its inputs, outputs, plugs and wires. In the early 1980s, with the emergence of HCI, we witnessed a renewed attack on computational metaphor and its concomitant assumptions. For example, Winograd and Flores (1986) utilised speech act theory in an attempt to underscore the social when thinking about how individuals 'interact' in and through computers, and Frohlich and Luff and others began exploring conversation analytic models which might be used to design interfaces to complex systems (Cawsey, 1990; Frohlich and Luff, 1989; Norman and Thomas, 1990). It is Suchman (1987) who, perhaps more than any other, has had the most profound impact on the ways in which we might consider human–computer interaction and the emergence of workplace studies in both the United States and Europe. In one sense, Suchman simply takes issue with the idea that action is determined by prespecified plans and goals, and provides an alternative way of exploring how individuals 'interact with' or use technologies. Her powerful critique of AI and HCI, however, coupled with her position within one of the world's leading system laboratories, namely Xerox PARC, transformed the debate and its academic and practical relevance.

Suchman begins her treatise by citing a well-documented distinction between European and Micronesian navigation. Since the Renaissance, European sailors have relied upon highly complex charts and plans to organise their voyages. Navigation consists of following the chart or plan, developed with regard to universal principles. In contrast, non-European sailors, such as the Trukese of Micronesia, use a rather different approach. They have no maps or plans, but rather utilise information provided by 'the wind, the waves, the tide, and current, the fauna, the clouds, and the sound of water'. They navigate in an *ad hoc* fashion, adjusting their speed and direction with regard to the circumstances at hand and the contingencies that arise. Suchman argues that the case provides an analogy to the ways in which cognitive science and related disciplines such as AI and HCI model human conduct. She suggests that the European navigator 'exemplifies the prevailing model of purposeful action found in cognitive science'. Human conduct is goal-oriented, and action is governed according to rules, scripts and plans. In attempting to achieve a goal, an individual may divide it into sub-goals and break down the task into a series of component actions. The individual identifies and invokes the appropriate representations, the relevant rules and plans, to meet the goal. It is this model which is perhaps best exemplified in the influential study of human–computer interaction by Card, Moran and Newell (1980, 1983) where they develop GOMS, a model developed on several layers and utilising a framework based on explicit goals, operators, methods and rules for selecting between options.

Suchman suggests that the goal-oriented, plan-based models of human conduct which inform HCI and cognitive science have a number of shortcomings. In the first place, they diminish the importance of the immediate context of action, and, in particular, the ways in which plans and schemes have to be applied and defeased with regard to the contingencies which emerge during the execution of practical actions. Secondly, she shows how the meaning of plans, scripts, rules and the like, is dependent upon the circumstances in which they are invoked; they do not so much determine conduct, but rather provide a resource through which individuals organise their own conduct and interpret the conduct of others. Thirdly, she argues that, by ignoring how individuals use and reason with plans and scripts in actual circumstances, human agency and the array of common-sense competencies on which it relies are cast from the analytic agenda. In one sense, therefore, she suggests that the Micronesian model of navigation provides a more suitable analogy for human conduct. More importantly, she demonstrates that formalisations, however detailed, are subject through and through to the contingencies which arise, and that rules, plans, scripts and the like depend for their accomplishment upon the ordinary abilities, practices and common-sense reasoning of individuals for their deployment and intelligibility. One of the implications of Suchman's argument is that we can only understand technologies, and the various formalisms which may be involved, by considering action with regard to the 'situations' in which it occurs.

Suchman's comments on the shortcomings of certain models in cognitive science draw from ethnomethodology and, in particular, Garfinkel's exposition of the indexical properties of practical action (Garfinkel, 1967; Garfinkel and Sacks, 1970). Throughout his writings, Garfinkel directs analytic attention towards the occasioned production and intelligibility of social action and activities, and explicates the common-sense knowledge and reasoning which inform the accomplishment of mundane events. Suchman's critique of cognitive science, and, in particular, its plan-based, goal-oriented models of human conduct, are nicely analogous to work by Wieder (1974), Zimmerman (1970) and others in which they demonstrate the shortcomings of the 'explanation by rule' in more traditional sociological theorising. For example, in his study of a halfway house in Los Angeles, Wieder reveals that, in contrast to more conventional explanations of organisational conduct, rules (both formal and informal) do not so much determine the actions of participants, but are rather constituted in and through mundane activities. The operation of the rules relies upon the participant's abilities to invoke and appeal to the rules, and to recognise action in accord with, or as an infringement of, the rules. Suchman's critique of cognitive science parallels debates within sociology and, more generally, social science, debates which have begun to direct analytic attention towards the practical accomplishment of organisational activities, and the ways in which formalisms, both 'social and technical' feature in day-to-day conduct.

Whilst Suchman's arguments have led to some debate, especially concerning what is meant by situated action and the status of rules and plans, her treatise has had a profound influence on research and thinking in a number of fields and disciplines (see Vera and Simon, 1993). For example, her critique of plan-based models of human conduct and their conception of mental processes and shared knowledge has contributed to the burgeoning debate within cognitive science concerning (social) action; a debate which is reflected in Still and Costall's (1991) contentious collection *Against Cognitivism* and the burgeoning body of research concerned with 'cognition in context' such as Lave (1988), Hutchins (1995), and, in a related way, Theureau (1992). Suchman's arguments have also had some influence within HCI and led to a growing recognition of the shortcomings of the theoretical and methodological assumptions which have informed a great deal of research on how individuals use computers. More importantly, however, Suchman's arguments have foreshadowed a growing body of naturalistic research by sociologists and social anthropologists concerned with the social and interactional organisation of technologically informed activities in complex work environments. Despite the long-standing interest in technology and work within sociology, Suchman's arguments and related debates in cognitive science, HCI and AI have had a profound influence on the emergence of ethnographic and ethnomethodological studies of work, interaction and complex systems; namely 'workplace studies'.

1.2   Technological innovation and collaborative work

The growing interest in the social and situated use of complex systems has arisen during a period of rapid technological and organisational change. Greater use of computer networks and electronic mail, rapid developments in the area of telecommunications and the growing ability to interweave different media have not only enhanced communications, but are providing the possibility of more richly supporting collaborative work. For example, it is argued that the numbers of users of electronic mail grew from 4.9 million in 1991 to 38 million in 1996.

Alongside these technological changes over the past decade, the business environment has been subject to radical change. Building on Pore and Sabel's (1984) influential treatise, Miles and Snow (1986), for example, suggest that new organisational forms are emerging which include vertical disintegration, the movement towards joint ventures and international licensing activities and business functions being performed by independent cells within a complex and relatively loose network of associations. Powell (1991) suggests that the decomposition of vertically integrated firms is leading to 'hybrid organisational forms' and Nolan, et al. (1988) further underscore the increasing necessity for organisations to be flexible and responsive to a constantly shifting and unpredictable market. Recent changes in organisational form have been facilitated by technological developments, but, at the same time, the transforming business environment is placing new and distinctive demands on information and communication systems.

In response to these technological and organisational changes, coupled with the growing dissatisfaction of more conventional research within HCI, we have witnessed the emergence of a new field, namely Computer Supported Cooperative Work (CSCW). The term appears to have been coined by Grief and Cashman in 1984 when they organised a small symposium which brought together a disparate collection of participants involved in such areas as distributed information systems, computer mediated communication and hypertext (cf. Bannon et al., 1988). Since these small beginnings, a burgeoning body of research has emerged, both 'technical and social', concerned with system support for flexible, collaborative activities.

It is interesting to note that technological developments in CSCW remain dominated by relatively crude notions of organisational conduct and human behaviour. For example, an important influence in CSCW research has been the attempt to develop technologies that support meetings, commonly known as Group Decision Support Systems (GDSS) (e.g. Vogel and Nunamaker, 1990). Such systems allow participants, who may be co-present or physically distributed, to share textual data, contribute to, and update, documents and to see and speak with each other. They can also include various large-scale public information displays, as well as private and public windows on individual workstations. The underlying concern in GDSS and a range of other CSCW systems, whether concerned with collaborative authoring, calendar management or work-team support, is the development of technologies to support 'group' activities, where organisational work is largely assumed to be synonymous with group work (hence the term 'groupware'). Even more sophisticated developments in CSCW research, such as media spaces, have tended to rest on a relatively conventional and limited conception of organisational conduct. Unfortunately, therefore, while early CSCW research has provided a vehicle with which to reconsider the 'interaction between the user and the system', there has been a tendency to replace the individualism found within HCI with group-based models of conduct found in certain forms of sociology.

As yet, it is generally acknowledged that CSCW systems have not met with a great deal of success. Indeed, it is sometimes argued that it is only more conventional computer applications for co-operative work such as shared databases, file stores and electronic mail which have met with widespread interest, and the responsibility for those systems can hardly be attributed to CSCW researchers. It is increasingly recognised that the relative paucity of successful CSCW systems does not simply derive from their technological shortcomings, but rather from the ways in which the systems fail to take into account how people in organisations work and interact with each other. Galegher and Kraut (1990) suggest, for instance, that the relative failure of the systems derives from their insensitivity to 'what we know about social interaction in groups and organisations'. A widely regarded example of the ways in which 'good' technologies can fail when deployed in organisations can be found in Orlikowski's (1992) study of the introduction of Lotus Notes into an international consultancy. She demonstrates that, despite the apparent advantages of Lotus Notes, to both management and the consultants themselves, the groupware system largely failed because it was out of keeping with the ways in which personnel worked both individually and in collaboration with each other. She argues that for the technology to work it would require a radical change in the consultants' frames of reference and in how work was distributed and paid for. The history of CSCW, like other disciplines concerned with the design and development of technology, is littered with examples of innovative and reliable technologies failing when deployed in actual organisations. Unfortunately, as Orlikowski points out, those responsible for the deployment of systems often assume that the work practices of personnel will change to accommodate the technology and that, in the fullness of time, all will recognise the benefits of the particular system. We have become increasingly aware, however, that, despite the dreams of both system designers and management, many technologies are underexploited, or even rejected, and those that survive can do a great deal of damage before personnel find a way of making the technology work.

The relative failure of such systems has become an important topic within CSCW. For example, Grudin (1988) has identified a number of key issues which may account for the failure of CSCW systems. These issues include: the disparity between who actually does the work and who receives the benefit from the system; the ways in which groupware and CSCW systems often formalise roles and responsibilities and are insensitive to informal organisation in the workplace; the fact that CSCW systems may be insensitive to the flexible and contingent character of work and organisational procedures; and the relative failure of management to recognise that in many cases the success of the system is dependent on wide-ranging organisational change. Underlying Grudin's analysis is, once again, the recognition that groupware and CSCW systems fail because their design and deployment does not take into account the social, situated and contingent character of collaborative work in organisational settings. Grudin and Palen (1995) go on to extend his analysis to examine deployments of groupware that have been successful. This, they suggest, has been due to the more sensitive design of recent versions of the systems and to 'peer pressure'.

In the past few years, there has been increasing effort to place a more sophisticated version of the social firmly on the agenda of CSCW. Various researchers, including Schmidt and Bannon (1992) and Robinson (1993), have begun to delineate a number of conceptual distinctions which they suggest are central to understanding co-operative work and providing appropriate computer support. Robinson, for example, argues that the use of even most basic procedure and technology requires 'articulation work'; bodies of practice and routine through which the formal procedures embodied in a particular system can be applied with respect to contingent and indigenous demands of doing the work. He argues that many CSCW systems inadvertently impoverish the activities they are intended to support through the ways in which they formalise rules and procedures. He goes on to suggest that 'CSCW applications should support the process of making distinctions, not the distinctions themselves' (Robinson, 1993: 45). Adopting a rather different approach, Schmidt and Bannon (1991) also argue for an understanding of co-operative work which radically departs from the narrow conception of the group and group behaviour which has undermined many CSCW systems. They suggest that we need to move away from the idea of groupware which demands the 'collectivisation of work' and in its place consider the ways we can support 'multiple individuals working together in a planned way in the same production process or in a different but connected process'. Their arguments draw our attention towards the diversity of co-operative work, and the importance of providing flexible support for a broad range of activities and forms of interaction. Like others, they conclude that CSCW systems are unlikely to meet with much success until we have a far greater understanding of the richness and complexity of collaborative work.

1.3   Naturalistic studies of work and technology

The burgeoning critique of more conventional approaches in HCI and cognitive science, coupled with the growing interest in developing systems to support collaborative work, have led to the emergence of a body of research, ethnographies, concerned with work, technology and interaction in organisational environments. These initiatives have been fuelled by technological failure and problems with the design and deployment of advanced systems. There is a widespread recognition that we need to find new methods for identifying the requirements for technology and develop more situationally sensitive strategies for their deployment; abandoning the long-standing assumption that complex systems will generate the (technologically) relevant change in work practice. These academic and practical concerns are of increasing importance in the light of the changing nature of both technology and organisations. The fragmentation and flexibility required for the 'new institutions' (Powell and DiMaggio, 1991), coupled with the enormous potential of information and communication technologies, provide an important momentum to readdress the 'interaction between human beings and computers' and explore its social and organisational properties.

There are, therefore, convergent developments in a number of academic and applied disciplines which place the situated and socially organised character of work and technology at the heart of the analytic agenda. In consequence, we are beginning to witness a (re)flowering of naturalistic studies of work and organisations, unparalleled save perhaps for the vivid ethnographies which emerged under the guidance of Everett Hughes in Chicago in the early 1950s. This new and growing body of studies is remarkable not least because of the diverse range of approaches which are being used to explore technologically informed organisational activities.

For example, perhaps one of the more interesting developments is emerging within cognitive science, with scholars in both Europe and North America increasingly concerned with the 'social', and in particular the 'situated' character of cognition (see, for example, Lave, 1988). The term 'distributed cognition' is increasingly used by a diverse range of scholars from cognitive science to demarcate a concern with (socially) shared representations and the co-ordination of action in organisational environments. There is some debate as to the provenance of the term distributed cognition, and some disagreement as to its domain of relevance, but Salomon (1993) provides a useful characterisation:

Traditionally, the study of cognitive processes, cognistic development, and the cultivation of educationally desirable skills and competencies has treated everything cognitive as being possessed and residing *in the heads* of individuals; social, cultural, and technological factors have been relegated to the role of backdrop or external sources of stimulation. This perception is fine as far as it goes, allowing us to examine in great detail some specific mechanics of information processing, problem solving, and learning. But once human behaviour is examined in real-life problem solving situations, and in other encounters with the social and technological surrounds, a rather different phenomenon emerges: People appear *to think in conjunction or partnership* with others and with the help of culturally provided tools and implements . . . The thinking of these individuals might be considered to entail not just 'solo' cognitive activities, but *distributed* ones. In other words, it is not just the 'person-solo' who learns, but the 'person-plus', the whole system of interrelated factors. (Salomon (1993: xii–xiii, author's italics))

Despite the ambivalence surrounding the definition of distributed cognition, it has provided the background for a broad range of interesting ethnographic work, much of which has been concerned with work and technology in organisational environments. Some of the most illuminating and influential research has been undertaken by Hutchins, whose studies of ship navigation, described in his splendidly titled monograph *Cognition in the Wild,* provide a flavour of the ways in which tools and technologies feature in situated cognition and the co-ordination of workplace activities (Hutchins, 1995). It is interesting to note that, alongside the commitment to explicating 'human cognition as a cultural and social process', Hutchins and others retain elements of models and metaphors which permeate more conventional research in cognitive science and HCI. So, for example, the idea of representation infuses the analysis of both individual and distributed cognition(s), and the computational metaphor informs the characterisation of tool-based cognition. Notwithstanding this slightly curious mix, the language of the cognitive peppered with the social, distributed cognition has provided the vehicle for a rich body of ethnographic work and an array of findings concerning the ways in which tools and technologies feature in individual and co-operative activity in organisational settings (see, for example, Agre, 1988; Gaver, 1991b; Norman, 1988; Rogers, 1992).

In passing, it is important to mention a parallel body of work which emerged in Europe over the past decade or so. Commonly known as 'course of action' analysis, a number of researchers in ergonomics in France developed an approach not dissimilar to distributed cognition. The approach, emerging in the light of the work of Pinsky and Theureau (1982, 1992) and Theureau (1992) is naturalistic, and is principally concerned with explicating the use of tools and technologies from within the courses of action in which they are embedded. The approach preserves a commitment to the cognitive whilst explicating the ways in which individuals interweave distinct courses of action, in and through tools and technologies. Like certain forms of distributed cognition, course of action analysis preserves the primacy of the individual and individual cognition, but powerfully demonstrates how representations and action are assembled and disassembled through co-operation and co-ordination.

A number of other analytic orientations have also informed workplace studies and begun to generate findings concerning technologically mediated collaborative activity. For example, symbolic interactionism, and in particular perhaps the work of Strauss (cf. Corbin and Strauss, 1993; Strauss, 1987; Strauss et al., 1964; Strauss et al., 1985) has informed a range of empirical studies and provided a number of conceptual distinctions which have permeated discussions of the social and technical in CSCW. As in other fields, such as education and literary criticism, there has also been a growing interest in drawing on, or revitalising, activity theory as a methodological and conceptual framework for the analysis of workplace activities (see, for example, Kuutti, 1991). Unlike other approaches, it is seen, perhaps, as offering a solution to the vexed problem of the 'micro and macro', which even haunts CSCW, a conceptual vehicle for interweaving the 'fine details of interaction' with the 'broader' organisational constraints and circumstances.

However, it is perhaps ethnomethodology and conversation analysis, more than any other analytic orientations, which have had the most prevailing influence on workplace studies and, more generally, social science research in CSCW. This is hardly surprising. Suchman's (1987) original critique of cognitive science and HCI drew on ethnomethodology and conversation analysis, and brought such work to the attention of an audience hitherto free from such incumbencies. Also, by virtue of her position at Xerox PARC, Suchman influenced the development of a series of workplace studies in North America and Europe which were supported (directly and indirectly) by Xerox and Rank Xerox.

At first glance, ethnomethodological and conversation analytic studies of new technologies in complex organisational environments do not appear significantly different from related work in distributed cognition, course of action analysis or symbolic interactionism. In the first place, almost all the studies are naturalistic, consisting of ethnographies based on extensive fieldwork and concerned in one sense with what Geertz (1973) characterised as 'thick description'. Similarly, most workplace studies, whatever their analytic standpoint, are principally concerned with explicating the situated character of practical action, and with taking the orientations of the participants themselves seriously, as a topic of inquiry. Thirdly, to a varying extent, almost all workplace studies are concerned with examining how participants co-ordinate their activities with each other, and with explicating the indigenous resources on which they rely. Despite these similarities, however, ethnomethodology and conversation analysis adopt a rather different approach to a number of key issues and concerns. For example, in contrast to related research, workplace studies informed by ethnomethodology and conversation analysis are not principally concerned with 'meaning' or 'representation', whether individual or shared; they are not concerned with cognition or learning (at least in its cognitive sense); and they do not focus on the ways in which situations shape human experience and activities. Rather, the recent array of ethnomethodological studies of work and technology, studies such as Harper's (1998) analysis of the International Monetary Fund, Button and Sharrock's (1994) description of engineering work, or Whalen's (1995) examination of emergency dispatch, directs analytic attention towards the socially organised practices and reasoning in and through which participants produce, recognise and co-ordinate their (technologically informed) activities in the workplace. They focus on the procedural, socially organised, foundations of practical action (Garfinkel, 1967; Garfinkel and Sacks, 1970). They examine the ways in which participants reflexively, and ongoingly, constitute the sense or intelligibility of the 'scene' from within the activities in which they are engaged. Technology, in the ways that it features in practical accomplishment of social action, is placed at the heart of the analytic agenda.

1.4   Technologies and social interaction

In doing sociology, lay and professional, every reference to the 'real world', even where the reference is to physical or biological events, is a reference to the organised activities of everyday life. (Garfinkel (1967: vii))

Our own approach also draws from ethnomethodology and conversation analysis. It is concerned with the *in situ* accomplishment of workplace activities and in particular with the methods and resources on which participants rely in the production and recognition of social actions and activities. It addresses the ways in which new technologies, such as information and communication systems, as well as more mundane objects and artefacts such as paper documents, feature in everyday practical activities in the workplace. It is concerned with delineating the practices and procedures which inform the concerted accomplishment of a range of everyday organisational activities and the use of a variety of tools and technologies which inform, and are informed by, those activities. In a sense, therefore, the studies in this book are directed towards explicating the resources on which organisational personnel rely to make technologies work in the production and co-ordination of the activities for which they are employed.

The studies discussed in the book address a diversity of organisational domains, including newsrooms, architectural practices, medical consultations and control rooms. They consist of snapshots, brief ethnographies, of workplace activities and the resources on which participants rely in their accomplishment. In one way they are selected to cover a broad range of technologies and to illuminate the very different practices on which personnel rely to accomplish particular tasks. They also provide a sense of comparison, and enable us to see how participants solve particular organisational problems and, in some cases, develop similar solutions. A number of the studies also illustrate rather different analytic standpoints. So, for example, in the following chapter, we consider the ways in which general practitioners read and write the medical record cards and the consequences of introducing computing technology. Later in the book, we discuss data gathered through experiments to reveal some of the interactional difficulties which arise in the use of more advanced communication technologies, namely media spaces.

Despite the diversity of approach found in the book, many of the studies are concerned with social interaction, and in particular the ways in which workplace activities are produced and co-ordinated in real-time interaction through talk and visual conduct. The studies are concerned with both face-to-face or co-located interaction, where participants share the same physical space, and with the production of activities which are co-ordinated between personnel who are located within different domains. In some cases, participants accomplish particular activities with regard to the real-time contributions of colleagues, some of whom are co-located, others only available by virtue of communication technologies such as the telephone, radio or video. Unlike many environments, the interaction which occurs within the settings discussed here does not necessarily consist of mutually focused encounters in which the participants are oriented to a particular topic or issue. Rather, personnel design particular activities at certain moments to implicate actions from others, or to allow colleagues to overhear or grasp a potentially relevant matter. For example, a critical aspect of the production of news stories within the editorial offices of an on-line news service, is the way in which journalists talk through stories as they are writing and thereby allow colleagues to catch the gist of tales which may be breaking. Or, for example, in the line control rooms of London Underground, personnel undertake various tasks whilst simultaneously shaping those tasks with regard to the concurrent actions and activities of colleagues within the domain. In almost all the settings we discuss in the book and elsewhere, it is found that the accomplishment of complex tasks, which may in principle be the responsibility of a particular individual in a setting, is 'ongoingly' co-ordinated with the actions of others. The 'situated' and contingent character of workplace activities derives from the ways in which the competent accomplishment of those activities is necessarily sensitive to, and thoroughly embedded in, the real-time actions of others. 'Situated' points to the emergent, moment-by-moment, production and co-ordination of workplace activities, and the ways tools and technologies feature, in their ongoing and collaborative accomplishment.

In order to address the interactional accomplishment of workplace activities, it is necessary to use data which provide access to the talk and visual conduct of the participants. All the studies discussed in the book involved extensive field work including observation and interview. Many of the studies also involved extensive video-recording of naturally occurring activities and events in the various environments. We have undertaken video-recording of architectural practices, medical consultations, newsrooms, media spaces, control rooms and many other working environments. So, for example, in London Underground control rooms we undertook successive periods of field work and video-recording, often leaving cameras to run up to eighteen hours of the day for a week at a time. The setting is particularly complex, involving 2 consoles, up to 6 personnel, and numerous screens and diagrams, so for some periods we used 4 cameras to gain access to both the participants and various tools and technologies on which they rely.

For research concerned with the interactional organisation of workplace activities, video has significant advantages over more conventional forms of 'qualitative' data (cf. Heath, 1997). In the first place, it provides access to details of talk and visual conduct which are unavailable through field observation, enabling the researcher to subject video-based versions of particular activities and events to repeated scrutiny, if necessary using slow-motion facilities and the like. Video-recordings also provide researchers with the ability to share data with colleagues, and to present and discuss materials on which observations and analyses are based. Furthermore, in public presentations, video-based data allow researchers to show the community the materials on which findings are based and make observations available for public scrutiny. As Heritage and Atkinson suggest:

In sum, the use of recorded data serves as a control on the limitations and fallibility's of intuition and recollection; it exposes the observer to a wide range of interactional materials and circumstances and also provides some guarantee that analytic considerations will not arise as artefacts of intuitive idiosyncrasy, selective attention or recollection, or experimental design. (Heritage and Atkinson (1984: 4))

Without video-recordings of the 'naturally occurring' events in the various settings, it would be difficult, if not impossible, to undertake analysis which examines the interactional production and co-ordination of workplace activities, and the ways in which personnel use tools, artefacts and various features of the local environment to accomplish the actions in which they engage.

None of this is to suggest that video-recording of workplace activities need not be accompanied by field observation. All the settings discussed in this book are highly specialised domains, in which personnel undertake complex tasks which rely upon extensive training and work experience. The settings also involve the use of various tools and technologies, some of which place intricate demands on the participants. Without a sense of the social and technical resources on which the participants rely, it would be difficult to understand many of the activities in which they engage. Some of these resources can be recovered through video, others require extensive observation and discussion with participants. Even in undertaking conventional field observation, video proved invaluable. It allowed us to show particular events to the participants and to discuss the reasons for particular courses of action or clarify what was happening on seemingly ambiguous occasions. It also allowed us to examine fragments, and discover, in the course of analysis, what further information we needed before we could develop our observations. In consequence, we organised data collection in almost all the settings by undertaking a period of field work, followed by video-recording, followed by field work, and so on. In the intervening periods, we undertook analysis of data and wrote draft reports on particular issues or phenomena. We could then use these observations and reports to pursue particular themes and clarify issues with the participants themselves.

With their concern with interaction, and the real-time production and co-ordination of workplace activities, almost all the studies discussed here, except the following chapter on the computerisation of medical record cards, draw on conversation analysis. Like ethnomethodology, conversation analysis is concerned with the methodological foundations of practical action, and in particular the resources through which social actions and activities are produced and recognised, that is 'accountable'. Conversation analysis, however, has become increasingly concerned with the sequential organisation of talk, both as a topic of, and a resource in, investigations. In the bulk of the studies discussed here, the sequential organisation activities in interaction, whether accomplished through talk or visual conduct, provide a pervasive analytic orientation and a vehicle through which the characteristics of technologically informed workplace activities are explicated. Moreover, the burgeoning body of observations and findings within conversation or 'interaction' analysis, provide a rich and varied body of resources with which to address the highly specialised and complex activities which form the focus of various chapters. In sum, therefore, video-recordings of workplace activities, coupled with certain methodological assumptions drawn from conversation analysis and ethnomethodology, provide the resources through which we explicate the practices, reasoning and procedures utilised by the participants themselves in the day-to-day practical accomplishment of their workplace actions and activities.

1.5   A note on an analytic orientation

The research discussed in this book, draws from ethnomethodology and conversation analysis, and in particular video-based studies of social interaction. It is driven by a number of analytic concerns and assumptions. Firstly, it is directed towards the investigation of the resources in and through which participants themselves produce their own actions and recognise the actions of others. Secondly, it treats talk, bodily conduct, the use of tools, technologies and the like, as ways in and through which participants accomplish actions and activities; actions and activities which rely upon, and embody, social organisation. Thirdly, it draws on the sequential and emergent character of social interaction to examine how participants orient towards each other's conduct and accomplish their practical activities. It may be helpful to expand a little on these assumptions and their background.

Ethnomethodology emerged through the pioneering studies of Harold Garfinkel and rapidly led to the development of conversation analysis through the contribution of Sacks and his colleagues, Schegloff and Jefferson. Unlike other forms of social science, ethnomethodology and conversation analysis do not provide a 'method', in the sense of a body of clear-cut sets of procedures that if followed will generate scientifically valid results or findings. However, they do involve a number of analytic commitments which have provided a foundation to a substantial body of empirical studies.

Garfinkel (1967) developed a distinctive approach to the understanding of human practical activity. He argues that we should place the methodological production of social actions and activities at the forefront of the analytic agenda and treat mundane events, even physical and biological phenomena, as socially organised accomplishments. At one point, he contrasts his recommendations with those suggested by Durkheim:

Thereby, in contrast to certain versions of Durkheim that teach that the objective reality of social facts is sociology's fundamental principle, the lesson is taken instead and used as a study policy, that the objective reality of social facts as an ongoing accomplishment of the concerted activities of daily life, with the ordinary artful ways of that accomplishment being by members known, used, and taken for granted, is for members doing sociology, a fundamental phenomenon. (Garfinkel (1967: vii))

Garfinkel suggests, therefore, that the 'ongoing and concerted accomplishment' of practical activities and events, the 'objective reality of social facts', should form a topic of sociological inquiry. He directs analytic attention towards the practices and reasoning, the methods in and through which social actions and activities are produced and recognised. He also notes that the methodological foundations on which participants rely in accomplishing action and activities are 'taken for granted', 'seen but unnoticed'; they inform the intelligibility of conduct, yet remain unaddressed and unexplicated, allowing individuals to confront, as an 'objective order of social facts', the very scenes and events they produce. This 'reflexivity' is an integral feature of practical activities and directs analytic attention towards the tacit, the 'seen but unnoticed' methods and reasoning on which people rely in accomplishing social actions and activities and 'confronting' normal scenes and appearances.

The pioneering research of Harvey Sacks and his colleagues, Emanuel Schegloff and Gail Jefferson, led to ethnomethodological studies becoming increasingly concerned with language use and social interaction. It was recognised that the analysis of social interaction, in particular talk-in-interaction, provided the possibility of developing a 'naturalistic observation discipline which could deal with the details of social action(s) rigorously, empirically, and formally' (Schegloff and Sacks, 1973: 233). Since its early beginnings, conversation analysis has led to a substantial corpus of empirical studies concerned with language use and interaction and delineated the organisation of a broad range of actions and activities in talk (see, for example, Atkinson and Heritage 1984; Psathas 1979; Sacks 1992; Sacks et al. 1974; Schenkein 1978). In recent years, the - original focus on 'conversation' has been increasingly enhanced by a growing body of empirical research concerned with talk in organisational settings including studies of news interviews, medical consultations, business meetings, counselling sessions and political oratory (see, for example, Boden, 1994; Boden and Zimmerman, 1991; Drew and Heritage, 1992).

The debate concerning the 'situated' character of practical action is reflected in Garfinkel's (1967) discussion of 'indexicality'. Indexicality points to the uniqueness of an activity or event, and drives analytic attention towards the ongoing, practical accomplishment of the rational, routine and mundane character of social actions and activities. The uniqueness of practical activities which informs ethnomethodology and conversation analysis is more radical than the notion of 'context' that is found elsewhere in social and cognitive sciences. Social actions and activities are treated as inseparable from, part and parcel of, the 'context at hand'; not as framed or influenced by prespecified characteristics of a context. The intelligibility of the scene, the character of the event, the sense of the local environment, the 'objective order of social facts' is for ethnomethodology ongoingly accomplished in and through the practical actions of the participants themselves; there is 'no time out' from the moment-by-moment, concerted production of the local order (and its array of social and physical properties). For conversation analysis, this radical treatment of context is reflected in the ways in which talk and, in particular, turns at talk or utterances are organised and addressed. Heritage, for example, suggests that turns at talk are both 'context shaped and context renewing'; a 'speaker's contribution is both designed with regard to the local configuration of activity and, in particular, the immediately preceding actions and contributes to the framework in terms of which the next action will be understood' (Heritage, 1984: 242). The step-by-step, sequential organisation of talk and interaction, whereby each subsequent turn or action displays an understanding of the prior, implicates subsequent action, both is an integral feature of the organisation of human conduct and provides an analytic resource for its investigation.

The double-edged element whereby sequential organisation is both an integral feature of the social organisation of talk and a methodological resource for its analysis remains a central and powerful tenor of conversation analytic research. As Sacks et al. (1974) suggest:

[It] is a systematic consequence of the turn taking organisation of conversation that it obliges its participants to display to each other, in a turn's talk, their understanding of the other turn's talk. More generally, a turn's talk will be heard as directed to a prior turn's talk, unless special techniques are used to locate some other talk to which it is directed . . . But while understandings of other turns' talk are displayed to co-participants, they are available as well to professional analysts, who are thereby provided a proof criterion (and a search procedure) for the analysis of what a turn's talk is occupied with. Since it is the parties' understandings of prior turns' talk that is relevant to their construction of next turns, it is their understandings that are wanted for analysis. The display of those understandings in the talk in subsequent turns affords a resource for the analysis of prior turns, and a proof procedure for professional analyses of prior turns, resources intrinsic to the data themselves. (Sacks et al. (1974: 728–9))

The emergent and sequential organisation of action and interaction is also relevant to how we examine visual conduct and activities in which tools, artefacts and the material environment feature. Gestures and other forms of bodily conduct arise in interaction, and, as we will see in the following chapters, tools and technologies, features of the physical environment and the like, routinely feature in collaborative activities within the workplace. Unfortunately, however, a substantial body of research traditionally concerned with visual and material conduct has assumed not only that gestures and the like are principally a reflection or embodiment of psychological or cognitive states, but that its organisation can be adequately explicated through experimental studies. As with cognate, naturalistic studies of interaction and bodily conduct, (see, for example, Kendon 1990), we are concerned here with how social actions and activities are accomplished in and through interaction, and the ways in which talk, visual and material conduct feature in the practical accomplishment of routine events. The sequential organisation of action in interaction is a critical resource in analysis.

Consider for instance the early research within conversation analysis concerned with the interactional organisation of a turn at talk (for example Goodwin 1981, and Heath 1986). A number of studies demonstrate how the production of single turn at talk, an utterance, may be co-ordinated with the conduct of the recipient. For example, Goodwin (1981) reveals how speakers can systematically delay the segments of projected utterances until they have secured an appropriate alignment from the co-participant, and how various resources, such as hesitation and self-repair, secure the gaze of the other. Elsewhere, it has been demonstrated that speakers may use various forms of gestural activity to shape, ongoingly, relevant forms of co-participation from other(s), and co-ordinate the production of an utterance with the alignment of the (potential) recipients (see, for example, Goodwin 1981, and Heath 1986). The actual utterance therefore, and the way in which it is understood sequentially, in the next turn, is the outcome of a complex interaction which includes both visual and vocal contributions by various participants during the very course of its production. In these and numerous other studies, it has been demonstrated how social actions, whether visual, vocal or a combination of both, emerge sequentially and implicate subsequent conduct. The ongoing, sequential development of action in interaction provides researchers with a resource with which to examine how the participants themselves are treating each other's conduct, and the ways in which they engender or encourage action from others.

However, whilst the sequential organisation of interaction remains an important resource for studies of visual and vocal aspects of *in situ* activities using video, it is recognised that it is not always possible to build a strong sequential case for the organisation of particular visual actions. For example, whilst a movement, such as an iconic or illustrative gesture, may appear to be an important aspect of a turn at talk, it can be the case that there is little evidence either in the next turn, or during the course of the utterance's production, that it is relevant, sequentially, to the accomplishment of the activity at hand. Similarly, studies of the use of objects and artefacts in interaction have tended to focus on instances where there is an explicit orientation by the participants themselves to the phenomenon in question rather than the more vague, less apparent, ways in which they might feature in the production of particular actions. Moreover, there is an increasing interest in using video to examine the organisation of activities which do not occur within 'focused communication', for example people in offices in a 'state of incipient talk' or individuals walking through public space, where it can be very difficult to demonstrate a strong sequential orientation by the participants to each other's conduct, even where their actions appear intimately interrelated. Finally, it is also recognised that in settings where activities require extensive specialised knowledge, such as control rooms or trading rooms in the City, analysis necessitates extensive field work and local expertise in order to begin to delineate the organisation of the participants' activities. Despite these difficulties, however, an important part of the richness and rigour of video-based studies of *in situ* social actions and activities derives from their continuing commitment to demonstrate how participants themselves are orienting to the organisation of activities described in the analyses. Building an analysis with regard to the sequential and interactional character of social action and activities whilst preserving a respect for context and describing participants resources remains a critical resource for these studies.

1.6   Observing a case

It is perhaps worthwhile considering an example. The fragment is drawn from a corpus of video-recordings of general practice consultations. It captures the first few moments of a consultation, where the patient enters the doctor's surgery, sits down and the proceedings proper begin. Aside from giving a flavour of the ways in which fragments are examined and presented in this sort of analysis, the particular example illustrates the ways in which a particular 'tool', in this case the medical record card, features in the activities and interaction of the patient and doctor.

The fragment is transcribed using the orthography developed by Gail Jefferson. Talk is laid out turn-by-turn, and the length of silences and pauses measured in tenths of a second and captured in parentheses, for example '(4.8)'. The colons, as in 'down::', indicate that the prior sound is stretched, the number of colons indicating the length of the sound. The underlinings, as in 'up', indicate that the word, or part of the word, is emphasised. '°' indicates that the following word is said quietly, and '=' that the following utterance is latched to the prior. '(.)' indicates a mini-pause, a pause or silence of two-tenths of a second or less. Double parentheses '((P. enters the surgery))' house transcribers' descriptions of actions or events.

Fragment 1.1   Transcript 1

((Patient, P, enters the surgery))
Dr: Do sit down::
      (5.5)
Dr: What's u̲p̲?
      (4.8)
P: I've had a bad eye::: (.) °in there=
Dr: =Oh: yeah
      (1.2)

As the patient enters the consulting room and walks towards the chair alongside the desk, the doctor utters 'What's u̲p̲?'. The utterance invites the patient to deliver his reason for coming. It projects a sequentially relevant next action for the patient, and, following a few seconds silence, the patient does indeed deliver the sequentially appropriate response, 'I've had a bad eye::: (.) °in there' (cf. Heath, 1981, 1986). In the case at hand, however, the patient withholds the reply for nearly five seconds. The silence may be a puzzle until we consider the visual conduct of the participants. A second transcript, capturing aspects of the visual conduct, may be helpful. The transcript presents the participants' conduct horizontally, with dashes capturing the length of silences and pauses, one-tenth of a second indicated by one dash. The transcript is accompanied by descriptions of particular actions or events.

Fragment 1.1   Transcript 2

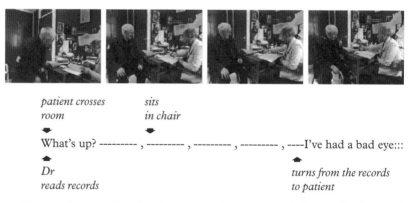

patient crosses   sits
room   in chair

What's up? --------- , --------- , --------- , --------- , ----I've had a bad eye:::

Dr   turns from the records
reads records   to patient

We can observe that the doctor continues to read the medical record cards after uttering 'What's up?' The last few entries in the records are routinely read at the beginning of a consultation to 'catch up' with the patient's recent medical history (see chapter two, and Heath, 1986). The patient withholds his reply until the doctor turns from the medical records to the patient. The shift of alignment by the doctor occasions the patient's response and progression into the business, namely the delivery and discussion of the reason for the visit. It may be the case that, by withholding a response to the query or 'topic initiating utterance', the patient encourages the doctor to, at least temporarily, finish reading the records and provide some further display that he is prepared and ready to listen.

There is further evidence to suggest that the patient is sensitive to use of the medical record and in particular the doctor's reading of the document. As he sits down, the patient momentarily glances at the doctor and then looks away just to one side. As the doctor looks at the record, he lifts his right hand and flattens the page. The gesture differentiates the doctor's reading, displaying a shift in alignment and, more importantly perhaps, the potential completion of the activity. As the hand presses the page, the patient looks up at the doctor and opens his mouth, as if to inhale before speaking. As the patient looks up, the doctor, rather than orienting towards the patient, looks down the page and continues to read. The patient immediately turns away and closes his mouth.

Fragment 1.1   Transcript 3

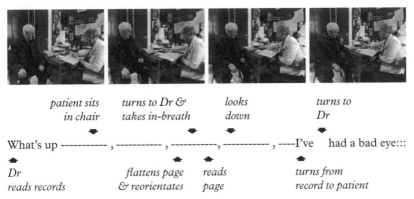

                    patient sits   turns to Dr &   looks   turns to
                    in chair   takes in-breath   down   Dr
                         ⬇   ⬇   ⬇   ⬇
What's up ----------- , ----------- , -----------, ----------- , ----I've   had a bad eye:::
    ⬆   ⬆   ⬆   ⬆
*Dr   flattens page   reads   turns from
reads records   & reorientates   page   record to patient*

In the case at hand, therefore, we can begin to see how the diagnostic phase of the consultation is established in and through the interaction, both vocal and visual, of patient and practitioner. We also gain a glimpse of how a relatively basic, organisational artefact, the traditional paper record, features in the beginning of the consultation and interaction between patient and doctor. The doctor takes the opportunity, as the patient enters the surgery and sits down, to glance at the medical records, and the patient orients towards the activity and its potential completion. In particular, the patient withholds response to the topic-initiating utterance until the doctor turns from the record to the patient; the absence of the sequentially relevant object, the patient's response, perhaps serving to encourage the doctor to realign his orientation. Moreover, within the pause itself, we find a complex 'negotiation' in which the patient 'monitors' the doctor's activity with regard to its possible completion, abandoning the production of an utterance in the light of the continued reading of the record. The fragment illustrates the moment-by-moment, step-by-step sequential organisation of the participants' conduct, both visual and vocal, and perhaps demonstrates how the use of a particular artefact arises in, and is consequential for, the action and interaction of both patient and doctor.

1.7   Summary

In the settings discussed in the following chapters, and in the case of many, if not most, organisational environments, work and the use of technologies are accomplished in interaction with others. In many cases, but by no means all, this interaction occurs between individuals who are physically co-located. Increasingly, however, our daily work involves dealings between people who are both co-located and physically distributed, the telephone and various other technologies providing the means through which the contributions of others feature in the ongoing production and co-ordination of workplace activities. Surprisingly, the interactional character of workplace activities, in particular their moment-by-moment 'collaborative' production, remains relatively underexplored and unexplicated. An analytic orientation, namely ethnomethodology and conversation analysis, coupled with a technology, video, provides us with an opportunity to begin to examine, in detail, the visual, material and vocal aspects of our work, and in particular the ways in which highly specialised, complex tasks are produced and co-ordinated in and through the social interaction of employees of organisations, and in some cases their clients.

The studies discussed in the following chapters are principally concerned with revealing the competencies, the social organisations, which allow individuals in very different circumstances to accomplish their work in concert with others, and to use, in whatever way they can, the tools and technologies found within the settings in which they work. The studies are first and foremost a collection of ethnographies; glimpses of the work to make technologies work. We hope they provide some sense of the complexity of even the most mundane actions and activities, of how individuals use various resources to accomplish, for practical purposes, their work, together in interaction, in contemporary organisational settings.

2 Documents and professional practice: 'bad' organisational reasons for 'good' clinical records

> It is a feature of the human predicament that we labour under two connected handicaps whenever we seek to regulate, unambiguously and in advance, some sphere of conduct by means of general standards to be used without further official direction on particular occasions. The first handicap is our relative ignorance of fact: the second is our relative indeterminacy of aim. If the world we live in was characterised only by a finite number of features, and these together with all the modes in which they could combine were known to us, then provision could be made in advance for every possibility . . . Everything could be known, and for everything, since it could be known, something could be done and specified in advance by the rule. This would be a world fit for 'mechanical' jurisprudence.
>
> Plainly this world is not our world. Hart (1961: 125)

2.1 Introduction

As Weber pointed out in his classic theory of bureaucracy, files and documents are an essential part of the modern organisation, in both the public sector and the 'advanced institutions of capitalism'. The modern medical organisation is no exception. Both time and money are devoted to documenting information concerning the activities of organisational personnel, especially in their dealings with the general public and, more particularly, patients. Perhaps the most important of these files and documents is the medical record. A great deal of time and energy, in both primary and secondary health care, is dedicated to documenting aspects of the medical history as it emerges in the patient's dealings with doctors and other medical staff. Over the past decade, there has been a growing commitment to take advantage of the benefits afforded by computing technology, and in the United Kingdom we have witnessed the widespread introduction of basic information systems into health care, particularly in general practices. Over the past few years, almost all health centres have introduced computing technology to enable and encourage general practitioners to abandon paper medical cards and record details

31

of the patient's medical history in electronic information systems instead. The computerised record has substantial advantages over the scruffy bits of paper and often 'illegible and haphazard' jottings that make up the traditional medical record card. Indeed, it was envisaged that the computerised system would replace the paper record for day-to-day work within a few years. However, despite the widespread deployment of the new technology, alongside their use of the computer general practitioners continue to update and rely upon the traditional paper record during the consultation.

In this chapter, we wish to consider why general practitioners persist in using the paper record despite the advantages of the computer-based system. In particular, we examine the socially organised practices and reasoning on which doctors rely in reading and writing the traditional paper record. We consider how the new information system fails to support the practices and practicalities of assembling and using clinical data within the framework of day-to-day medical consultations. The case of general practice does not simply provide a vehicle for considering how a particular system fails to support the work of a particular professional group, but raises more profound issues which bear upon contemporary research in disciplines such as HCI and CSCW. It allows us to begin to reveal the intricate and complex social arrangements which surround and inform the use of even the most mundane of human artefacts, and shows how seemingly 'individual' and 'cognitive' abilities, like reading a line of clinical data, are embedded in socially organised procedures and conventions.

It has been argued that, despite their seeming contribution to organisational life and bureaucratic work, basic information systems have generated as many problems as they have cured (Landauer, 1995). Certainly the 'paperless office' now seems to be a dream which only the most optimistic believe will enhance our working lives. Few of us would have anticipated the extraordinary ability of paper to survive the onslaught of advanced digital technologies. In our own research, for example, we have been continually surprised to find that in each of the settings we have examined, settings which have been transformed by the introduction of technologies to support organisational activities, paper continues to remain an essential and integral feature of the daily work and interaction of the participants. Consider, for example, journalists working in the production of broadcast news. Despite the development of computer editing systems, personnel continue to print off and distribute stories on paper. Or consider London Underground control rooms where the paper timetable, despite the introduction of complex multimedia technologies, is a critical resource for dealing with problems when they arise. Moreover, the recent history of computing technology is littered with examples of the problems, and on some occasions disasters, which emerge when an organisation attempts to replace a traditional paper-based system with electronic media. The introduction of Computer Aided Dispatch into the London Ambulance Service, or the aim to replace paper certification in the London Stock Exchange, mentioned in the last chapter, are two of the more costly examples. The persistence of the paper medical record card in general practice may perhaps throw a little light on a more generic and potentially intriguing problem.

A system designed to support the production, storage and retrieval of clinical data would seem to provide a case *par excellence* for the application of the methodological and conceptual framework which informs a significant part of research in HCI. There is, for example, a substantial body of research which has undertaken experimental studies of 'subjects' including medical practitioners 'interacting' with both basic and 'intelligent' systems (see, for example, Shortliffe, 1976, and the review by Berg, 1997). Medical systems provide an intriguing domain for exploring the abilities and competencies of the 'user', and the ways in which these are brought to bear to operate a computer system, particularly to perform complex diagnostic tasks. Many of these tasks are performed by an individual, often alone, or with a patient who lacks the relevant expertise to comprehend the specialised forms of activity undertaken by the medical practitioner. In consequence, it would seem reasonable to suggest that detailed experimental work of practitioners using such systems would provide a rich domain with which to identify and examine the generic and specialised cognitive skills on which users rely. Given the wide-ranging debate concerning the relationship between clinical expertise, medical models and the like, and their relationship to the comprehension and analysis of particular cases, the use of basic and intelligent systems in the area of medicine would seem to provide an important opportunity for explicating the 'interaction' between information and cognitive representations.

In this chapter, however, we would like to take a rather different tack. We wish to show that, whilst reading and writing a medical record card is indeed an individual activity, and presumably involves cognitive abilities or competencies, it rests upon a body of socially organised practices and conventions which inform both the production and the intelligibility of the records. These practices and conventions, the indigenous reasoning, we suggest, are bound into, and part of, the practicalities of everyday medical practice, and perhaps are more accessible through observation and field work rather than experimentation. Moreover, the relevance of these observations to our understanding of the interaction between

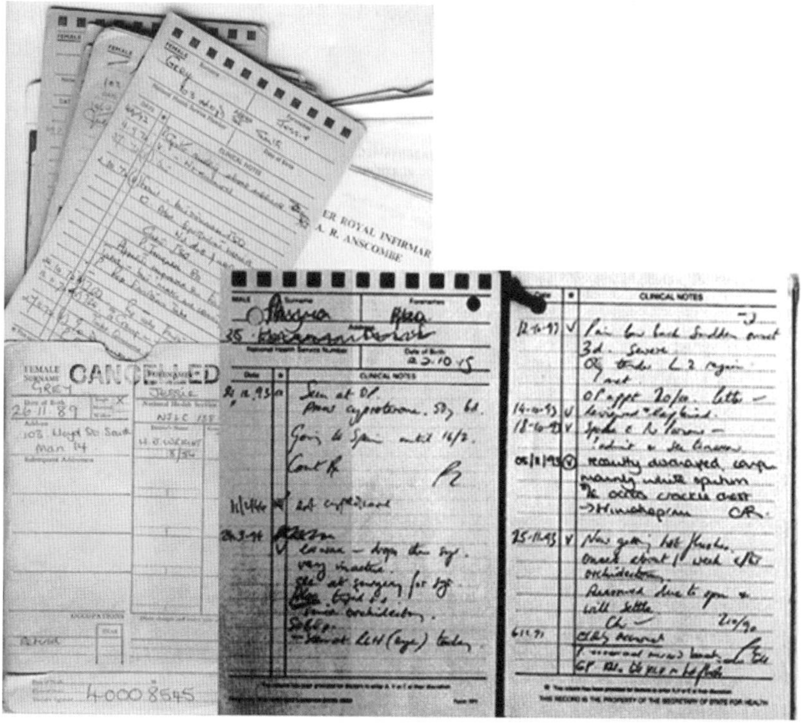

Figure 2.1 An example of a National Health Service Medical Record Card and detail of the contents.

computers and human beings may be not only of 'scientific' interest, but of relevance to the design and deployment of complex systems.

2.2   The traditional medical record card

One has reached the conclusion that the key to good general practice is the keeping of good clinical records. Time and again one has seen that a quick glance through a well kept record provides either the diagnosis or an essential point in the treatment. (Taylor (1954: 36))

The traditional paper medical record used in general practices in the United Kingdom consists of an A5 envelope (about $7'' \times 5''$, or 18×13 cm) containing a number of cards and various pieces of paper such as referral and discharge letters, and notes containing the results from tests. On the envelope is written the patient's name, address, date of birth and National Health Service (NHS) number (Figure 2.1).

The cards consist, in large part, of descriptions of consultations; each

and every consultation requiring a single entry on the medical record
card. The records are stored and made available to the doctor whenever
he or she consults with a patient, whether it is in the surgery, at home or in
hospital. The records follow the patient, and only the death of the patient
can result in the deletion of a record. Even then the record is kept for up to
six months in case any contingencies or enquiries arise. The following
extracts are drawn from various patient records:

28.9.85   c.   Vomited ×2 in night
               Maxolon 10bd (300 m)

11.8.95   c.   Not good – irritable
               Pain better, but drowsy in morning
               restart diary

22.5.95   a.   Diary OK for 1wk
               R elbow pain
               -less tender
               ↑ Doth to 150

24.2.95   c.   all test normal
               feeling low tearful fragile
               start Prozac
               see 10d
               for inj R tennis elbow

12.1.86   v.   Died 12.30 am
3.12.86   c.   Dog bite
               Rf (......)
               Tetanus Toxoid 0.5 ml

22.4.86   c.   cold
               also rheumatism
               cert 1/52 Paracetamol

At first glance, the entries in the record appear brief and unsystematic
and one wonders why so much trouble is dedicated to their upkeep.
Certainly researchers in the social sciences and epidemiology have long
complained about the quality of information kept in the records and
argued that they fail to provide a secure foundation for reliable analysis.
Despite the apparent quality of the paper records, doctors go to some
effort to maintain the medical documents. The records play an important
part in day-to-day professional practices, not simply in providing a
bureaucratic dossier that documents the contact between doctors and
their patients, but actually in the organisation of the consultation. Both
diagnosis and prognosis are often inextricably linked to information
which is documented in the patient's medical record card.

For example, before beginning a consultation the doctor glances at the patient's medical records normally turning to the most recent entry. This reading allows the doctor to assess whether the patient is returning with an illness which has already been discussed. If this is so, the document provides the resources with which to tailor the beginning of the consultation (cf. Heath, 1981). Or, for example, when faced with a problem for which the diagnosis is unclear or ambivalent, a doctor will often read the record in order to see whether there are any previous illnesses which explain the current difficulties. As well as a resource for hints or ideas, the records also provide the doctor with factual versions of the patient medical biography, so that previous treatment programmes, allergies and the like can be checked and confirmed by a brief glance at the record. For doctors, therefore, the records provide a reliable source of information which is adequate for the uses it serves in the day-to-day consultative activity.

Doctors therefore rely upon the records to accomplish their professional work. They expect the records to contain certain sorts of information and to be adequate for the uses to which they are put during the consultation. Given that a patient can consult any doctor within a particular practice, and that records follow patients if they happen to move to a new area, the entries in the record have to be intelligible to any general practitioner, and relevant to an unpredictable range of circumstances. The reliability of the records, despite their seeming idiosyncrasies, would suggest that the doctors rely upon a powerful and generic body of practices which allows them to read the document in the relevant ways and to produce entries in a systematic and conventional fashion. The organisation which informs the production and use of medical records is not formally specified. Rather, it consists of a set of tacit, taken-for-granted conventions, a community of practice, which informs both the production and intelligibility of the record; both the ways in which entries are written and how they are read. We wish to suggest that the tacit and taken-for-granted practices on which doctors rely in reading and writing the records are relevant to understanding the relative success or failure of particular systems and more generally may facilitate the design technologies to support collaborative work in primary health care. Before considering the computer-based system, therefore, it is necessary to consider the traditional medical record in more detail.

2.3   The mapping of category items

Entries in the medical records consist of standardised elements, or better, classes of particular items. For example, consider the following relatively brief entry.

29.2.85   c. 'feeling tired'
              Depressed
              Librium (30) (5 mg)

This record consists of the following: the date and location of the consultation ('c' for consultation being held in the surgery, 'v' for a home visit); the patient's presentation of the problem or symptoms; the practitioner's diagnosis or assessment; and the treatment, its strength and the amount. A single entry in the record therefore consists of distinct classes of items: the occasion of the consultation; a description of the complaint or illness; and the management or treatment of the complaint or illness. These classes include different categories of item. The patient's complaint can include the patient's presentation of their symptoms such as 'sore throat', and/or the doctor's diagnosis such as 'Depressed'. The management of the complaint can consist of drug treatment such as 'Librium (30) (5 mg)', referrals such as 'rf ....', certificates such as 'Cert 1/52', and the like. None of this is to suggest that items are documented for each category in each class for every consultation. However, if a category of item is not recorded, then various sorts of inference can be drawn. For example, a doctor might conclude that his colleague was unable to form a diagnosis, or presumed that given the symptoms 'anyone' could be expected to draw the appropriate conclusion.

Critical to the writing and reading of the medical record are the ways in which entries are internally organised, and ordered with regard to each other. The geography of a single entry is particularly important. The respective items are presented across and then down the page, providing a serial or even sequential order. The position of each item, with respect to the surrounding items, provides an important resource with which to recognise what a particular item means. For example, 'Depressed' in the entry cited above gains its status as an assessment or diagnosis by virtue of its position, following 'feeling tired'. If 'depressed' was the first item, and say 'paranoid' the second, then 'paranoid' would constitute the assessment, whereas 'depressed' would become the presenting complaint or symptoms. Similarly, 'paranoid' could be the patient's presentation of the complaint, if followed by, for example, 'exam tension' or 'difficulties at work'. The sense of the descriptive elements within an entry is not intrinsic to the particular items, but rather is assembled with regard to where, in what order, and with what, it is co-located. Similarly, the temporal organisation of entries in the record is embodied in the textual order, working backwards, the last being the most recent. As we will discuss later in the chapter, on occasions, items within a particular entry can gain their determinate sense by virtue of their relationship to previous entries. The geography of items within the record is a critical resource in both reading the entry and making sense of its constituent items.

2.4   Descriptive economies: interclass defeasibility

In writing entries in the records, doctors orient to a descriptive economy. They largely avoid repetition of particular items and information, and exploit a competent reader's ability to draw the necessary inferences from particular items and their configuration within an entry. An adequate description of a consultation relies not so much on an extended description of the event and its findings, but rather on a few brief words and letters assembled to give a particular impression. The adequacy of a description relies upon what is both recorded and retrievable by a competent reader, that is, a fellow general practitioner. To enable us to discuss the ways in which practitioners assemble a coherent and economic description and provide readers with a particular impression, it is useful to introduce the idea of 'defeasibility'. We draw the term from H. L. A. Hart and others within the philosophy of jurisprudence. It describes the ways in which any rule or law, no matter how precise its formulation, will inevitably confront circumstances where, despite its potential relevance, it is rendered inappropriate with regard to the contingencies 'at hand'.

Consider the following entries drawn from various patient records.

10.2.73   c.   Tonsilitis
            Apsin (30) (250 mg)

14.3.84   c.   'Fed up'

13.2.73   c.   Feeling sick
            Depressed.
            Valium (15) (5 mg)

In the first instance, we find no details concerning the patient's presenting complaint or symptoms. 'Tonsilitis' would be treated as the diagnosis, especially given that the following item refers to antibiotics, which suggests there is evidence of an infection. However, any competent reader confronting this entry would be able to infer the symptoms suffered by the patient given the diagnosis. These would normally consist of a sore throat, a temperature and perhaps associated headaches and drowsiness. Given the diagnosis and the recommended treatment, there is therefore no need for the practitioner to document the patient's symptoms. As for 'fed up' in the second example, its character coupled with the single inverted commas would lead one to assume that the item is one of the presenting symptoms of the patient. The absence of a diagnosis and any treatment allows the reader to assume that, following the appropriate medical enquiries, the practitioner was unable to formulate an assessment or diagnosis. Indeed, standing alone, the item suggests that the patient has not only presented a trivial complaint, but is perhaps someone of whom colleagues should be wary. Finally, 'Depressed' constitutes a diagnosis; the assessment is further confirmed by the treatment that the practitioner has recommended to the patient, namely antidepressants. The patient's symptoms are largely excluded, presumed to be retrievable from the diagnosis. However, note 'feeling sick'; a symptom, again marked by inverted commas, which is perhaps documented since it is not characteristic of the diagnosis in question. It might also suggest that the doctor is covering himself in case the illness turns out to have a physical foundation.

In writing an entry, therefore, practitioners write an entry in the records with regard to the reasoning and inferences that a colleague would ordinarily be expected to draw. They can rely upon colleagues reading certain information into a description and thereby avoid producing redundant or potentially irrelevant material. The descriptions in the records are designed with regard to 'what any competent' reader would discover within the assembly of items; doctors expect their colleagues to bring their expertise and experience to bear in reading the records and thereby draw the relevant inferences. The descriptions are designed for a particular class of recipient, namely general practitioners. In their production of the records, doctors orient to the uses to which the information is regularly put and the knowledge and competencies that suitable qualified colleagues will bring to bear on the text. Without the relevant knowledge and experience, the entries in the record do indeed appear haphazard and idiosyncratic, as a hapless report of the events in question.

2.5   The description as a whole

The defeasibility of items may occur not only within a particular class, but also across classes within an entry. For example, the presence of an antibiotic 'Apsin' in the entry above gives further support to the categorisation of 'Tonsilitis' as a diagnosis rather than simply a presenting symptom of the patient. Consider the following examples which include various forms of intraclass defeasibility.

14.4.83   c.   lower abdomen tenderness
                    soft faeces. muscle spasm?
                    probanthine 15 (40)
                    does not want to go to MRI for tests

12.7.85   c.   vomiting, stomach pains,
      .   cannot sleep, weak and unstable
                    difficulties at home.
                    r/f AA

3.12.87   c.   tired and weepy
                    'cannot work', mild pains in l/shoulder
                    r/f GC

The first entry is rather interesting. The symptoms themselves do not appear particularly serious and the doctor provides a candidate diagnosis. Even so, the reference to MRI (the local hospital) suggests that the doctor believes his assessment may be incorrect and that there may well be something more seriously wrong with the patient. The doctor has deliberately designed the entry ambivalent to reveal his ambivalence, and, by attempting to encourage the patient to undergo further tests, attempts to cover himself should problems emerge in the future. In the second example, we find no diagnosis, and a number of symptoms which could reasonably point to different kinds of assessment. For making sense of what the doctor is considering, however, the critical entry is 'r/f AA'; an attempt to have the patient contact 'Alcoholics Anonymous'. Finally, an entry with a curious collection of symptoms with no assessment or diagnosis. However, the reference to 'r/f GC' would allow any doctor in the practice to know that their colleague had referred the patient to the psychiatric social worker, and in this was not only able to gain a second opinion, but believed that the patient may be suffering from psychological or social problems.

The production of an entry therefore, that is the writing of the record, does not consist of following a set of clearly formulated rules or procedures as to what information should be gathered into an entry. Rather, entries are written with respect to the overall impression of the patient's illness and the doctor's management of it. An entry is not so much a précis of what happened in the consultation, but rather a brief sketch involving a few sharp strokes which provide a particular image of the event. The consultation is documented by interrelating components in such a way as to provide a certain impression. Each item is dependent for its meaning on the other items within an entry, and the sense of the whole emerges from the interrelationship of the various components. The ways in which the medical records are assembled (both in writing and reading) are not unlike the hermeneutic circle discussed by Husserl or the *Gestalt* contexture described by Gurwitsch:

Between the parts or constituents of a Gestalt contexture there prevails the particular relationship of Gestalt coherence defined as the determining and conditioning of the constituents upon each other, In thoroughgoing reciprocity the constituents add to, and derive from one another, the functional significance which gives one its qualification in a concrete case. (Gurwitsch (1964: 134))

2.6   Intra-entry defeasibility

The description of a consultation may be produced not only with regard to the mutual dependence of items within an entry, but also with consideration to other entries within the patient's medical record cards and in particular the immediately preceding consultations. For example, the following entry neither presents a complaint, nor a professional assessment, nor a diagnosis. Furthermore, whilst treatment is mentioned, namely an eye ointment, it does not provide an adequate basis with which to infer the symptoms or character of the patient's problem. Standing alone, it looks as if a doctor would be unable to retrieve potentially relevant information concerning the consultation.

3.12.80   c   eye now appears virtually normal
Neospurin

The absence of relevant information within the entry, would encourage any general practitioner to turn to the previous entry to see whether it casts light on the subsequent consultation. In the case at hand we find:

26.11.80   c   Conjunctivitis
Albacid 10%

Given the proximity of the two events, some eight days between each consultation, the reader could assume that the most recent entry reported a return visit; a consultation which was principally concerned with the progression of a problem which patient and doctor had discussed on a previous occasion. In such circumstances, the practitioner knows that the diagnosis and the treatment details will be found in a previous entry and that there is no point (re)documenting the same information on each occasion. In the case at hand, the reader might also assume that the eye was taking some time to clear up, and this would account for the change of treatment during the subsequent consultation.

Similarly, entries such as:

12.4.84   c. Breathlessness and pain on exertion 6/52
sleep as usual. weight 12 st 9 lb, pallor cyanosis, oedema-nil,
mildly hyper resonant-liver dullness
soft systolic murmur all areas BP 165/105
Angina Pectoris. Trinitrin

16.4.84   c. Tablets relieve pain. weight same. C 2/52

18.11.84   c. Admitted MM via 999

are written with regard to each other and provide a competent reader with the resources to retrieve the information that they would ordinarily expect to find within a single entry. The very brevity of the entry, the omission of certain categories of item, coupled with the presence of some mentioned treatment, serves as an embedded instruction to the reader to turn to previous entries in order to retrieve the relevant information. The practices that doctors use to assemble the records, and the various economies to which they orient, are the selfsame practices on which they rely in reading the records. They provide for a delicate and subtle range of inferential work through which conventional sorts of information concerning a consultation and a patient can be found or discovered.

The defeasibility of items across two or more entries is not simply a matter of saving the doctor time. By designing an entry so that a colleague turns to read other, related entries, a practitioner provides a sense of the career, or course, of a particular illness and the ways in which various consultations featured in its development. It also provides a resource for a practitioner to determine wherever an upcoming consultation is itself an event within the progression of an illness. In such circumstances, the beginning of the consultation and its overall shape are tailored with regard to the particular illness with which the patient is 'returning'. By defeasing items across entries and assembling the text with regard to an impression of how this event is related to previous meetings concerning this particular illness, doctors produce careers or trajectories of illnesses. The records reflect and embody the routine progression of particular problems and the ways in which the proper management of illness by the members of the profession attends to, and of course (re)produces, the routine progression and cure of particular troubles. The design of the text therefore, the ways in which items are described and assembled, provides instructions as to its span of potential relevancies and what information within the document potentially features in this *Gestalt* of the particular illness. As Garfinkel (1967) suggests, however, on any subsequent occasion the record may be examined with regard to the contingencies which demand a retrospective recharacterisation as to what is indeed relevant to some (emergent) particular trouble.

A clinical record does not have this character. A subsequent entry may be played off against a former one in such a way that what was known then, now changes complexion. The contents of the folder may jostle each other in bidding to play a part in a pending argument. It is an open question whether things said twice are repetitions, or whether the latter has the significance, say, of confirming the former. The same is true of omissions. Indeed, both come to view only in the context of some elected scheme of interpretation. (Garfinkel (1967: 204–5))

2.7   The computerisation of clinical records in general practice

The computer system most widely deployed in general medical practice in the United Kingdom is known as VAMP (for 'Value-Added Medical Products'). This is an application which works on a standard personal computer that is intended to be placed on the doctor's desk and used during consultations. VAMP provides a computerised record system for the documentation and retrieval of medical biographical information and a facility for issuing prescriptions. It also includes a database for information concerning available drugs and treatments. The aim of the system is to provide more accurate, flexible and accessible clinical data concerning patients, overcoming many of the shortcomings of the paper medical record card, and to provide wide-ranging, up-to-date information concerning available treatments, their side effects and the like. It was assumed that within a year of its deployment the system would largely replace the traditional paper medical record.

In order to rationalise certain aspects of the paper records, the system has made a number of relatively small changes to the ways in which diagnostic and prognostic information is documented and presented to the general practitioner. Whilst these changes appear relatively minor and would seem to enhance the clarity of information, they are consequential to the ways in which doctors are able to use the new clinical records within the consultation.

Unlike the paper record, the details of each consultation are no longer written into a single entry. With VAMP, diagnostic and prognostic information are stored separately, in distinct locations or files, and cannot be accessed simultaneously. One file, called the 'medical history', contains information concerning the date and location of the consultation, the patient's presenting symptoms and a diagnosis, the results of any tests, and any additional comments by the practitioner. The second file, known as the 'therapeutic history', contains information concerning treatment. It includes details of drugs, their names, amount, dosage and frequency, appliances, dressing and information concerning any referrals.

The medical history file stipulates both the type of information which is entered and the amount of information. It is divided into two sections; the assessment or diagnosis and a section for 'free text'. In the original version of the system, each section consisted of no more than one line of ten characters. The information entered into the diagnostic section has to use a fixed set of diagnostic categories drawn from an established system known as Oxmis, though this has recently been replaced by an alternative system known as the Read classification. Free text can be entered with the diagnosis if the practitioner wishes to describe the patient's symptoms or elaborate on the assessment or diagnosis (see Figure 2.2).

The therapeutic file is also sub-divided into two files. One file details information concerning repeat prescriptions, for example relating to chronic difficulties. The second file details therapy for acute problems (see Figure 2.3). With VAMP, it is not possible to view both files simultaneously. The system also includes a number of other features which,

```
                        HISTORY DISPLAY


LANGDALE      JEANETTE        51y    Female Permanent 12 HIGH ST, BATTERSEA
MEDICAL HISTORY    Checked     by              3yr exam:Eligible 28/11/83
1      1950     FRACTURE NOSE       D                            3  DM
2 17/10/60      NORMAL LABOUR       D         M 8LB 70Z          3  DM
3 25/01/64      NORMAL LABOUR       D         F 7LB 5OZ          3  DM
4 29/11/71      PSORIASIS           O      O                     1
5      1982   S MENORRHAGIA         R GYN  1                     3
6      1983     HYSTERECTOMY        D         BENIGN PATHOLOGY   1  CD
7 21/07/87    S HYPERTENSION        O         140/85            1  DM



TRANSACTION:

   Date    Type Problem Description    Outcome    Comment         Prt

Enter required Transaction, H for Transaction options, <ESC> to exit
```

Figure 2.2 Illustration of a medical history page from VAMP (1993).

```
                        THERAPY REPEAT


   CADE       JAYNE             43y    Female Permanent 42 ARUNDEL ROAD HORSHAM
THERAPY HISTORY  Repeat till 14/06/88 days/script 21     3yr exam:Completed 15/07/91
   Date  Pharmaceutical name        Frm  Strength  Dosage    Days Qty  op  Rp  Is
1 27/05/88     BETNOVATE            CRE    0.10    PRN                 1   6   2  SP
2 29/06/88     TRILUDAN             TAB   60.00    1BD        28           6   1


SELECT LINE

Allergy/Int:  ALLERGY SEPTRIN
```

Figure 2.3 Illustration of a prescription page for repeat prescriptions
from VAMP (1993).

whilst again seeming insignificant, are consequential to the use of the computerised clinical records in the consultation.

Information entered into the system through the keyboard is ordered by a series of prompts which require the practitioner to move progressively through a series of options. For instance, in order to issue a prescription the doctor must first enter the relevant file in the system. The system then displays details of past prescriptions, and a series of prompts which require particular types of information to be entered in particular fields in a serial order. The prompt line requires such details as the name, form, strength, dosage and quantity of the drug being prescribed and each field has to be recompleted for each drug which is prescribed. The doctor normally uses the alphanumeric keys to type in abbreviations of the relevant information. After details of the form and strength have been entered, the system will then attempt to match the details to check whether the appropriate quantities are available in the on-line dictionary of drugs, appliances and dressings. In working through the sequence of prompts, the doctor presses the carriage return key to move to the next field, or the control key in conjunction with a character key to return to a previous field. After exiting the final field, the system prints out a prescription and updates and displays the patient's recent treatment history roughly corresponding to the last five consultations.

2.8   Some unanticipated consequences of the system

The computer-based system reproduces many of the classes and categories of information that are ordinarily used in the paper medical record card. It also provides additional facilities, integrating pharmaceutical information traditionally held in handbooks into the system itself. However, a number of small changes in the ways in which information is entered and accessed have had profound consequences for professional practices and the use of the computer during the consultation.

By separating an entry into two overall files, one containing information concerning the medical history, the other containing the therapeutic history, doctors are no longer able to interweave information which would ordinarily be defeased across the two classes within a particular entry. With VAMP, information has to be entered into both files, and can only be read separately. So, for example, the type of interclass defeasibility we found in:

14.4.83   c.   'badly bruised'
           cert 1/4
           r/f Brook Centre

is no longer possible, nor is it possible to defease items across entries, as in:

3.12.80   c   eye now appears virtually normal
           Neospurin.

The economies of intraclass and interentry defeasibility are removed by the system, as are the ways in which doctors can generate particular inferences, and even produce deliberate ambiguity by omitting or including particular categories of information.

The system also separates the therapeutic files into long-term, repeat prescriptions and information concerning the management of more acute problems. The two files cannot be opened simultaneously and read together, nor can information be entered whilst the doctor views both files. Whereas with the paper records doctors could draw a range of inferences concerning the patient by glancing at the variety of treatments that the patient is receiving, the separation of the acute and chronic treatment files means that this inferential work and, in particular, assembling an overall picture of the patient, here and now, is more difficult to achieve. Moreover, the doctor cannot tailor his description of a patient's treatment, with regard to a colleague reading all the information together.

The introduction of a restricted body of diagnostic categories, coupled with limitations on the amount (and range) of free text, can also undermine the doctor's ability to provide the particular impression he wishes to sketch concerning a patient and the consultation. The doctor can no longer create a professional assessment, or rely upon the juxtaposition of treatment and symptoms to hint at, but avoid commitment to, a particular diagnosis. It also undermines the doctor's ability to leave things open for the time being and see how the patient's illness has developed, or not, by the follow-up consultation. It precludes the doctors' ability to embed a certain ambivalence in the diagnosis or assessment of the complaint or to avoid a diagnosis. Limitations on the amount of free text can also inhibit more discursive entries which often, for example, accompany consultations in which patient and doctor have discussed more psychological or social problems.

The system also generates a number of additional, seemingly minor problems. For example, within a practice, the handwritten entry provides a rich array of resources for the 'competent' reader. Colleagues will recognise at a glance the author of a particular entry in the records and will, if necessary, draw all sorts of inferences concerning the treatment and even diagnosis that the patient received. In one particular practice with which we are familiar, one practitioner was particularly 'interested' in the psychological foundations of a patient's illness, and colleagues, in consequence, would treat certain details in the records with some scepticism. Handwriting also allows, as we have seen in the entries discussed above, the writer to use various stylistic devices to give a certain flavour to statements that they included in the medical records. So, for example, we saw how inverted commas were used to display that a particular item was the patient's characterisation, rather than the doctor's, and it is not unusual to find all sorts of punctuation, such as commas, exclamation marks, underlinings, crossings out and the like used by doctors to flavour the ingredients which make up an entry. Moreover, there are certain practices which may be frowned upon, and yet are essential to giving a certain cast to an entry, or even simply making the working day a little more entertaining. A case in point is the liberal use of acronyms and abbreviations. It is not unusual to find doctors within a particular practice developing various expressions which give colleagues a sense of the patient and what to expect. So, for example, we have come across items such as 'SEN' (Sub-normal even for Norfolk), 'AWF' (Away with the Fairies), and 'CTL' (Close to ley-lines – areas in England where some of the more unusual Churches have established centres). The introduction of the computerised system has removed these resources, and, whilst formalising the record, created an impoverished document.

The computerised system therefore removes the tailorability, economy and *Gestalt* which are essential to the production of entries within the paper record and to the ways in which entries are read and interpreted. Doctors are no longer able, nor encouraged, to defease categories of information, within or between classes and entries, but have to laboriously complete each section and field. They can no longer delicately tailor or flavour the information they provide, so that the reader can discover 'more than is said in so many words', or recognise that the doctor is uncertain about the nature of the illness or the ways in which it should be managed. Perhaps more importantly, the system, as it is organised at the present time, fragments an entry into different files, so that doctors can no longer assemble, or read an entry or a series of entries as a 'whole'; the descriptive *Gestalt* as a representation, or embodiment of a particular consultation(s), is undermined by the system.

Of course, there are various ways in which the system could be enhanced which would allow more flexibility to the ways records are written and read. Indeed, in subsequent versions of the system doctors were given more space in which to construct their 'free text' and fewer restrictions were placed on which files could be accessed at the same time. These improvements may ameliorate some of the worst problems with VAMP, and yet the overall design leaves in place critical distinctions that undermine how individual items, classes of items and sequences of entries can be written and read.

In chapter eight, we return to the medical record card to consider how the requirements for a technology for general practitioners could be rethought. Although mindful of the needs for using the records for other financial and bureaucratic purposes, we focus on the requirements of the practitioners during the consultation. This leads to the consideration of quite distinctive kinds of technologies to the typical systems, operated through keyboard and screens, which are currently found in doctors' consultation rooms. We consider how we might draw upon the study, outlined in this chapter, of the detailed practices through which records are assembled, as well as the difficulties doctors and patients encounter when utilising both computer and paper-based systems, in order to provide a technology that is sensitive to both the reading and writing practices of doctors, and to the ways in which this activity is embedded within an ongoing consultation between doctor and patient.

2.9   Medical records and the interaction between patient and doctor

Both the paper and computerised record are primarily used during the actual consultation. The doctor refers to the record to retrieve information concerning previous illnesses and the their management, and often documents diagnostic and prognostic details as he talks to the patient. Moreover, just as the paper prescription is written during the final moments of the consultation, its exchange often forming the end of the encounter, so the computer is used to produce prescriptions. The paper documents and the computer therefore are an integral feature of the interaction between patient and doctor; various activities rely upon the use of these tools and artefacts, and their use is embedded in the ongoing co-ordination of actions and activities between the participants. The fragment discussed in the previous chapter gives a flavour of how the paper record can feature in the interaction between patient and doctor, and it is perhaps worthwhile considering another example before briefly discussing the use of the new system during the consultation. The following fragment is drawn from Heath (1986) and once again involves the beginning of a consultation.

Fragment 2.1   Transcript 1

> *((knock on the door))*

Dr: Come in
        (1.5)
Dr: Hello
P: Hello
        (3.4)
Dr: Err:: (.) How are things Mister (0.6) Arman?
P: Erm:: (0.5) all right (.) I just er:: (1.0) come to (0.7) have you look you know about er::: (0.7) have you got any information from the hospital?
Dr: No:: (0.3) I don't think so.

The doctor glances at the records as the patient enters, and, finding that it is a return visit, asks Mr Arman how he is. As the patient begins to reply, the doctor begins to look through the records to see whether there is any information from the hospital. The patient's reply is hesitant; he pauses a number of times, produces 'ers' and stretches various sounds. In various ways, then, the gist of the utterance is delayed, but then appears to be forthcoming with 'come to have you look you know about'. During the first part of the utterance, the patient is looking towards the doctor. A moment before the patient begins to produce what appears to be the gist of reply 'have you look you know about' he turns away and crosses his legs.

Fragment 2.1   Transcript 2

patient turns away
crosses legs
➡

Patient: err:: ---------- come to ------- have you look you know about err ----
                                               ◆   ◆
                                          Dr turns   *Dr turns back*
                                          from records   *to records*
                                          to patient

As he crosses his legs, the patient's knee rises towards the doctors field of vision, and in particular the records. As he looks up, and ceases to read the document, the patient continues, producing a coherent and unhesitant stretch of talk. He stalls, right at the moment the doctor turns back to the record.

Patients therefore are sensitive to the use of the paper record during the consultation and may attempt to co-ordinate their own actions with the doctor's reading or writing. Indeed, as we saw in fragment 1.1, despite their limited visual access to the paper record, and understanding of what the doctor may be doing as he is looking at it, they discriminate actions and potential boundaries with the activity of say reading, and co-ordinate their own actions with the document's use. Moreover, as the two fragments reveal, patients are not without resources in (re)shaping how doctors might align to their talk and provide rather different, and perhaps more suitable, forms of co-participation. Reading or writing the record therefore has to be accomplished with regard to ongoing demands and activity of patients, where patients are highly sensitive to the moment-by-moment accomplishment of the document's use.

Parallel considerations arise with the use of the computer system during the consultation. Like the paper record, the patient has limited access to the computer system. He may be unable to see what is being written or read, and may have limited understanding of relevance to his complaint. He can however see and hear, the doctor using the keyboard, and can discriminate where the other is looking and even what he may be looking at. As in other settings, co-participants can use whatever may be available to them to make sense of the activity of the other, and, in surprisingly delicate yet systematic ways, will attempt to produce their own actions with regard to the real-time accomplishment of the activities of others. In the case at hand, for example, we have found that patients may attempt to co-ordinate production of their utterances with the quick, bleating sounds of the printer, or treat visible screen changes as potential boundaries within the doctor's use of the system. Or, for example, consider the following fragment, drawn from Greatbatch et al. (1995), in which the patient juxtaposes an utterance with the doctor typing.

Fragment 2.2   Transcript 1

```
Dr:    . . . is all connected (0.2) with uhm (0.7) with ⌐all this this
P:                                                      ⌊(          )
Dr:    this worry and stress. °hhhhhhhh uhm
       (3.1)
P:     You see if I could – I'd be all right if I could just – you know sleep.
```

The doctor enters information into the system as he summarises the underlying reasons for the patient's symptoms, namely 'worry and stress', and continues to slowly type through the ensuing in-breath and silence. Towards the end of the silence, the doctor presses the carriage return key with his right hand and gazes at the keyboard. As he releases the key, the doctor lifts his right hand and turns away from the keyboard. Just as the key is released and the hand raised, the patient produces his utterance 'you see if I could . . .'; an utterance which raises an important aspect of his difficulties and hints to a particular solution.

Fragment 2.2   Transcript 2

Dr strikes   Dr raises hand
key   from keyboard

```
Dr:    hhh uhm ----------, ----------, ----------, -
P:                                     You see if I could I'd be a
```

As with the paper record, both patient and doctor are not only sensitive to the use of document, but sensitive to how the other orients to its use. In the following fragment, for example, not only does the patient co-ordinate his contributions with the doctor's use of the system, but the doctor himself is sensitive to the patient's attempt to talk whilst he enters information.

Fragment 2.3   Transcript 1

```
P:    I did occasionally go to him:: (.) for: (0.2) sleeping tablets::
Dr:   Ye⌈rs:
P:       ⌊(hh)but not often.
Dr:   Ri:ght
      (0.6)
P:    And °er. (0.3) then again it was only prescription for: (0.2) maybe
      a weeks::: (0.6) supply just to get me back into ⌈(0.2) so: . . .
Dr:                                                    ⌊Okay: . . .
```

As we join this fragment, the doctor has begun to enter the details of a prescription for the patient. As the patient utters 'occasionally' the doctor's left hand rises from the keyboard, and the patient begins to turn to the doctor, as two keys are hit. As the patient pauses, the doctor appears to delay further key strokes until the patient continues, and then just as the word 'sleeping' begins to be uttered, the doctor continues to type. In the transcript, the key strokes are represented by '❑'.

Fragment 2.3   Transcript 2

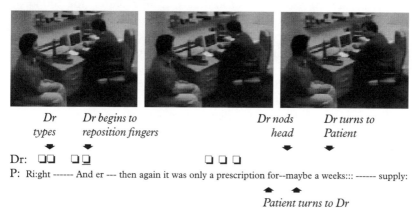

| Dr | Dr begins to | | Dr nods | Dr turns to |
| types | reposition fingers | | head | Patient |

```
Dr:  ❑❑    ❑❑                    ❑ ❑ ❑
P:   Ri:ght ------ And er --- then again it was only a prescription for--maybe a weeks::: ------ supply:
```

Patient turns to Dr

On the word 'right' the doctor produces a sequence of 4 key strokes. The key strokes have a rhythm: 2 quick, 2 slow, the first 2 projecting the second 2, and the fourth as final stroke. The strokes project the completion of the sequence on the fourth, and on the fourth stroke the doctor begins to reposition his fingers. Just as the sequence is hearably complete and the doctor begins to lift his fingers, the patient produces 'And', projecting continuation. The doctor continues to type whilst the patient is uttering 'prescription'. On the word 'maybe' the patient begins to turn towards the doctor. As he does, the doctor stops typing, and, whilst retaining his orientation towards the screen, nods. Despite the typing being arrested and the head nod, the patient withholds further talk, and the doctor turns from the screen, to the patient. At that moment the patient continues with the word 'supply'.

The patient therefore is able to anticipate potential boundaries in the activity of the doctor, and juxtapose talk with the developing course of the computer's use. The doctor is not insensitive to the patient's attempt to co-ordinate his talk with the activity. It is interesting to note that the doctor himself treats the patient's pause as demanding some form of alignment, and with the head nod failing to encourage further talk, temporally orients away from the computer to the patient.

With both the paper and computerised record, therefore, we find patients developing practical discriminations concerning the developing course of the activity with the document, and in various ways attempting to co-ordinate their own conduct with its use. Moreover, the document's use, that is the ways in which it is read and 'written' is highly sensitive to the patient's conduct, and the sort of ongoing demands for co-participation he or she may (attempt to) place on the doctor. The two artefacts are not, however, equivalent in this respect. Their use requires different types of action, and the separation of keyboard from monitor, the sound of typing, the particle visibility of the screen and the like, all provide different sorts of resources for making sense of the doctor's activity, or for that matter accomplishing the activity in interaction with a co-participant. Moreover, unlike the paper record, the computer is an 'active' domain; indeed, some doctors suggest that is not unlike having a third participant in the consultation. Consider the following example. We join the action as the doctor begins entering details of the prescription.

Fragment 2.4

Dr:	Right.	*Dr types, then as a screen-*
	(4.7)	*change occurs, turns to the*
		paper records
Dr:	Well your blood-pressure is absolutely perfect	
	at the moment. I mean providing that you're	
	not getting any- any problems with the	*Screen changes*
	medication I think you should continue-	
	continue them now.	*Screen changes end*

P: Oh yes (⌐)   *Dr turns to screen*
         └*((Computer Beep))*   *Patient looks at screen*

Dr: Do you need the GTN tablets today or not.   *Dr points to screen*
      (.)
Dr: Have you got enough or
P: Well I've got some
      but I've had them or- uh=   *Dr looks at screen*
P: =(⌐)
Dr: └ Right well I -
      throw- throw those ones   *Dr types*

The delivery of the doctor's favourable comments on the patient's blood-pressure is juxtaposed with the beginning of a series of screen changes. The completion of these changes and the accompanying beep draws the doctor's gaze from the patient to the computer. The sound and the doctor's response interrupts the patient's reply. Rather than developing the discussion concerning the improved blood-pressure, the doctor's enquiry concerning the GTN tablets is occasioned by the next item and prompt appearing on the screen. Thus, as soon as the system is ready for the entry of further information, the doctor turns to the monitor and shifts the topic to request the information necessary for the completion of the prescription. The doctor's actions, and the information he requests from the patient, are organised with regard to the operation of the system rather than discussion of the patient's illness and its management.

In co-ordinating their conduct with the computer, doctors exhibit a curious ability to anticipate the completion of certain system functions. For example, in fragment 2.4, it is interesting to note that the doctor returns his gaze to the screen to coincide with the completion of the various changes that have occurred. The change in orientation anticipates, rather than responds to, the screen change. The precision timing involved in such cases may be based on not only becoming familiar with just how long it takes the computer to perform particular functions, but also the doctor's ability to remain sensitive to screen changes whilst simultaneously looking at the patient. Indeed, the ability to remain peripherally aware of the computer, and in particular the screen, whilst engaged in seemingly unrelated activities, is an important aspect of the ways in which practitioners become increasingly able to use the computer during the consultation itself.

While both the paper record and the new system are used within the consultation, and inform the ways in which patient and doctor interact with each other, the computer raises one or two additional issues. In the first instance, its lack of mobility, in particular the difficulty in positioning the computer to enable it to be read or written with regard to the ongoing demands of the interaction, undermines the possibility of 'background-ing' activities with the record. Secondly, the separation of keyboard and monitor, dividing the domain where information is entered from where it is read, introduces additional demands when information is being entered into the system. It requires the doctor to successively glance between the keyboard and the screen to determine whether there are any mistakes or errors. Thirdly, and perhaps most importantly, unlike the paper record, the computer, in particular the screen, is an 'active' domain. The screen not only changes appearance when it undertakes some operation, sometimes catching the eye of the patient or occasioning action from the doctor, but the entry of information is organised through a series of 'prompts' offered by the system itself. These prompts can serve to encourage the doctor to complete the next action in a sequence of system actions, and in consequence undermine his ability to listen to the patient and participate in the coherent development of talk on a topic. It is not surprising, therefore, that doctors complain that having the computer is almost like introducing a third party into the consultation. The system is constituted by the participants as an active domain within the local environment of activity which places constraints on their own conduct.

2.10   Formalising the 'informal'

These textual and interactional difficulties are not simply the product of a poorly designed system. Indeed, one can see that the system in question was carefully designed to reproduce many of the properties of the paper record. Whilst inevitably using conventional hardware, a keyboard and screen, the system preserves the classes and categories of items within an entry which are ordinarily found in the traditional medical records. It builds in a certain economy to an entry, restricting the amount of free text and providing abbreviations for prespecified diagnostic categories. It also provides an important distinction between treatments for chronic and acute troubles so that the general practitioner can differentiate the status of the various illnesses that a patient might be suffering. However, the system formalises the components that are routinely found in, or retriev-able from, the paper record. It attempts to tidy or polish the record, to make certain that each entry does indeed include the information that practitioners routinely expect to find in the record, namely details con-cerning diagnosis and management, information which it is widely accepted is essential to good general practice. In formalising the contents of the record, and removing the inconsistencies and ambiguities found in the traditional paper card, the computer system has begun to produce a database that some might believe is more reliable and consistent, which might provide reliable information for research and on which to base managerial and financial recommendations and decisions.

In trying to improve the medical record, the design of the system ignores the practical reasons which account for the messy and seemingly idiosyncratic character of the original paper documents. In a sense, the design of the system reflects a rigorous, but limited, requirements analysis; an analysis which is insensitive to the ways in which the documents are written and read within the practicalities of the consultation. The relevant classes and categories of information have been identified, but the practices through which the document is written, read and used within the consultation have been largely ignored. By ignoring why the record is as it is, the design fails to recognise that the very consistencies and inconsistencies which have been identified are themselves the products of systematic and socially organised practices. By ignoring these practices, the design not only discounts the indigenous rationality oriented to by the doctors themselves in their producing and reading of the records, but fails to recognise that such practices are themselves inextricably embedded in the day-to-day constraints of *in situ* medical work. This is not to suggest that doctors cannot change the ways in which they produce and read records, indeed, that is just what they are trying to do in using the system at the present time. Rather, it is to argue that the troubles they encounter in using the system may themselves be a consequence of attempting to introduce procedures which are insensitive to the local, practical constraints of professional medical work and the ways in which information in the medical records is used in the consultation.

VAMP was developed and deployed in the United Kingdom during the 1980s. The Government at that time was attempting to curtail expenditure on the National Health Service and encourage private funding for new initiatives. Consistent with this programme, the funding for VAMP did not derive directly from government but rather was a private initiative supported indirectly by major pharmaceutical companies. The VAMP system was provided free of charge to doctors in exchange for a commitment by doctors to use the technology for a certain period, following the various strictures embodied in the system, and to make the patient data, duly anonymised, available for sale by the company. Little needs to be said about the potential value of the data in question. VAMP, for a substantial cost, could not only provide pharmaceutical firms with a generalised database concerning the disease distribution and prescribing habits of Britain's general practitioners, but also identify trends in particular practices. Unfortunately, however, the design of the system was subject to two, almost incompatible, demands: to provide, on the one hand, a technology which would enhance the everyday consultative practice of individual general practitioners; on the other, a system which would generate systematic and consistent data, easily manipulated into the relevant categories for a database. To reverse Garfinkel's (1967) famous dictum, we find 'bad' organisational reasons, for 'good' clinical records.

The computerised record undoubtedly provides, in one sense, a more consistent and seemingly reliable record. Each entry does indeed contain an assessment or diagnosis, and treatment information contains all the relevant details concerning the name, strength, quantity and frequency of a particular drug. Whether the data are more accurate or reliable than the information contained in the paper record is open to question, since practitioners are no longer able to preserve the uncertainty and ambivalence which is central to much medical decision making, even in general practice. The formal categories of information are used, but whether they reflect a true, or more reliable, incidence of disease, is a moot point. More importantly, by subjecting the design of the system to demands which are extraneous to the practicalities of day-to-day medical practice, VAMP fails to support the ways in which practitioners use the record in their day-to-day dealings with patients.

In this light it is unfortunate, though not surprising, to find that in many practices doctors continue to use the traditional medical record. Whilst they document the formal diagnosis and prescription details on the computer, they use the paper record to add small items of information which clarify or provide particular impressions of the consultation. They also read, and continue to use information, from the paper record during the consultation; indeed it remains in many cases an important resource for diagnosis and treatment. Unfortunately however, the necessity to use the computerised system, given free of charge, in exchange for providing the relevant data, has begun to undermine the reliability of the information gathered in the paper record. In particular, the presence of the alternative system has introduced more variability into the production of the entries for the paper records, so, whilst practitioners can rely upon their own entries, the types of information gathered by colleagues may not necessarily be consistent. These problems are exacerbated by the commitment to using the VAMP system to issue prescriptions and thereby log treatment details. Doctors also do not necessarily enter treatment details on the patient record, so that intraclass defeasibility and the *Gestalt* of the traditional entry is not necessarily available. Sadly, therefore, despite attempting to preserve the traditional record in the face of the difficulties encountered by the system, the possibility that some information may be omitted undermines their potential usefulness for everyday consultative practice.

Above all, it is desired that folder contents be permitted to acquire whatsoever meaning the readership can invest them with when various documents are 'combinatorially' played against and in search of alternative interpretations in accordance with the reader's developing interests on the actual occasion of reading them. Thus the actual event, when it is encountered under the auspices of the possible use to be made of it, furnishes, on that occasion, the definition of the document's significance. Thereby, the list of folder documents is open ended and can be indefinitely long. Questions of overlap and duplication are irrelevant. Not only do they not arise but questions of overlap cannot be assessed until the user knows, with whatever clarity or vagueness, what he wants to be looking for and, perhaps, why. (Garfinkel (1967: 204))

2.11 Discussion

Writing and reading medical records in general medical practice relies upon a body of procedure and reasoning through which doctors are able to economically assemble a body of clinical data which is of practical import to their day-to-day consultative work. The ways in which the records are produced parallel the ways in which they are read, or rendered intelligible, and the data which are gathered are designed to flexibly serve a variety of practical problems and consultative concerns. General practitioners have 'entitled use of the records', the socially organised competencies to produce an intelligible and inferentially rich document which is of practical relevance to their working lives. The materials gathered in the medical record cards, at least until recently, were indeed of little use to researchers, or to managers who wished to develop more rigorous methods of allocating financial resources. This is not to suggest that the paper records were ideal, or that developments in computing technology cannot serve to enhance professional practice and provide a more reliable and wide-ranging body of data for diagnosis and the management of illness. Far from it; as we will discuss in chapter eight, even a brief consideration of the practical ways in which doctors assemble and read the records within the framework of everyday consultative work can suggest a range of considerations for the requirements or design of more interesting, useful and less disruptive technology. By identifying the categories and classes of information which occur or can be found in the medical record card, whilst treating the practices and reasoning for its production and intelligibility as epiphenomenal, VAMP attempts to formalise the informal, and undermines the very activities which in part it is designed to serve. The very fact that practitioners are prepared to increase their work load, by continuing to update the paper record alongside the computer-based system, perhaps reveals, more than any other observation, the impoverished environment provided by the computer system.

VAMP is a practical problem for the general practitioners, and over the past few years, despite the various attempts to improve the system by adding extra facilities and 'windows', we gather there is still some dissatisfaction with the system and a reluctance to abandon documenting both diagnostic and prognostic information of the paper records. VAMP also points to some rather interesting academic issues with regard to the ways in which we examine and understand the interaction between human beings and computers. Simply with respect to method, it is unlikely, for example, that either experimental research, or interviews with general practitioners, which were undoubtedly undertaken as part of the requirements process for VAMP, would reveal the indigenous practices and reasoning which inform the (unremarkable) production and intelligibility of the medical record. Indeed, in our own experience, whilst general practitioners have a rough idea, if you ask them, concerning how they use and assemble the medical records, they are largely unable to explicate just how they write and read clinical data or use them in interaction with patients. Such practices are indeed 'tacit', 'taken for granted', 'seen but unnoticed', and yet an essential and accountable feature of everyday professional medical work.

It is also not clear that other approaches which might develop more 'intelligent' systems to support medical work, through techniques like 'knowledge elicitation', 'knowledge analysis' and 'knowledge engineering', would reveal such socially organised and indigenous practices and reasoning which appear essential here. Even in developing less complex systems, like VAMP, developers make use of a model of human conduct, particularly in terms of a user's tasks or goals, or as critiqued by Suchman (1987), of 'plans', that is common within AI and HCI. Such an orientation is based upon the idea that the 'user', in this case the general practitioner, is a creature that follows certain prespecified rules.

It would appear that the VAMP system reflects a model of human conduct and the 'user' which permeates a range of complex technologies and academic approaches to both requirements analysis and human–computer interaction. It presupposes that the individual general practitioner follows a stable set of rules to produce a particular goal, namely a reliable and consistent body of medical data; the entries in the record. The goal, the ideal outcome, and the rules rely on the data which one might ordinarily find in the record. A number of issues arise. In the first place, as we hope to have shown, producing entries in medical records does not simply consist of following a collection of prespecified rules, but rather involves the use of a complex set of practices which are fundamentally oriented to the ways in which the 'data' will be read and used. Secondly, the ways in which the entries are assembled, with regard to particular circumstances and the 'contingencies at hand', are treated as epiphenomenal when considering the conduct of the 'users'. Thirdly, the ways in which 'rules', 'procedures' and 'reasoning' are thoroughly embedded in the practicalities of everyday medical work, rather than being seen as generalised cognitive abilities, also disappear from view. In this way, therefore, we can see the way in which VAMP, and one suspects certain approaches in AI and HCI, may not simply misconceive the user, ignoring a complex array of professional and common-sense competence that he or she brings to bear in reading and writing a document, but, in Garfinkel's (1967) terms, treats the general practitioner, the user, as a judgmental or cultural dope:

By 'cultural dope' I refer to the man-in-the-sociologist's society who produces the stable features of the society in compliance with pre-established and legitimate alternatives of action that the common culture provides. The 'psychological dope' is the man-in-the-psychologist's-society who produces the stable features of the society by choices amongst alternative courses of action that are compelled on the grounds of psychiatric biography, conditioning history, and the variables of mental functioning. The common feature in the use of these 'models of man' is the fact that courses of common sense rationalities of judgement which involve the person's use of common sense knowledge of social structures over the temporal 'succession' of here and now situations are treated as epiphenomenal. (Garfinkel (1967: 68))

It is likely that, in both practical and academic research, the problems of methods for system design and development, and in AI and HCI, cannot be separated from the misconception of the user. By paying only cursory attention to the circumstances in which computers will be used when developing 'requirements', or in arguing that science can only be achieved through the application of experimental methodology, conventional system design can, in large part, ignore how technologies are used in the everyday practical circumstances of the workplace. Circumscribing the domain in this way, treating the everyday world as beyond consideration, allows AI and HCI to preserve their commitment to, and ultimate aim of describing, generic cognitive abilities which are insensitive to the practicalities of particular tasks and activities. The circumstances of use have been cast from the analytic domain, and, in consequence, the socially organised, situationally sensitive, practice and reasoning which feature in the production and intelligibility of mundane activities, such as reading a record card, disappear from view.

Indeed, in this light it is unclear whether it is appropriate to maintain too narrow a focus on the interaction between a computer and the single human user. In the medical consultation, there are various other relationships which need to be considered: not only the real-time 'interactions' of both doctor and patient with the computer, but also the interrelationships of activities between doctors made possible at different times through the paper and electronic documents. Taking these relationships into account necessitates a recharacterisation of the ways in which human–computer interaction is usually considered. It may also imply some novel technological considerations that go beyond the design of interfaces between a computer and an individual user. In particular, reflecting upon the socially organised practices and reasoning of participants in real-world settings may suggest more radical considerations when developing technologies to support both asynchronous and real-time collaboration between individuals.

With the emergence of CSCW, we have witnessed a growing interest in 'social' aspects of technology, though, at present, there is a strong commitment to the 'group' and, to a lesser extent, to conventional role theory. One danger for CSCW is that, in preserving a version of the 'social' as characterised by group behaviour and role fulfilment, the individual 'interacting' with a single, stand-alone system remains the provenance of HCI. The medical record cards in general practice, and the difficulties associated with the deployment of VAMP, perhaps raise additional issues which are of relevance to CSCW and illuminate ways in which the use of a technology, whether paper or digital, even where the 'user' is alone and 'unconnected' to others, is a collaborative and socially organised activity. In the case at hand for example, the production of the record is oriented to a particular category of recipient, or 'entitled user', namely fellow general practitioners, and the conventions which inform its production are sensitive to the ways in which the information will be read, and used, by others. The record's production is accountable, socially sanctioned and sanctionable, and the achievement of a community of practice and reasoning. The very reading of entries in the record, the ability to make sense of the materials with regard to the circumstances at hand, to be able to find 'more than what is said in so many words', to disambiguate the record, discriminate fact from opinion and the like, relies upon, and is inseparable from, socially organised practice and procedure. We can also add the use of the record, whether paper or digital, within the developing course of consultation, and the ways in which reading and writing (or typing) are embedded in, and co-ordinated with, the interaction between the patient and practitioner. To dismiss these socially organised and indigenous practices and conventions, whether for the purpose of 'scientific research' or the design and deployment of computing technology, would appear foolhardy, as if, to corrupt Garfinkel's moral, we 'ignored the walls when trying to find what's holding the roof on'.

3   Animating texts: the collaborative production of news stories

> The fact is that when the listener perceives and understands the meaning (the language meaning) of speech, he simultaneously takes an active, responsive attitude towards it, and understanding live speech, a live utterance, is inherently responsive, although the degree of this activity varies extremely.   Bakhtin (1986: 68)

3.1   Introduction

It is increasingly recognised that recent developments in digital communications and broadcast technologies will have a wide-ranging impact on conventional news media. For example, we have already witnessed new, experimental television programmes in which on-line audiences can actively participate in programmes, and agreements are currently in place to facilitate new forms of co-operation between national broadcasters, newspaper publishers and telecommunication companies. In the short term, perhaps the clearest example of the ways in which digital technologies are affecting the 'media' is illustrated by the enthusiasm with which conventional newspapers, such as the *Daily Telegraph*, *Le Monde* and the *New York Times* are providing on-line new services alongside their conventional broadsheet. These services place considerable demands on those responsible for producing the news. Journalists and editorial staff have to produce new and attractive products; they have to shape news produced for one medium, such as newspapers, for another and, increasingly, they have to tailor, in some cases the same, material for particular types of reader.

For some companies, providing electronic on-line news services for a heterogeneous readership is by no means new. There are a number of major international companies which have provided real-time, on-line news services for some years. Although their services have not been available to the general public, they have had to address many of the problems which now face their colleagues in the conventional news media. For example, they have had to consider how stories need to be designed to enable material to be read off-screen rather than from a newspaper. They have also developed services which tailor the news for a highly differentiated readership, so that the 'same' story will be received in very different forms by different readers. It is recognised that such innovations place considerable demands on personnel, and in particular require the real-time management, co-ordination and delivery of a complex array of material by journalists and editorial staff.

In this chapter, we consider the work of journalists in the financial section of one such company, namely Reuters in London. The section consists of a number of 'desks', each desk specialising in particular types of financial news. Desks receive particular stories from bureaux throughout the world, and journalists edit the material using a basic information system. They then transmit those stories to particular customers primarily based in financial institutions in London and elsewhere in Europe. Journalists edit the material alone, and yet it is critical that they remain aware of stories being handled by other journalists and on other desks in the newsroom, and, where necessary, inform colleagues of potentially relevant items they may have received. We consider how journalists co-ordinate their activities with each other and provide a coherent and satisfactory news service. In particular, we explore the ways in which journalists and editorial staff render textual material 'visible' to others within the local milieu, and remain sensitive themselves to stories being handled by their colleagues.

The type of information system used in Reuters and other companies is principally designed to allow certain forms of data to be produced by particular individuals and passed on to others, who, in turn, may add to or modify the material. The system does not support the real-time collaborative production of textual materials, nor does it allow journalists to view stories as they are actually being edited or rewritten by colleagues. To use an expression common in CSCW, the system supports 'asynchronous', not 'synchronous', interaction between individuals. The system is operated through a conventional workstation including a standard keyboard and a 14- or 21-inch monitor. The system and its conventional hardware, therefore, localises information and the activities in which journalists are engaged. The stories are read and written on screen, and it is difficult, even impossible, to see what a colleague is looking at or editing at any moment, even a colleague sitting alongside at the same desk. In a sense, therefore, the journalist would appear to be an example *par excellence* of the individual and skilful 'user' often discussed in research on human–computer interaction.

We suggested in the previous chapter that, despite their limited access to the computer-based activities of the doctor, patients would attempt to co-ordinate their contributions with the use of the system. Related issues arise within the newsroom. While colleagues may themselves attempt to 'second guess' the activity in which another is engaged, journalists can take it upon themselves to inform colleagues of potentially relevant stories, and in particular stories which may be of interest to other 'desks'. In various ways, text is transformed into talk, and talk can itself engender the production of text. Materials localised to the screen, and thereby inaccessible to others, are rendered visible, or better perhaps audible, to others within the domain, colleagues who may have some sort of professional interest in a particular story or set of events. The newsroom therefore provides an interesting opportunity to explore the relationship between talk and text, and to consider the competent use of a particular computer system which relies upon the individual's ability to co-ordinate his or her actions, in real-time, with the contributions of others. Indeed, competent use of the system necessarily involves socially organised resources through which text is written, read and co-ordinated with the contributions of others; contributions which are both 'synchronous and asynchronous'.

3.2   The setting

A number of international news agencies provide real-time, on-line information to the financial sector as well as to other customers, including television companies and newspapers. These include Blomberg, Nightrider and Reuters. Reuters is by the far the largest concern and has the most customers. It has offices in most major cities throughout the world and co-ordinating centres in London, Tokyo and New York. In London, the Financial News Section of Reuters is divided into four desks, each with its own editor, journalists and sub-editor(s). These desks are Money and Capital, Equities, Oil and Minerals, and Commodities. The desks are positioned near each other in a large open-plan office.

The principal customers of the news are the members of the major financial institutions in London and other major cities. Aside from providing a general financial news service, the aim of the editorial section is to deliver reliable and timely information of relevance to dealers and traders working in particular areas, such as in oil and minerals. Journalists on particular desks are expected to identify relevant stories for their particular customers and to tailor the news with regard to the practical interests of the members of the respective financial institutions working in particular areas. This commitment to discriminating the newsworthiness of material with regard to the interests of a particular audience is a critical feature of the journalists' work. Indeed, a few years ago Reuters introduced a practice whereby each journalist is expected to spend one day a month with one of its customers in order to become more familiar with their interests and concerns.

The desks in the editorial section receive stories from the various offices throughout the world. The journalists based in the outlying bureaux provide topic codes for the stories which allocate the material to particular desks. In this way, even before the editorial section receives a story, a journalist has made a preliminary assessment of its potential newsworthiness with regard to a particular audience. The stories are also given a priority code, which in certain circumstances involves journalists in the editorial section in London having to 'turn the story around' in less than sixty seconds. The coding allocates the story to one of the desks, where it appears in a 'basket' on the editorial screen. Journalists take stories from the basket, check their topic coding and edit the headline, the 'header' and the story. The edited story is then sent directly on-line to the relevant customers or, in the case of longer pieces, say a couple of pages or so, is passed to the sub-editor for a final check.

Individual journalists working on the various desks have a fair amount of discretion in coding, editing and prioritising stories. They largely work on stories alone, and in many cases it is unlikely that the material and its coding will be seen by colleagues before it is sent to customers. All the same, journalists are expected to remain sensitive to the potential relevance of stories to colleagues and their customers working in other areas, and to inform their fellow journalists if material is received which might bear upon their respective domains. For example, a news story addressed to Money and Capital, might also be of interest to the customers served by the journalists in Equities. In many cases, different desks will transmit different versions of the same story, even though the original material was received by one desk. At the morning editorial meetings, which review the previous day's work and discuss the more important upcoming stories of the day, budgets, possible interest-rate announcements, government defections and the like, it is not unusual for editors to criticise their colleagues for failing to inform each other of potentially relevant stories. A case in point was a press release from a company called Kleeneze concerning innovations in battery technology. The story was handled by Money and Capital, but it was felt that it also should have been picked up by Oil and Minerals, since it had important implications for lead consumption and sales. It is also assumed that journalists in outlying bureaux will often miscode, or fail to recognise the implications of particular stories for a range of other areas, and the editorial section is largely held responsible for recoding and rewriting incoming stories. Hence, the journalists in London have to assess the potential newsworthiness of a particular story with regard to both their own customers, and customers served by other desks.

The journalists therefore face an interesting problem. They receive stories which in many cases may not be received by other desks, coding and editing the story with regard to their customers and area of specialism, and also they have to consider the potential relevance of the story for colleagues and customers who have very different concerns in fields in which the journalist may have little experience or knowledge. Moreover, the stories are received on-screen, a screen the size of the monitor on a conventional personal computer, and are not visible to colleagues on one's own desk let alone those working on desks some distance away. Each desk in the editorial section receives a substantial number of stories each day, and during peak hours, say between nine and twelve o'clock, the desks may be receiving three or four stories every 5 minutes or so, some of which need to be 'turned round' in less the 60 seconds. There is not much time for consultation, and colleagues engaged in rapidly rewriting and editing stories, as one can imagine, may not necessarily welcome queries and suggestions concerning potentially relevant stories.

Journalists also need to co-operate with colleagues on their own desks. For example, in passing stories on to sub-editors it is often necessary to provide instructions concerning the ways in which the story should be handled; or, in editing a particular item, it may be important to inform colleagues of how the news is potentially relevant to other stories in the basket or news which has broken earlier that day. Decisions to make major changes to a story, its priority or topic coding, often are also done in consultation with colleagues. A case in point is when to delete a story, or 'spiking', a term still used in the electronic office. Journalists will often talk through stories with colleagues on the same desk before deciding to spike a story. Like their colleagues on other desks, however, journalists will be handling a range of different stories, dealing with problems and issues which have arisen, and may not appreciate unnecessary interruptions or interventions.

On the one hand, therefore, journalists work alone, rewriting and editing stories with regard to the interests of their particular customers, and attempting to tailor materials with regard to a distant audience. On the other hand, journalists need to work closely with colleagues, informing them of important events, and passing on stories which may be of relevance to other desks and their respective customers. This balance has to be achieved in the face of a substantial amount of material, which is received in real-time, on-screen, localised to particular desks and individual screens, and which is largely unavailable and invisible to others for whom it might be relevant within the domain. This has to be accomplished so as to not bombard colleagues with information which may be irrelevant to their readers, or may have been dealt with under the guise of another story. The fact that journalists in Reuters provide a news service which is timely, coherent and relevant, given the substantial amount of news pouring into the four desks in London, is no mean achievement.

3.3   Giving voice to the news

Given the ways in which stories are localised within the editorial office, one possible solution for journalists might be to simply call out to colleagues to inform them when particular stories are breaking. This practice is perhaps best exemplified in dealing rooms in financial institutions, where traders will, on occasion, shout important information across the dealing room, for anyone to hear (cf. Heath et al., 1994–5). Very occasionally, when major news events occur, journalists will follow a similar practice. However, whilst such a practice may seem a relatively efficient way of distributing important information rapidly to a large number of people, it is by no means the most appropriate or successful method. In the first place, it is obtrusive, especially for personnel who are engaged in writing and editing stories, and a generalised announcement does not necessarily mean that the person, or even the desk, for whom the story is relevant necessarily picks up on the news. Secondly, the relevant information cannot always be summarised in a single statement as in the dealing rooms – for example, 'Hanson on the bid' (cf. Heath et al., 1994–5) – but, rather, consists of textual stories, some of which can be quite lengthy. Thirdly, stories are not necessarily relevant to all desks and their respective customers, so that in attempting to distribute information, journalists need to be sensitive to who, within the editorial section, may have an interest in the event. Stories are analysed with regard to their potential relevance to different types of customer. In consequence, they rely on more delicate and interactionally sensitive methods of informing others of potentially relevant news stories.

Consider the following example. Things are relatively quiet in the newsroom and, as he works on a story about a fall in Israeli interest rates, Peter begins to make a joke of the text he is editing on-screen. Peter's remarks, which are produced in a pronounced Jewish accent, are not explicitly addressed to colleagues on his own desk (Money and Capital), nor to those on the adjoining desk, Equities. Whilst talking aloud, he continues to look at his monitor and edit the story.

Fragment 3.1   Transcript 1

Peter: <u>Ban</u>k of (.) <u>I</u>srael interest ra(i)te dro<u>ps</u>.
          (0.3)
Peter: Down, down, down.
          (0.4)
Peter: Didn't it do this last week.
          (13.0)

In talking aloud, Peter gives voice to the story on which he is working. Peter's remarks are loud enough to be audible to colleagues sitting on the adjoining and surrounding desks. By talking aloud, he renders aspects of the text that is documented on his screen 'publicly' accessible, or at least audible to others within the immediate location. In so doing, he does not simply talk through the text, but provides a selective rendition which animates aspects of the story, giving it the character of a joke. Interestingly, the way in which the story is voiced and animated, its light-hearted rendition coupled with Peter's continuing orientation to work on the text, does not demand that his colleagues respond, or even acknowledge, what has been said. It places no one under an obligation to respond, or, more technically, to produce a sequentially appropriate response. It identifies neither a particular recipient nor an appropriate next action or activity. The question, 'didn't it do this last week' is rhetorical, it elaborates the joke, and perhaps provides a framework for Peter's remarks, but does not demand, nor encourage, a response. In some sense, Peter's remarks render the materials on which he is working selectively 'visible' to his colleagues within the local milieu, but, through the ways in which this is accomplished, it places no one under any particular obligation to respond.

Peter continues to work on the story. Roughly twelve seconds later, Alex, who is sitting some six feet away at the Equities desk, momentarily changes his orientation. He glances towards Peter and then turns back to his own monitor. Peter appears to treat the action as relevant to the story that he voiced some moments ago. He utters 'er:::' and after pausing for one second, perhaps to relocate the potentially relevant part of the text, tells part of the story on which he is working. In the illustrations, Peter is on the right, and Alex second from the right (see transcript 2).

Peter's talk is now addressed specifically to Alex. He no longer makes a joke of the story, nor characterises the text on which he is working, but rather delivers a quote from the material itself. The quote provides a more precise and potentially factual report of the events. Peter's delivery

Fragment 3.1   Transcript 2

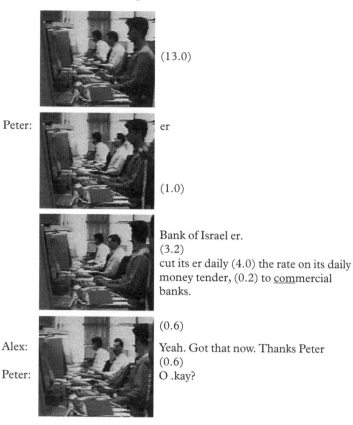

(13.0)

Peter: er

(1.0)

Bank of Israel er.
(3.2)
cut its er daily (4.0) the rate on its daily
money tender, (0.2) to <u>commercial</u>
banks.

(0.6)

Alex: Yeah. Got that now. Thanks Peter
(0.6)
Peter: O .kay?

sharply contrasts with the earlier version. It is not rendered as a joke or as a précis, but rather as part of the original, authentic story. The ways in which the talk is produced, coupled with the accompanying visual conduct, provide colleagues with the resources to differentiate the status of the two renditions and in particular their 'relationship' to the textual version of the story.

The exposition of the story is occasioned by Alex's momentary orientation to Peter. Peter treats Alex's action as requesting further information concerning the story, particularly its relevance and potential newsworthiness. Although the original joke is not specifically addressed, the informing is designed to enable Alex to receive accurate and authentic information concerning the recent change in Israeli interest rates.

It looks as if the telling is over following Alex's acknowledgement of the story with 'Yeah. Got that now. Thanks Peter.' However, some seconds later, Peter reads aloud the sentence that describes the actual fall in interest rates. By pausing in the delivery of the sentence, Peter momentarily renders the description problematic, and, on completing the sentence, he goes on to correct the story. The correction involves the speaker realigning his position to the text, from narrator to commentator. Peter differentiates his version from the original text and publicises, at least across the two desks, the editorial correction.

Fragment 3.1   Transcript 3

Peter: Half a percent, (1.2) to eleven percent.
         (0.2)
Peter: I think they mean a half a percentage point
         (15:04)
Peter: Ser̲v̲ice Jerusalem (0.5) with a <u>drop</u> copy to Nicosia, right?
         (0.7)
Alex: Yes

Finally, Peter marks the completion of the handling of the Israeli Interest Rate story by checking with Alex as to which Reuters' bureau should receive copies of the corrected version.

What begins as a joke therefore, turns out to have some serious import for news production. The Israeli Interest Rate story gets publicly corrected, distributed to more than one desk and subsequently to the customers of both Money and Capital and Equities. It also features in, and is referred to in, other stories that are handled by the two desks on that day. The story achieves its wider circulation by virtue of Peter's joke. The joke is delicately designed to establish these possibilities. It does not demand that others abandon the activities in which they are engaged or even take up the story. Rather, Peter's joke renders visible the gist of the story which he is currently editing. It momentarily displays the activity in which he is engaged. It provides colleagues with news concerning the Israeli Interest Rates, but does not project a response. The talk is produced by Peter (and treated by his colleagues) as if devoid of sequential relevance and yet invites others to consider the import of the story with respect to their own activities and responsibilities.

In gaining some indication that a colleague is interested in hearing more of the story, Peter transforms the way in which he presents the text to the others. Instead of continuing the joke, he provides an authentic rendition of the text, (re)presenting the change in interest rates. The speaker therefore differentiates the informing by virtue of the ways in which he presents the text, though in both cases it is as if he is simply reading outloud the story on the screen. In the final part of the informing, the speaker once again alters his standpoint *vis-à-vis* the text, visibly locating and correcting an error in the original copy. In rendering his activity visible, the speaker exploits, through the ways in which he talks through the story, differential standpoints with respect to the text itself. In this way he ongoingly tailors the sequential significance and sense of the story for those within the local milieu.

In this way a textual story, located temporarily on the screen, is transformed into talk, and rendered visible to others within the local domain. It informs the activities in which the journalists engage both individually and collaboratively.

3.4   Apostrophic readings

In the previous example, a journalist talks aloud as he is working on a story. In the light of a relatively innocuous action by a colleague, the journalist delivers a more detailed exposition of the story. The exposition contrasts with the humour of the reading; the exaggerated Jewish accent is abandoned as Peter provides his colleague with details of the story and in particular the specifics of the ways in which it may be of particular relevance to the Equities desk. Peter, therefore, does not simply make visible, through reading and explicating the story, the text on which he is working and the activity in which he is engaged, but, rather, through the talk, differentiates elements of the text with regard to participation of the (potential) recipient.

The next fragment illustrates the ways in which a story is characterised, even when the characterisation is itself a quote or rendition from the text, and may be transformed, not only through successive utterances, but within the developing course of a single turn at talk. Differentiating and transforming the text in this way, is embedded in, and co-ordinated with, the actions of the potential recipient(s) and the ways in which they participate in the text's rendition.

In fragment 3.2, Peter returns to the desk after his lunch break. A fellow journalist on the Capital and Money desk begins to tell Peter what he is working on.

Fragment 3.2   Transcript 1

((*Peter sits down*))

Jan: I'm looking at this <u>Nigeria Crisis</u>. (.) I don't think it (.) tells us anything we don't know already.
         (4.2)
Jan: There's people saying i(t). it's unclear why the Government has opted for new elections.

Peter: Well then spike it. It's crap.
Jan: erm (0.8) I fear the way things are going, said a cigarette vendor.
          (.)
Peter: A cigarette vendor?
          (0.2)
Peter: He's one of the er major analysts we spoke to?
Jan: He's one of our key sources.

          .
          .
          .

Jan: No I don't think we need this.

Jan announces that he is working on the Nigerian crisis and raises a question concerning the story's newsworthiness. He receives no response from Peter, and continues by giving a flavour of the story which reveals perhaps why it might not be worthwhile sending it out. Although Jan's utterance serves to suggest that he is continuing with the exposition, Peter takes up the possibility raised in the introduction, namely, deleting or spiking the story. At the same time, Peter remains oriented towards his own screen and appears reluctant to engage in further discussion concerning this story of the Nigerian crisis.

Despite Peter's response, and his seeming lack of commitment to participating further in the exposition, Jan attempts to encourage his colleague to listen to further details concerning the story. He produces 'erm', suggesting perhaps that he is about continue, but withholds the projected utterance. Roughly one-third of a second into the pause, Peter lifts his hands from the keyboard and turns from his own monitor towards Jan.

Fragment 3.2   Transcript 2

J   P

Erm   I fear the way things are going

Jan treats Peter's actions as displaying his willingness to listen to the story. He continues to talk about the Nigerian crisis but transforms the way in which the text is rendered visible within the talk. Rather than describe, in his own words, what the story says, Jan quotes a quote from the text. The talk achieves the character of a quote by virtue of the way in which Jan conducts himself both vocally and visually. He remains oriented towards the monitor, even after Peter has turned towards him, and appears to read the text. Moreover, the way in which the text is spoken of – in particular, the use of the first-person pronoun, the present tense and the expression 'I fear' – displays to Peter that the quote is itself a quote from the story. In the way in which Jan talks, therefore, he appears to produce a seemingly authentic version of the text itself; a quote that is presented as a simple, unsoiled voicing of the voice quoted in the story.

Jan, however, transforms the story and his own standpoint towards the text. The ascription of the quote to a cigarette vendor delightfully changes the telling into a joke. It not only underscores retrospectively the absurdity of the quote, but also reconfigures the speaker's position *vis-à-vis* the talk he has produced; it even renders questionable the authenticity of the quote which it now turns out was delivered 'tongue in cheek'. The joke, of course, turns on the idea that a quote from a cigarette vendor would feature in a Reuters's story and is 'newsworthy'. Through the ascription, the speaker's voice is reconstituted retrospectively, and prospectively reconfigures the nature of the activity and its sequential relevance.

Transforming the telling into a joke undermines the newsworthiness of the story. It is no longer relevant, at least in the next turn(s), for the co-participant(s) to address the import of the story with respect to its newsworthiness, but rather to recognise and respond to Jan's joke. Rather than deal with the organisational relevancies of the story, Peter takes up the joke delightfully, juxtaposing 'cigarette vendor' with 'major analyst', with Jan in turn producing 'key sources'.

Although Jan's remarks may appear more concerned with telling a funny story than dealing with the news, like fragment 3.1, the exchange has some relevance for the work in which the participants are engaged. It not only informs Peter what story Jan is working on, but also allows Peter to know which story he should take next from the basket. Moreover, Jan's remarks provide Peter with a characterisation of the story, a characterisation that suggests that the story might be worth spiking and invites Peter's response. Although Jan may be more concerned than Peter with whether the story is worth salvaging, he establishes Peter's support in spiking the story if he so wishes. By the completion of the episode, not only is the story spiked, but all those working on the desk know that it has been spiked and know why. In one sense, therefore, no matter how jocular or trivial Jan's remarks might seem, they provide the foundation for a collaborative decision not to transmit a news story concerning the ongoing crisis in Nigeria. This might seem unimportant to us now, but for those in the trading floors in the City of London, financial services and elsewhere at that time, the decision to spike the story may well have been consequential. It is not surprising, therefore, that you might seek the thoughts of your colleagues, however indirectly, before taking such a decision.

The articulation of the story is accomplished progressively, in the light of both the speaker's ability to establish particular forms of co-participation and the recipient's willingness to co-operate as an interested listener. An important feature of the story's articulation is the speaker's shifting alignment to the on-screen text displayed within the talk. The different standpoints that the speaker adopts in relation to the story and particular components within the material, including reported speakers and their utterances, are contingent on, and accomplished with respect to, the (co-) participation of a colleague(s). Moreover, in the light of particular forms of co-participation, the speaker not only can articulate particular 'voices' and reconfigure these 'voices' retrospectively but, in so doing, transforms, within the articulation of a single utterance, the activity in which he is engaged. In consequence, the sequential and interactional import of particular actions, and the trajectories of conduct which emerge therein, transform as Jan shifts the way he voices the text.

These observations are of potential relevance not only to our understanding of the ways in which computing technologies feature in the conduct of individuals who are working together in the same location, but also to other, less 'practical' concerns. For example, in recent years, we have witnessed a growing recognition, in various disciplines, of the importance of the work of Bakhtin (1986) on our understanding of text, language and social interaction. Bakhtin's rich and insightful descriptions of the 'active listener' have had a profound influence on literary criticism and increasingly are informing work in social psychology (see, Iser, 1985; Wertsch, 1986). In the case at hand, we can see other ways in which the 'active listener' is critical to language use and interaction. The articulation of talk as it emerges, and its rendition of a text, are sensitive to, and co-ordinated with, the conduct of the listener, just as the conduct of the 'recipient' is 'responsive to', and co-ordinated with, the actions of the speaker. The 'product' of the actions and activities in this fragment, the story's telling and the deletion of the material, is the outcome of complex and emerging interaction between the participants.

3.5   Viewing stories together

In some cases, journalists encourage colleagues not simply to listen to a story on which they are working, but to look at, even read, the text with them. These collaborative viewings are a recurrent feature of the journalists' work, seemingly more concerned with generating a discussion concerning particular stories rather than actually working on the text together. Consider the following example. It is drawn from the Equities desk and begins with one of the journalists, Paul, noticing that IBM have just announced massive lay-offs.

Fragment 3.3   Transcript 1

Paul: °hhhh <u>We</u>ll th<u>at</u> certainly is (a) <u>de</u>finition of do<u>wn</u>sizing.
          (0.7)
Nick: What thirty five thousand?
          (.)
Paul: Yeap
          (0.3)
Nick: How many,⌜out of. how
Paul: ⌞ <u>Fifty</u> <u>thousand</u> in a(v) (.) le<u>ft</u> or committed to leaving in
          ninety three an through actions taken today(.) another <u>thir</u>ty five
          thousand (.) are leaving I.B.M.
Nick: Bloody Hell
Viv: What is that in terms of . . .
              .
              .
              .
Paul: It used to be three hundred and fifty thousand (.) it may

Nick is reading some material on his screen. Rather than bluntly announcing the story and risk interrupting the activity in which his colleague is engaged, Paul attempts to delicately seek Nick's commitment as a recipient, before telling the tale. A moment or so before remarking on the lay-offs, Paul firstly turns towards Nick and then towards Nick's focal domain his colleague's screen. Producing a loud in-breath, Paul then returns his gaze towards his own monitor.

Paul's actions occasion a shift in orientation by his colleague. Nick turns and looks at Paul, just at the moment that Paul's gaze arrives at his own monitor, where the story is based. As Nick turns, Paul begins to speak. Without interrupting his colleague, Paul then establishes a potentially willing listener even before he begins to speak. He also establishes a listener oriented towards a potential speaker who is looking at his own screen, thereby revealing perhaps that whatever is going to be said is related to on-screen material. Having encouraged Nick to temporarily abandon the activity in which he was engaged, Paul delivers a comment on the story displayed on his monitor.

Having secured Nick's alignment towards the initial remark, Paul's comment may itself be designed to secure his co-operation in a more detailed exposition of IBM's cutbacks. The comment 'We<u>ll</u> th<u>at</u> certainly is <u>de</u>finition of do<u>wn</u>sizing.' has the flavour of what Sacks referred to as a story preface, an utterance which projects a story, gives a flavour of its interest and attempts to secure the relevant alignment of a recipient (see Sacks, 1992). Whilst revealing that he has seen the figures, Nick's response ('What thirty five thousand?') elicits confirmation from Paul. He then momentarily glances at Paul's screen, and asks for further information 'How many, out of. how'.

In this way, Paul establishes a recipient who is not only prepared to listen to the details of IBM's decline but is also visually oriented towards him. Paul exploits the recipient's commitment by delivering an extensive quote from the story. Even so, as the quote emerges, the perturbation 'a(v) (.) le<u>ft</u>' encourages Nick to shift how he participates in the exposition. In juxtaposition with the perturbation, Nick turns and looks at his colleague's monitor, the source of the story.

Paul therefore successfully secures the co-operation of a colleague, not only to listen to the story, but also to actually look (or rather attempt to look) at the material on the screen. In the following frames, Paul is on the left, and Nick is second from the left.

Fragment 3.3   Transcript 2

Paul: <u>hhh</u>h <u>Well</u> <u>that</u>

certainly is (a) <u>defi</u>nition of do<u>wn</u>sizing.

(0.7)

Nick: What thirty five thousand?

Nick's conduct provides a foundation for the story's exposition. In turning towards the screen, temporarily abandoning the activity in which he is engaged, Nick displays an interest in, and commitment to, listening to the story. Moreover, by turning towards the text, and not looking at the speaker, Nick avoids placing his colleague under an obligation to return the gaze, and thereby undermine Paul's ability to read the material out loud (cf. Heath, 1986). Mutual alignment towards the text provides an appropriate interactional environment for one participant to read aloud to another and thereby tell the story.

Towards the end of 'thirty five thousand', Nick begins to turn back to his own monitor. Paul momentarily pauses in the telling of the text. The next component 'are leaving IBM' is produced with a downward intonation and as a potential completion of the relevant or interesting part of the story. Nick's shift in orientation perhaps encourages Paul to complete the informing, and, in response, he mumbles, 'Bloody Hell'. It is left to Viv (the editor on the desk) to develop the discussion; she elicits further information about the story and they go on to discuss its implications. Viv elicits just the information that Nick was asking for earlier, namely what proportion of IBM's work force is being sacked. As the discussion continues, Viv announces that Paul should write a feature on the IBM story.

So, whilst the original telling may simply be concerned with pointing out a certain irony concerning the behaviour of IBM and the stock market, the voicing of the text brings the story to the attention of others on the desk and leads to a feature which may not otherwise have been written. This moment of 'small-talk' turns out to have some significance for the organisation of the work in which the participants are engaged, particularly in collaboratively deciding what to do with a story. Many of the tellings have this sort of character. In various ways they render textual material, based on-screen and largely unavailable to others within the newsroom, 'visible' in particular ways. These outlouds, informings and renditions do not simply allow others to have an idea of the activity in which a colleague is currently engaged, though this can be important, but rather flavour the stories in ways that are potentially of interest to the conduct of others. In many cases, such tellings may simply lead to a story being spiked, and recognisably so, but, in other instances, it may lead to news which would not otherwise be available being transmitted to customers or, as in the last case, features being written on topics which otherwise would remain passing news items. So, whilst these tellings might appear slight, they can have a profound impact on the production of news and in turn the behaviour of the market.

3.6   Forestalling a rendition

Occasionally speakers fail to establish an appropriate orientation from a colleague for the exposition of a story. Consider the following example in which Barry talks through a story he is working on: a typhoon which is gathering in Argentina. Meanwhile, Celia, his potential recipient, is hurriedly editing a piece on tin mining.

Fragment 3.4   Transcript 1

Barry: I've <u>got</u> a bit <u>more</u> on the:: erm,
          (1.0)
Barry: This
          (.)
Barry: the Typhoon. It's going to (con) <u>su</u>per typhoon,
Celia: Oh <u>God</u>.

          .
          .
          .

Barry: Um yeh.
          (9.0)
Barry: °a hundred and forty knot winds

Barry and Celia sit alongside each other on the Commodities desk. Whilst Celia is typing, Barry begins to talk. The utterance 'I've got a little more on the typhoon' suggests that it is being built to secure a recipient prior to delivering the gist of the story (cf. Sacks, 1992). Although Barry is unable to see exactly what Celia is working on, he positions his utterance so as to maximise the possibility of gaining some commitment. It is juxtaposed with Celia momentarily removing her hands from the keyboard.

Unfortunately, as Barry begins to speak, Celia once again begins to type. Barry, however, does not abandon his attempt to tell Celia about the typhoon gathering in Argentina. Rather, he attempts to encourage Celia to temporarily suspend the activity in which she is engaged and to participate, at least minimally, in the exposition of the tale.

Barry leans sideways towards Celia while simultaneously exaggerating his orientation towards his own monitor. His bodily movement appears to display his attention to the text, whilst bringing his colleague within the auspices of the ecological frame defined by his physical orientation (see transcript 2).

As Barry refashions his orientation with regard to Celia and the local environment, his colleague shifts posturally towards his monitor. However, she continues with the activity in which she is engaged, typing and looking at her own screen. Celia's bodily reorientation appears

Fragment 3.4   Transcript 2

Celia   Barry

Barry: I've <u>got</u>   a bit <u>more</u> on the:: erm,

delightfully to respond to Barry's demands, providing some indication that she is prepared to listen, whilst simultaneously allowing her to continue the activity in which she is principally engaged.

Fragment 3.4   Transcript 3

Barry reorients

--I've <u>got</u> a bit <u>more</u> on the:: erm,--------this-the

Celia ceases   *Celia reorients*
and again   *'dividing' her physical*
starts typing   *reorientation*

Celia's attempt to divide her orientation, continuing to edit the story whilst providing Barry with some display that she is prepared to listen to his exposition, fails to satisfy her partner. He attempts to secure more commitment from his colleague. Prior to completing the preface to the story Barry stretches the word 'the::', produces an 'erm' and pauses.

Such perturbations within the delivery of an utterance are utterly conventional devices through which speakers attempt to secure alignment from their recipients (cf. Goodwin, 1981; Heath, 1986). However, in the case at hand, neither the sound stretch nor the 'erm' serves to encourage Celia to provide a more wholehearted commitment to listening to the story. She continues to type and remains oriented towards her own monitor.

In the light of the recalcitrance of the potential recipient, Barry pauses, withholding the projected item and the upcoming story. Roughly half a second into the pause, Barry momentarily glances at Celia's screen. The glance may be more concerned with encouraging her to orient towards him, rather than assess the state of her current activity. As he returns his gaze to his own monitor, Celia produces a series of staggered taps on the return key, which suggests an upcoming boundary or completion point in her current activity.

Barry exploits this potential opportunity, and begins to speak precisely on the projected break in Celia's activity.

Rather than simply tell the story, Barry once again attempts to encourage Celia to upgrade her commitment to the news. He temporarily delays telling the tale, and thrusting his head towards his monitor, utters the word 'this'. Barry's visual conduct, coupled with the demonstrative pronoun, appears to be designed to show the source of the story and simultaneously encourage Celia to turn and look at his monitor (and in consequence temporarily suspend the activity in which she is engaged).

Barry's attempts to encourage his colleague to participate more fully in the exposition of the story fail. Celia once again begins to type.

Barry returns to the prior activity and completes the preceding utterance; replacing the word 'this' with 'the typhoon'. However, rather than follow his initial turn with the story it projects, a detailed exposition of the text that he has on-screen, Barry produces a description of the typhoon which attempts to make it sound even more exciting: 'it's going to (con) super↑ typhoon'. Not only does Barry's utterance delay his entry into the narrative, thereby avoiding an exposition of the story without having secured the alignment of the recipient, but the utterance itself appears to be designed to tempt Celia to abandon her activity and find out more about such an alarming typhoon. Thus, Barry produces a description of the event which potentially foreshadows more to follow if the recipient(s) were to display more commitment.

Celia's response, 'Oh God', whilst suitably appreciative of the seriousness of the typhoon, fails to provide Barry with encouragement to enter into the full-blown details of the troubles facing Argentina. Celia continues to type and look at her monitor as she delivers her reply, and gives Barry little indication that she is prepared to abandon the activity in which she is engaged to hear the tale. In the light of Celia's seeming lack of interest, Barry returns to work on, rather than regale his colleague with, the story.

Sadly, some nine seconds or so later, Barry quietly utters, under his breath, 'a hundred and forty knot winds'. Whilst this may well be the quote for which he was attempting to establish a suitable audience, by the time it is delivered, it fails to even secure an acknowledgement.

We can begin to see, therefore, that the telling of stories in the news-room is the outcome of a complex negotiation between journalists. Expositions of texts, stories and the like are not simply off-loaded, but articulated with regard to the concurrent behaviour of colleagues and their seeming interest in the materials which may be discussed. Tellers even differentiate components of the story with regard to the co-partici-pation of the recipient, and systematically attempt to secure particular forms of alignment for specific elements of the story. In the case at hand, whilst the utterance which prefigures the story is co-ordinated with a potential break in the recipient's activity, the speaker does not, at that moment, demand an immediate commitment to the telling. However, even prior to the completion of the story's preface, it is apparent that the successful articulation of the tale is contingent upon the recipient provid-ing a more intensive display of participation. In particular, given the ways in which the speaker co-ordinates his utterance and visual conduct with regard to Celia's own work on a story, Barry is most likely seeking a tem-porary suspension of his potential recipient's activity. The speaker's suc-cessive failure to establish the relevant (sought for) co-participation at specific junctures within the developing course of the activity, finds him transforming and then largely abandoning the telling.

Within this step-by-step negotiation, it is interesting to note that the teller systematically attempts to co-ordinate specific elements of his talk with his colleague's activity. The problem, however, is that Celia's activity is only visible by virtue of her orientation towards the monitor and use of the keyboard. Barry can neither see the text she is editing on-screen nor know, in any specific way, what she is actually doing, or where she is, when working on the material. Despite his limited access to Celia's activity, Barry attempts to co-ordinate aspects of his talk, and the production of the story, with his co-participant's work. In particular, he attempts to maximise the likelihood that Celia might be prepared to temporarily delay her own commitments to listen by co-ordinating the onset and delivery of utterances with potential boundaries within the activity in which she is engaged. For example, Barry positions the onset of the initiating utterance with regard to an upcoming boundary within Celia's activity; a boundary which is projected by virtue of a particular sequence of key strokes and the use of the return key. And, a little later, he produces

the key word, or topicaliser, 'the typhoon', right at the point at which
Celia momentarily reorients her body towards Barry's monitor. So, whilst
the details of Celia's actions are largely unavailable to Barry, embedded
within the concerns and practicalities of the materials on which she is
working, he attempts to systematically co-ordinate the production of the
telling with whatever he can retrieve from the 'visible' elements of his colleague's conduct.

Whilst Barry fails to establish an appropriate audience for an exposition of the story, the item he mentions does not pass unnoticed. A minute
or so later Carol seeks further information about the item from Barry,
clarifying how it fits with some weather news within another story which
has entered the basket. Some fifteen minutes later, as Barry leaves the
desk to go home, Carol asks where he put the typhoon story and to whom
it was sent. So, whilst Barry's story does not meet with much apprecia-
tion, and remains largely unexplicated, it does not turn out to have some
relevance for the production and co-ordination of news that afternoon.
The very mention of the story, and the events it describes, provide
resources to colleagues with which to deal, or even to interpret materials
which are received later that day. So, whilst the story may not be of interest at some moment in time, or at least warrant delaying an activity in
which you are engaged, the very fact that it has been displayed and overheard can provide colleagues with a way of seeing and managing subsequent stories. Indeed, not unlike the medical records, materials which are
animated at some point during the day can gain a determinate sense and
relevance with regard to subsequent events, events which might more or
less be anticipated but are largely unknown until they arrive in someone's
tray. Momentary exchanges or tellings, or simply catching someone
reading aloud parts of a story, can retrospectively be found to have some
import for an activity in which you are engaged some time later.

3.7   Discussion: texts in interaction

The production of a timely and comprehensive news service in Reuters
relies upon journalists on the editorial desks keeping each other informed
of particular stories and events. The incoming news stories are addressed
to particular desks, and it is the responsibility of journalists on those desks
to read those stories with respect to not only their own customers, but the
customers and interests of their colleagues. The journalists have to envisage who might have an interest in the stories they have received, and the
circumstances under which those stories might become relevant for
others, even though, at this moment, they would not appear to have any
bearing on their own practical concerns.

The news stories are received by particular desks, on-line. The stories are not publicly visible and the technology localises the stories to material on the screens; material which is largely invisible to others on the same desk let alone elsewhere in the editorial section. On occasions journalists will shout out information they received on-line or take the trouble to walk across the room and chat to a colleague about some potentially relevant or interesting events. In many cases, however, such direct informings are neither practical nor desirable. Journalists receive numerous stories each day and, especially during peak times, they have neither the time nor the inclination to specifically inform their colleagues of some potentially relevant news. Indeed, if journalists were to take it upon themselves to announce every story that might have some bearing on the work of their colleagues then the noise and successive interruptions would provide little time for the principal task at hand, reading, editing and transmitting the news. Moreover, it should be added that a technology, even a large screen placed in the editorial office, which simply displayed the 'headers' of all the incoming stories, would hardly help, since journalists have to read and analyse the story in order to assess whether it might be of relevance to colleagues on different desks. Even recent experiments with intelligent systems designed to analyse the incoming stories and distribute them to the appropriate journalists and customers have failed to enhance the news service. The practical intelligence and discrimination of journalists in analysing and distributing stories is critical to the successful production of the news.

The journalists selectively render visible or animate the texts on which they are working. The texts located on-screen and largely inaccessible to their colleagues are animated with regard to the practical interests of colleagues and customers. The materials are animated in such a way that, whilst journalists might themselves believe a story is critical to the practical concerns of other desks, their colleagues are given the autonomy and responsibility for deciding on the relevance, the newsworthiness, of the materials. In rendering stories visible in this way, journalists preserve the territorial and organisational rights of colleagues so that their colleagues do not necessarily have to respond to, or make anything of, the story they are being told. The ways in which journalists therefore give voice to stories have a lightness of tone. They do not demand a response, but rather provide their (potential) recipient(s) with the opportunity to reply if they so wish. They provide a gist, a sense of the news, without bombarding colleagues with information. They seek the interest and commitment of a colleague before revealing the details of a particular story. Even then, the materials are often explicated in cursory and passing fashion. It is hardly surprising that journalists often render texts visible through jokes and quips. Such objects can be treated lightly. They allow the tellers to distance themselves from imbuing the talk with unwarranted relevance, and the (potential) recipients to ignore the story if they so wish. In animating texts, journalists preserve the integrity of the activities in which others are engaged, and respect the organisational responsibility of colleagues to decide on the newsworthiness of particular stories.

It is not surprising, therefore, that in animating texts journalists are sensitive to the willingness of colleagues to listen to the story before delivering the news. Many of the tales are prefigured by a story preface or a joke which gives the flavour of the news, even whether it is important or not, before telling the tale (cf. Sacks, 1992). The preface or quip is itself often positioned with regard to the current activity, as far as it can be inferred of the potential recipient, the speaker anticipating upcoming boundaries which might avoid interruption and maximise the possibility of a colleague listening to the exposition. Failure to elicit a response or appropriate alignment from a potential recipient, can encourage a speaker to abandon a story even before its delivery.

The teller is sensitive to the conduct of the recipient not only prior to the delivery of a story, but also during its exposition. We have seen the ways in which tellers progressively establish the particular form of co-participation they require within and across utterances. So, for example, a teller might seek to establish the alignment of a recipient towards the text for the delivery of a quote, whereas a précis of the story might be delivered whilst the 'co-participant' is looking at his own monitor and editing a separate story. Moreover, in failing to secure relevant co-participation for the accomplishment of a particular type of action, such as a reading, the teller may transform the projected activity and deliver the news in a different fashion than suggested in the preceding talk. Journalists not only render particular activities in which they are engaged visible to others within the local milieu, but develop selective characterisations of stories, differentiating the various forms of co-participation they require for different parts of those renditions. Quotes, précis, readings, summaries are differentiated in the talk itself and systematically accomplished with respect to different forms of co-participation from the recipient(s). The accomplishment of the tellings, the step-by-step production of (a characterisation of) a story, are produced with respect to the current conduct of the co-participant and, in particular, his or her orientation to different components of the characterisation during its articulation. On the other hand, the characterisation itself, and the ways in which the textual story is rendered visible, are contingent on the co-participation of the recipient during the course of its production.

The relationship between the informings and the text is both curious and complex. In the production of an informing, tellers differentiate the status of different components of the characterisation with respect to the original text. The text itself, the existence of an authorised and written account, is exploited in the telling in a variety of ways. It is used to produce and present the factual version of some set of events to enable others to build or transmit stories that will have a significant impact on the behaviour of particular markets. It is used to make political comments or to ridicule the journalism of colleagues. Within each fragment, we find the teller systematically displaying the relationship between the informing and the text, and demarcating his own standpoint or 'voice' with regard to the original author and even sources within the text itself. So, for example, we can observe the ways in which the teller can display that he is rewriting that story within the course of its telling and retrospectively recast the authority of the text. Or, for example, we can see how tellers prospectively establish a quote of a quote and display their own alignment towards the relevance of the story for news production. The text is selectively rendered visible. It is revealed within the talk and through the ways in which the teller animates or embodies the text. The developing rendition, the ways in which the talk embodies the text, is dependent on, and embedded in, the emergent interaction with others within the local milieu, and in particular the teller's ability to establish and sustain particular forms of co-participation during the production of a telling. The text, therefore, or at least the text displayed on the monitor, does not so much 'mediate' the interaction, but rather is ongoingly constituted in the interaction.

The characterisation, the animated versions of particular elements of the story, the quotes and summaries, does not simply transmit or present the text, but rather constitutes the text within and with regard to the activity 'at hand'. The co-participants' access to the story, even when they look at the screen with the speaker, is constrained both by what they can see and their understanding of the contents of the piece. A colleague's talk constitutes the text and the ways it is seen on this occasion, its intelligibility and its sense here and now. In constituting the text, personnel provide a sense of their current work and the activities in which they are engaged. Access to the story is 'asymmetrical'. It is not simply that co-participants may not necessarily be able to see the same story, but rather what they know of the text, even during the course of a collaborative reading, is permeated through, and embedded in, the ways in which the teller is concurrently characterising the text. The reading is interactionally constituted, not only in the sense through the author's relationship with the reader (Iser, 1985), but also in and through the interaction between teller and recipient. The talk elaborates the text and the text elaborates the talk within the developing course of the interaction.

The observations discussed here provide further support to the critique of the conduit metaphor of communication, the idea that communication is simply a channel through which individuals exchange information. The critique developed by Bakhtin (1986) and others, such as Wertsch (1991), elucidates the dialogic nature of talk and shows how activities arise in and through the communication of the participants. In the case at hand, we can begin to see how text is interleaved with talk and, following Bakhtin (1986) and Volosinov (1973), can consider the ways in which talk reproduces and relies on a particular textual genre (news reporting) which may be theoretically distinct from the current context and yet forms an integral part of retelling and editing stories within the newsroom. But the character of the dialogicity and textual rendition discussed here goes beyond the idea of genres characterised so profoundly by Bakhtin and developed in diverse ways by Todorov (1990), Lodge (1990) and Goffman's (1974) frame analysis of talk. In particular, we find that the delivery of a piece of news to a colleague, itself a selective rendition of a textual report, is produced with respect to the shifting alignment and participation of the recipient. How the text is (re)produced is thoroughly embedded in the activity at hand, as that activity emerges in and through the interaction of participants. The relationship between the speaker and the author, the report and the original text, and the distinction between *de dicto* and *de re* (cf. Coulmas, 1986) is thoroughly contingent on, and embedded in, the emergent interaction between the participants, even during the shifting course of a single utterance and textual rendition.

In recent years, there has been a growing interest in how individuals produce and sustain language and interaction in institutional settings (see, e.g. Drew and Heritage, 1992). An important feature of institutional conduct, which has served as a central focus of such research, is the asymmetrical relationship between the participants. So, for example, there has been a burgeoning body of studies concerned with how a patient and doctor orient to, and preserve, the distribution of knowledge, expertise, power and status ordinarily associated with incumbents of the two roles (see e.g. Heath, 1992; Parsons, 1951; West, 1985). In the editorial section of Reuters, we find rather different forms of asymmetry. Here, whilst the journalists may stand on 'equal footing' with each other, they have particular access to certain stories, and the materials on which they work are largely invisible or unavailable to colleagues. Screen-based technologies localise the activity; the text is received and read on-screen, changes are typed on the keyboard and the computer cannot be easily passed between individuals like a piece of paper. Stories can be sent to others, though interestingly this largely occurs when journalists have already discussed a story, and agreed to pass it on to another desk. In a sense, therefore, the sorts of practice that we have discussed in this chapter are ways in which journalists deal with asymmetrical access to each other's activities and the materials in which those activities are embedded or on which they are based. By selectively rendering their screen-based textual materials visible to each other, journalists systematically provide their colleagues with relatively unobtrusive ways of receiving information which may be of relevance to their work and responsibilities. Written stories are exposed and made public in and through the journalists' talk.

In animating news stories, rendering them selectively visible in and through talk, journalists attempt to co-ordinate their actions with the conduct of their colleagues. As suggested, to a large extent receiving, reading and editing stories on-line localises the other's activity, and conceals the particular actions from colleagues within the domain. So, for example, though one can see that a colleague is typing, and one may even know which story he or she is working on, what the journalist is actually doing at some particular moment is largely unavailable. Despite limited access to the conduct of others, journalists attempt to co-ordinate their spoken contributions with the real-time actions of colleagues. In various ways, journalists use whatever is available of a colleague's conduct in order to juxtapose and produce their own activities. So, for example, prefaces and jokes may be positioned with regard to a pause in the use of the keyboard, or a couple of taps on the return key coupled with a shift in visual orientation might be used to assume that a colleague has nearly finished editing a particular story. Journalists appear to become adept in recognising junctures and boundaries in each other's work through the ways in which they read and type. In many cases, a colleague's contribution is immediately juxtaposed with the onset of a break in another's activity, suggesting that individuals are able to prospectively assess just when a break in an activity might arise. However, it should not be forgotten that in noticing a colleague noticing what you are doing, or in hearing another begin to speak, a journalist may very well momentarily suspend or shape an activity to enable him or her to listen to a projected exposition. Talk may be geared to the use of the computer, just as the use of the computer may be sensitive to the talk of colleagues.

The use of the editorial system in Reuters, therefore, is thoroughly bound into and inseparable from the interaction and collaboration between journalists. Journalists have, for example, developed various ways in which textually embedded on-line stories, received by particular desks, can be rendered selectively visible within the domain, to enable colleagues to see or at least hear for themselves whether it is worthwhile to pick up on particular news items. Journalists have developed practical solutions to the ways in which the technology and its accompanying organisational arrangements localise information to particular individuals and desks. Stories are read and edited with regard to the interests of colleagues and their respective customers, and journalists are able to keep each other informed with respect to the more relevant and amusing stories which might be breaking. Even so, in animating stories, journalists are sensitive to the concurrent activities of colleagues, activities which are themselves produced in and through their 'interaction' with the system. These activities have limited visibility within the domain, and journalists use whatever they can to retrieve information from their colleagues' use of the technology and to position and co-ordinate their own contributions. An individual's 'interaction' or use of the system is co-ordinated, ongoingly, with his or her interaction with colleagues within the local milieu.

4   Team work: collaboration and control in London Underground line control rooms

4.1   Introduction

It is hardly surprising that attempts to build technologies to support collaborative work draw from more traditional sociological models of the 'team' and the 'group'. Such models continue to permeate the social sciences and with their formal description of roles and responsibilities, task specifications and the like, they provide a set of principles which can be embodied in complex systems. In consequence, the concept of the 'group' played an important part in CSCW, and still underlies the thinking behind a range of technological innovations. To an extent, therefore, CSCW has replaced the individual and cognitive model of human conduct found within HCI with a socialised being, an incumbent of organisational rules who follows formally prescribed procedures to achieve particular ends. It is increasingly recognised, however, that, despite the substantial contribution of such models, to both our understanding of human conduct and the design of technology, certain organisational arrangements do not readily lend themselves to descriptions which attempt to characterise conduct in terms of formal roles and responsibilities. The newsroom at Reuters may be one such example.

Other forms of organisation may be rather different. Take, for instance, command and control supported by safety critical systems. Power stations, military surveillance centres, railway control rooms and the like are settings in which there is a clear allocation of tasks and responsibilities, coupled with a detailed and formal specification of the procedural organisation of particular activities. Safety critical technologies support, and are supported by, the relevant task specifications and accompanying division of labour, so in some sense one might speak of a 'socio-technical system'. Such domains involve team work, in which a group of personnel produce and co-ordinate actions with regard to formally prescribed practices and procedures; an organisation which not only generates the relevant service efficiently, but, for all practical purposes, minimises risk and danger to human life. In principle, therefore, the organisation of work in such settings should illustrate, perhaps more than most, the group or teamwork model which has permeated CSCW and its attempts to build systems to support collaborative work.

In this chapter, we wish to examine a setting which involves, *par excellence*, 'team work'. The setting, a line control room on London Underground, houses between four and six personnel whose responsibility is to oversee traffic movement and deal with problems and difficulties when they arise. Within the control room, there is a relatively strict division of labour which to some extent is formally prescribed in various documents and reflected in training manuals and the like. We wish to show however that a description of the formal characteristics of the team or the group, with its emphasis on clearly delineated tasks and responsibilities would fail to resonate with the flexible and emergent character of the participants' work, and in particular with the ways in which their activities are thoroughly interdependent and interactionally co-ordinated with regard to the contingencies 'at hand'. In particular, we wish to show how work and collaboration within the line control rooms of London Underground, like work in the other settings we have examined, relies upon a tacit body of practices and reasoning in and through which the participants produce, make sense of and co-ordinate their activities with each other. To attempt to formalise such practices into roles and responsibilities, task descriptions and the like would not only do analytic injustice to the richness and complexity of the activities in question, but provide an unreliable foundation for the design and deployment of systems to support co-operative work.

One of the most important, though often implicit, aspects of the ways in which both social and cognitive scientists conceive of work and the use of technology, is with regard to the notion of task. Certain forms of cognitive science (and HCI) conceive of task in terms of individual information processing oriented towards certain goals and plans which are enacted through patterns of behaviour. For social science, the notion of role, or patterns of action associated with categories of organisational personnel, permeates a range of analytic approaches, where, for example, expectations and dispositions, coupled with formal rules, allow individuals to produce and co-ordinate actions with regard to particular goals. In attempting to reconsider the concept of task with respect to its contingent and socially 'situated' character, perhaps the most critical considerations are the ways in which specialised forms of organisational activity, that is tasks, are accomplished interactionally and contingently. Rules, prescriptions, routines and the like are ongoingly subject to the real-time contributions of others; others who may be co-located or based outside the immediate domain. In the following two chapters, building on the discussion of the editorial section at Reuters, we wish to explore the ways in which specialised tasks, 'belonging' to particular personnel, are accomplished in and through interaction with others, and implicate, in the very course of their production, action and activities by colleagues.

A second, related issue also informs some of the following discussion. In recent years, there has been a growing recognition amongst both social and computer scientists of the importance of 'awareness' in collaborative work. Awareness has been subject to investigation in field studies of the workplace, and has also informed the design of complex systems, especially those designed to support real-time distributed working (cf. Benford et al., 1996; Gaver et al., 1995; Heath et al., 1995). The idea of awareness which informs some contemporary research in CSCW appears akin to the idea of 'peripheral vision' (e.g. Fisher et al., 1981). Individuals are assumed to have an ability to monitor aspects of the physical and behavioural environment outside the focus or direct line of their regard. In this sense, an individual's ability to remain aware, and the domain of his or her awareness, is treated as remaining stable over time, if only for the duration of a particular activity. In this and the following chapter we explore how 'awareness', or, better perhaps, how 'figure' and 'field', or 'foreground' and 'background' are ongoingly accomplished by participants in the developing course of their activities. In other words, 'awareness' is momentarily produced in and through the action and interaction of the participants themselves; it is not an ability, but a socially organised and contingent achievement.

One final consideration before turning to the materials. There is a growing body of contemporary research within the social sciences and CSCW concerned with 're-embodying' social action, reconceptualising conduct with regard to its material environment. So for example in different ways Varela et al. (1993) and Robertson (1997) draw on Merleau-Ponty to argue that 'the body as a lived experiential structure and the body as a milieu of cognitive mechanism' should be placed at the forefront of the analytic agenda. An important aspect of the re-embodiment of action is embedding action within the immediate physical environment; an aspect which forms the focus of certain approaches to situated action. Building on some of the observations which arose in the previous chapter, by looking at the line control rooms of London Underground, we can begin to consider the ways in which, in and through their actions and activities, personnel render relevant, at some 'here and now', particular features of the local environment in momentary specific ways. The character and relevance of an object, an image, an artefact or whatever, is reflexively constituted within the action and interaction, and provides resources for recognition and interpretation of

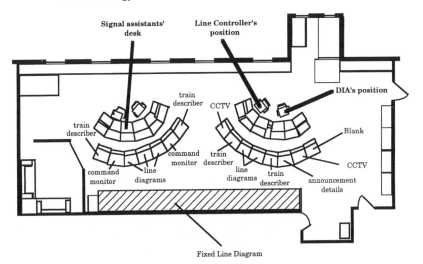

Figure 4.1: The Bakerloo Line Control Room.

conduct (cf. Heath and Hindmarsh 1997). In the case at hand, the environment, a complex 'multimedia' milieu, is a resource in, and constituted through, the production, recognition and co-ordination of conduct.

4.2   The technology in the control room

Whilst drawing on materials from a number of line control rooms on London Underground, we focus in particular on the Bakerloo Line. The Bakerloo Line Control Room has recently been modernised. Manual signalling has been replaced by a complex computerised system which is operated centrally by signal assistants who are based in the line control room. The line control room now houses the line controller, who co-ordinates the day-to-day running of the railway, the Divisional Information Assistant (DIA) whose responsibilities include providing information to passengers through a public address (PA) system and communicating with station managers, and two signal assistants who oversee the operation of the signalling system from Queens Park to the Elephant and Castle, the busiest section of the line. It is not unusual also to find a trainee DIA or controller in the control room or a relief controller when problems and crises emerge. Figure 4.1 shows the general layout of the control room whilst Figure 4.2 gives a general view of the room from behind the controller's desk.

The controller and DIA sit together at a semicircular console which faces a tiled, real-time, fixed line diagram which runs nearly the entire

Figure 4.2 A general view of the Bakerloo Line Control Room. The DIA is on the left with two controllers to the right.

length of the room. The diagram indicates the location of trains on the Northbound and Southbound track between Elephant and Castle and Queens Park; lights illuminate on the board when the trains pass over different sections of the line. The console includes a radio phone system for speaking with drivers, the public address control keys, the headset and microphone, closed-circuit television (CCTV) monitors for viewing station platforms and their control keys, three monitors showing line diagrams and traffic, and a monitor listing the actual running times of trains. The console also contains two touch-screen telephones which are operated by the user touching parts of a display of numbers and personnel names shown on the monitor (see Figure 4.3). On occasions a trainee DIA (tDIA) or a second controller (Cii) will sit at this console. The signal assistants sit at a similar console alongside the controller and DIA (see Figure 4.4). They also have access to monitors showing real-time graphic displays of the line and its traffic, listings of running times, input monitors for making changes to the scheduled service, and touch-screen telephones.

The Underground service is co-ordinated through a paper timetable

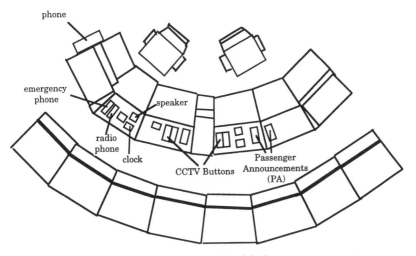

Figure 4.3 Line controllers' and DIAs' desk.

Figure 4.4 A view from behind the controller's desk, showing the fixed line diagram in front.

which specifies: the number, running time and route of trains; crew allocation and shift arrangements; information concerning staff travel facilities; stock transfers; vehicle storage and maintenance, etc. Each underground line has a particular timetable, though in some cases the timing of trains will be closely tied to the service on a related line. The timetable is not simply an abstract description of the operation of the service, but is used by various personnel including the controller, DIA, signalmen and duty crew managers, to co-ordinate traffic flow and passenger movement. In the line control room, controllers and other staff use the timetable in conjunction with their understanding of the current operation of the service to determine the adequacy of the service and, if necessary, initiate remedial action. Indeed, a significant part of the responsibility of the controller is to serve as a 'guardian of the timetable'. Even if he is unable to shape the service according to the timetable's specific details, the controller should, as far as possible, attempt to achieve its underlying principle; a regular service of trains with relatively brief intervening gaps.

Despite important differences in the formal specification of the responsibilities of the controller and DIA, the various tasks they undertake rely upon close collaboration. Indeed, control room personnel have developed a subtle and complex body of practices for monitoring each other's conduct and co-ordinating a varied collection of tasks and activities. These practices appear to stand independently of particular personnel, and it is not unusual to witness individuals who have no previous experience working together, informally, implicitly, yet systematically co-ordinating their conduct with each other. (It should be noted that, in the setting which has formed the comparative part of this project, the line control rooms on the RER in Paris, the work force is actually organised in teams which only work shifts that include the same colleagues (Darfel et al., 1993; Filippi and Theureau, 1993; Joseph, 1995).) One element of this extraordinary interweaving of sequential and simultaneous responsibilities and tasks is an emergent and flexible division of labour which allows the personnel to lend support to the accomplishment of each other's tasks and activities and thereby manage difficulties and crises.

4.3   Assessing the service

On London Underground, like other rapid urban transport systems, passengers rarely schedule their journey with reference to the official timetable, but use the railway on the assumption that trains will travel between particular locations at frequent and predictable intervals. On the Bakerloo Line, for example, trains run approximately every two and a half minutes during the 'peak' period and between five and seven minutes at other times of the day. The DIA orients to the ways in which passengers organise their travel with London Underground and provides information when particular problems arise in the 'normal' operation of the service. Such problems may vary from a slight delay as a result of absent staff, through to a major evacuation caused by the discovery of a 'suspect package'. The nature of such information varies with respect to the circumstances at hand, however these public announcements reveal recurrent characteristics.

Fragment 4.1   Transcript 1

DIA: Good Morning this: is Bakerloo Line Information↑ (0.3)
DIA: The next train (just) left from Regents Par:k↑ (0.6) (an)
        well be with you at Ba:ker Street (in) one minute (0.3)
        Marylebone (0.6) three minutes:, (.) Paddington in
        approximately six minutes:.
        (1.2)
DIA: (Our) next train just left from (.) Regents Par:k↑ (1.2)
        destination Harrow an Willsdo(w)n.

The actual advice is routinely foreshadowed by a series, or package, of actions which successively align the potential recipients to the upcoming information. In this instance, the package consists of a greeting and an identification of the speaker and source of information. The rising intonation at the end of the initial sentence, coupled with the pause, also encourages the passengers to listen to the actual announcement. The advice itself provides specific information to particular passengers, namely those who are waiting at Baker Street, Marylebone and Paddington, and who may be waiting because of a delay in the service. The announcement appeals to the current or prospective experience of passengers and gains its significance by virtue of the ways passengers organise their use of the Underground service. Thus, even though the announcement is addressed to the 'general public', it achieves its performative impact, its relevance, through its design for specific categories of passengers; namely those waiting at this moment at the particular locations on the Bakerloo Line who are suffering a delay.

To produce timely and relevant information, the DIA monitors the service and transforms his observations into carefully tailored announcements. In the case at hand, the DIA glances at the fixed line diagram and switches the CCTV monitor to the northbound platform at Regents Park (see Figure 4.5). He sets the PA system, and as the train begins to leave the station, delivers the announcement. The specific advice the DIA gives is co-ordinated with the train's departure from a particular station, and is

glance at fixed   ▶   set PA   ▶   coordinate announcement
line diagram   with train movement

Figure 4.5 Assessing the state of the service.

based on the anticipated time it takes for a train to travel between the stations in question. The DIA's announcement is achieved by utilising
various technologies in the control room. The fixed line diagram allows
the DIA to assess the state of the service and, in particular, to notice any
gaps or intervals between the trains, and the CCTV monitor provides
access to a particular train itself, at least as it appears on the screen, and
allows the DIA to co-ordinate and design the announcement with the
'actual' movement of the vehicle.

4.4   'Monitoring' and discriminating action

Whilst the DIA does have independent access to various forms of information concerning the operation of the service, such as the fixed line diagram
and the CCTV screens, the assessments he makes and the various actions
he undertakes are often dependent upon the actions of his colleagues, particularly the line controller. It is relatively unusual, however, for the line
controller, the DIA or the signal assistants to explicitly provide information to each other concerning the problems they have noticed or the interventions they have made. Indeed, given the demands on these personnel,
especially when dealing with emergencies or difficulties, it would be
impossible to abandon the tasks in which they are engaged in order to
provide information to their colleagues as to what they are doing and why.
However, it is essential that both controller and DIA (and others) remain
sensitive to each other's conduct, not only to allow them to co-ordinate
specific tasks and activities, but also to enable them to gather appropriate
information concerning the details of the current operation of the service.

   To produce timely and relevant information for passengers, the DIA
systematically monitors the service and the actions of his colleagues, and
transforms these bits and pieces into carefully tailored announcements
for passengers who are using the service at some moment in time.
Consider the following instance, where the DIA delivers an announce-

ment to warn the passengers at a particular station that their next train will be delayed.

Fragment 4.2   Transcript 1

DIA: Hello: and good afternoon La(d)ies an Gentlemen↑ (.)
        Bakerloo Line Information↑ (0.3) (°hhh) We have a
        sli:ght gap in our sou:th bound Bakerloo Line Service↑
        (.) towards the Elephant an Castle, (1.6) Your next
        South Bound train:↑ (0.6) should depart from this:
        station in about another three minutes::.(0.2) The next
        South Bound train↑ (0.2) should depart from this
        station in about another three minutes::. ·

The announcement emerges in the light of the DIA overhearing the controller's conversation with the driver, or operator (Op), and assessing its implications for the expectations and experience of travellers using the service.

Fragment 4.2   Transcript 2

C: Control to the train: at Charing Cross: South Bound,<do you receive?
      (6.3)   *((Controller switches CCTV monitor to platform))*
C: Control to the train at Charing Cross South Bound, do you receive?
      (1.0)
Op: ((   )) (°two four O:) Charing Cross S:outh Bound
C: Yeah two four O:: <we got a little bit of an interval behind you, (.) could
      you take a couple of minutes: in the platform for me please?
Op: ((   )) Over
C: Thank you very much Two Four O:
      (5.2)

↘

DIA: Hello: and good afternoon La(d)ies an Gentlemen↑ (.)
        Bakerloo Line Information↑ (0.3) (°hhh) We have a
        sli:ght gap in our sou:th bound Bakerloo Line Service↑
        (.) towards the Elephant an Castle, (1.6) Your next
        South Bound train:↑ (0.6) should depart from this:
        station in about another three minutes::.(0.2) The next
        South Bound train↑ (0.2) should depart from this
        station in about another three minutes::.

The DIA transforms the controller's request into a relevant announcement by determining which passengers will be affected. In the case at hand, those waiting at Charing Cross will suffer a short delay. A little later, the DIA produces a second announcement (not included in the transcript above) to inform passengers who have recently arrived on the platform of the delay.

The DIA does not wait until the completion of the controller's call before preparing to take action. As the controller begins his first attempt to contact the driver, the DIA glances at the fixed line diagram, as if to seek an account for the controller's intervention (frame 2.1). As the controller begins his second attempt to contact the driver, the DIA moves to a seat nearer the console and in reach of the PA system (2.2). On the phrase 'couple of minut<u>es</u>:', where the specific implications of the intervention become apparent, he begins to set the PA system to make an announcement to the passengers at Charing Cross (2.3). The DIA monitors the controller's actions as they emerge in interaction with the driver, and, using the various technological sources of information, particularly the fixed line diagram, is able to make sense of the controller's intervention and assess its implications for passengers at a certain location.

Fragment 4.2   Transcript 3

Ci tDIA   DIA   Ci   DIA   Ci   DIA

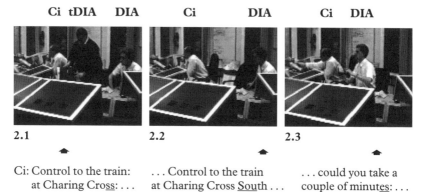

2.1   2.2   2.3

Ci: Control to the train: ... Control to the train   ... could you take a
    at Charing Cro<u>ss</u>: ...   at Charing Cross <u>South</u> ...   couple of minut<u>es</u>: ...

The DIA overhears the controller's emerging intervention and transforms his request for the driver to 'take a couple of minutes' in the platform, into a public announcement informing passengers that there will be a slight delay before the train continues its journey. The announcement 'reproduces' certain features of the request to the driver, providing an explanation – 'a <u>sli:</u>ght gap in our <u>sou:</u>th bound Bakerloo Line Service↑' – which foreshadows the specific advice 'Your next South Bound train:↑ (0.6) should depart from this: station in about another <u>thr</u>ee minutes::'. The controller's intervention, therefore, engenders a specific activity by the DIA; an activity which systematically reformulates features of a conversation between two colleagues and presents the information to a particular category of passengers.

Despite the necessity to monitor the conduct of the controller, the DIA maintains a certain 'social distance', providing his colleague with what Hughes (1958) once characterised as 'the elbow room with which to fulfil his colleague's particular duties'. As the DIA begins to 'track' the call to the driver and prepare to make an announcement, he neither looks at the controller nor watches the activity of his colleague. Moreover, as he changes position and moves closer to the controller, he avoids making his own activity visible or noticeable to his colleague; rather the actions appear to be accomplished independently of the call to the driver, as if the DIA is engaged in some unrelated business. Through his bodily comportment and the ways in which he warily accomplishes his actions, the DIA preserves a careful balance of involvement, overhearing the controller and monitoring his colleague's actions on the 'periphery' of the visual field, whilst avoiding overt attention to the controller's conduct.

Certain phrases or even single words addressed by the controller to a driver or signalman on the telephone are often enough for the DIA to draw particular inferences and undertake relevant action. For example, in fragment 4.2 the request to 'take a couple of minutes' allows the DIA to infer that the controller is attempting to reduce an interval on the southbound service; a problem that it is unlikely to have been noticed until the controller called the driver. The DIA overhears the call, develops an account for intervention and assesses its implications for his own conduct.

In the following instance, the DIA, who is apparently engrossed in updating his own timetable, grabs the phone and calls the station manager at Piccadilly Circus on hearing the word 're:verse:'.

Fragment 4.3   Transcript 1

C: Controller↑ to South Bound Two Three Three,
     <do you receive?
     (8.2)

Op: Two Three Three receiving pass your message (...) (0.3)
     over↑

▶ C: Yeah Two Three Three: (.)
▶   I'd like you to re:verse: at Piccadilly:, (.)
▶   an: you'll also be re:formed there: >
     I'll come back to you:: when you get to Piccadilly:. over.
     (1.2)   ((Radio noise (0.3)))

Op: O:kay >thankyou very much Controller: (0.2) erm: (.)
     can you ma(ke) (0.2) er:: (.) i(s)it er: possible to make
     announcement (to the people) (when I get there) over?
     (0.7)

C: Yeah: the D I: A:: will make announcements for: you, (.)
     Can you confirm you've just left Re:gents:?

Op: Er:: Roger (.) no (I think) (I'm er::) (0.2) still at Ba:ker
     Street, Over on the:: (.) on the (—) South Bound, Over?

C: hh Yeah:: we've received driver thanks: very much,
     I'll tell the D I A:: (who) will monitor you down: te
     Piccadilly.
     (0.3)

DIA: Ye ah (.) Bakerloo Line Infor<u>mation</u> Two <u>Three</u>
       <u>Three</u> is going to reverse with with you:, (0.2)
       South to North:,
       (2.0)
DIA: Two <u>Three</u> <u>Three</u>. He's at Baker: Street now::.

((roughly 3 minutes later))

DIA: Good morning Ladies and Gentlemen↑ (.) Bakerloo
       Line Infor<u>mation</u>↑ (1.0) This train is for:: (0.4)
       Piccadilly Circus:↑ only.(1.2) This tr<u>ain</u> (.) for: (.)
       Piccadilly Ci<u>rcus</u>↑ only.

*((Successive announcements made at each station as the train in
question arrives.))*

Before the controller has finished speaking to the driver, the DIA calls
the station manager at Piccadilly and warns him that the 233 is to be
'detrained'. On completing the call, the DIA then produces a series of
public announcements on each southbound platform between Baker
Street and Piccadilly, warning passengers that the train is 'for Piccadilly
only'. The following frames will provide a sense of the ways in which the
DIA produces a series of actions on overhearing the controller's request
to the driver.

Fragment 4.3   Transcript 2

3.1   **3.2**   **3.3**

C: Yeah Two Three Three (.)
                 I'd like you to <u>re:verse:</u> at Piccadilly:,
                            (.) an: you'll be <u>re:formed</u> there:

The DIA, therefore, overhears the controller's intervention and assesses
its implications for both staff and passengers. The controller's request,
and in particular the word 'reverse', engenders sequentially relevant
actions from the DIA; firstly to warn the station manager of the upcoming
events, and, secondly, to inform passengers who may join the train at a
number of stations prior to Piccadilly that its presupposed destination has
been changed. The driver himself is sensitive to the implications of

'turning early' for the passengers, and asks the controller to have the DIA make the relevant announcements. The controller relies upon the DIA undertaking a specific set of sequentially appropriate actions with respect to particular types of action that he, the controller, may undertake. Indeed, in the case at hand, if the DIA failed to warn the station manager or provide the appropriate passenger information, the absence of such actions would be noticeable and accountable.

It is not simply that DIAs happen to remain attentive to the local environment of activity and are able to draw the relevant inferences from the actions of their colleagues. Rather, personnel within the control room organise their conduct so that whilst engaged in one activity, they simultaneously monitor or participate in the activities of others. This double-edged element of accomplishing these specialised tasks within the line control room, is an essential feature of their 'collaborative work', demanding that participants design their activities so that whilst undertaking one task they remain sensitive to the 'independent' actions of their colleague(s).

Producing an activity whilst simultaneously participating in the activities of another, has implications for the ways in which personnel utilise the various tools and technologies within the line control room. So, for example, the DIA may switch his CCTV monitor to a particular platform to enable him to read a number from the front of a train for the controller, even though the DIA is engaged in delivering a public announcement and only happens to overhear that problems are emerging concerning the identity of particular trains. Or, for example, it is not unusual to find the controller or DIA switching the telephone handset to the other ear, to enable his colleague to overhear a conversation with a member of the Underground staff based outside the line control room. Almost all tasks within the line control room are produced by the DIA or controller as they simultaneously participate in the concurrent activities of their colleagues. The various tools and technologies which are provided to support these tasks, are shaped, corrupted and even abandoned, in order to enable control room personnel to participate simultaneously in multiple activities which more or less involve each other.

In both fragments 4.2 and 4.3 we can see the ways in which phrases or even single words serve to engender particular actions and activities for colleagues within the control room itself. These words or phrases, whilst featuring in the accomplishment of specific actions in interaction on the radio phone, simultaneously embody particular activities for the DIA and allow him to produce sequentially appropriate conduct and provide a co-ordinated response to a problem or crisis. The DIA is not the 'principal recipient' of the controller's telephone talk, and yet is able to retrieve the necessary bits and pieces of information to enable him to produce 'sequentially' relevant actions and activities. The production of conduct by the DIA (and others such as the signal assistants) relies upon a body of procedures and conventions which provide for, and engender, the relevance of particular actions given specific types of activity undertaken by the controller. The very intelligibility of the scene for the DIA and his colleagues derives from their use of, and orientation to, a body of practice which informs the production, recognition and co-ordination of routine conduct within the line control room. So, for example, it is not simply that the DIA remains peripherally aware and sensitive to the whole gamut of 'goings on' within the control room, but rather that he discriminates the local environment of conduct with respect to, for example, the routine implications of specific types of events for his own conduct. Interventions such as turning trains short, closing stations, delaying trains, taking trains out of service, and so on, in their different ways implicate specific trajectories of action for the DIA (and others). The procedures and conventions oriented to by the DIA and his colleagues in producing and co-ordinating actions inform the ways in which they 'monitor' and discriminate each other's conduct and remain sensitive to the local environment of 'goings on'.

4.5   Rendering activities visible

Whilst relying on each other mutually to monitor their conduct and to draw the relevant conclusions, even when they are engaged in seemingly distinct and unrelated activities, the DIA and controller employ various devices to keep each other informed of changes to the operation of the service. Activities such as telephone conversations with personnel outside the room, tracking a particular train with the CCTV, or discussions with line management concerning the state of the service, are, at least in part, publicly visible within the local milieu, and ordinarily the bits and pieces available can be used to make sense of what is going on.

Other sorts of activities may be less visible, and yet it is critical that personnel within the line control room maintain a sense of what each other is doing. One of the most important activities in this regard surrounds the use of the timetable. The timetable is a resource not only for identifying difficulties within the operation of the service, but also for their management. For example, the controller will make small adjustments to the running times of various trains to cure gaps which are emerging between a number of trains during the operation of the service. More serious problems such as absenteeism, vehicle breakdowns or the discovery of suspect packages often necessitate 'reformation' of the timetable; a process through which the line controller reschedules trains and crews in order to maintain a coherent and even service. The controller marks the changes on the relevant pages of the paper timetable, as do the signal assistants and DIA when they hear of the changes which have been made. In order to facilitate reformation, the pages of the paper timetable are covered with cellophane or laminated sheets to enable the personnel to mark changes and to remove them with a cloth when the events have passed. Since the organisation of the service is dependent on the timetable, and the various information systems rely upon the viewer knowing the relative ordering of trains, it is critical that reformations are known by all staff within the control room and indeed some personnel, such as duty crew managers, who are located elsewhere. If this information is not available, personnel will draw the wrong conclusions from the fixed line diagrams and monitors and take inappropriate action. Reforming the service, however, is an extremely complex task, which is often undertaken during emergencies, and it is not unusual for the controller to have little time explicitly to keep his relevant colleagues informed.

One solution to this potential difficulty is to render features of their individual reasoning and actions 'publicly' visible by talking through the reformations whilst they are being accomplished. The solution is analogous to the ways in which journalists handle the news in Reuters. The controllers talk 'out loud', but this talk is not specifically addressed to a particular colleague within the control room. Rather, by continuing to look at, and sketch changes on the timetable, whilst producing talk which is 'addressed' to oneself, the controller avoids obliging anyone to respond. Talking through the timetable, whilst rendering 'private' activities publicly visible, avoids establishing mutual engagement with colleagues which would undermine the ongoing accomplishment of the task in question.

Consider the following fragment in which the controller finishes one reformation and then begins another.

Fragment 4.4   Transcript 1

> *((... Controller (C) reads his timetable ...))*
> C: <u>It's</u> ten seventeen to (↑) °hhhhhhh
>   (4.3)
> C: (Rr:) <u>ri:ght</u> (.) tha<u>t's</u> that one d<u>one:.</u>
> C: hhh °hhh (.) hhh
> C: Two: O: <u>Six::</u> (.) For:ty S<u>ix::</u>
>   (0.7)
> C: Two Two <u>Fi:</u>ve
>   *((... the DIA begins to tap on his chair and he and the trainee begin a*
>   *separate conversation. As they begin to talk C ceases talking out loud ...))*

Whilst looking at the timetable, the controller announces the completion of one reformation and begins another. The controller talks numbers, train numbers, and lists the various changes that he could make to the 206 to deal with the problems he is facing, namely reform the train to 246 or to 225. As the controller mentions the second possibility, the DIA begins to tap the side of his chair, and a moment or so later, discusses the current problems and their possible solutions with a trainee DIA who is sitting by the DIA's side. As soon as the DIA begins to tap his chair and displays, perhaps, that he is no longer attentive to his colleague's actions, the controller, whilst continuing to sketch possible changes on the timetable, ceases to talk aloud. Despite therefore, the controller's apparent sole commitment to dealing with specific changes to the service, he is sensitive to the conduct of his colleague, designing the activity so that, at least initially, it is available to the DIA and then transforming the way the task is being accomplished so that it ceases to be 'publicly' accessible.

Whilst talking out loud may primarily be concerned with providing co-present colleagues with the necessary details of changes made by the controller to the running order of the service, it is interesting to observe that a great deal more information is made available in this way than simply the actual reformations. As in fragment 4.4, talking to oneself whilst engaged in a potentially 'private' activity seems designed to accomplish more than simply providing the facts of the matter. Rather, the controller renders visible to his colleagues the course of reasoning involved in making particular changes. The natural history of a decision, the controller's reasoning through various alternative courses of action, is rendered visible within the local milieu, and provides colleagues with the resources through which they can assess the grounds for and consequences of 'this particular decision' in the light of possible alternatives. While the controller is talking out loud, it is not unusual to find the DIA and signal assistants following the course of reasoning by looking at their own timetable, and where necessary sketching in the various changes which are made. In this way, the DIA, controller, signal assistants and whoever else might be present assemble the resources for comprehending and managing the service, and preserve a mutually compatible orientation to the 'here and now', and the operation of the service on some particular day. The information provided through the various tools and technologies, including the CCTV monitors, the fixed line diagram and information displays, is intelligible and reliable by virtue of this collaborative activity.

On occasions, it may be necessary for the controller to draw the DIA's attention to particular events or activities, even as they emerge within the management of a certain task or problem. For example, as he is speaking to an operator or signalman, the controller may laugh or produce an exclamation and thereby encourage the DIA to monitor the call more carefully. Or, as he turns to his timetable or glances at the fixed line diagram, the controller will swear, feign momentary illness or even sing a couple of bars of a song to draw the DIA's attention to an emergent problem within the operation of the service. The various objects used by the controller and DIA to gain a more explicit orientation from the other(s) towards a particular event or activity, are carefully designed to encourage a particular form of co-participation from a colleague, but rarely demand the other's attention. They allow the individual to continue with an activity in which they might be engaged, whilst simultaneously inviting them to carefully monitor a concurrent event.

4.6   The production of convergent activities

Personnel within the line control room are continually and unavoidably 'monitoring' and 'discriminating' the local environment of conduct, and, by virtue of a body of indigenous practice and procedure, co-ordinating particular actions and activities with each other. Through these practices, personnel produce and preserve the mutual intelligibility of emergent events and activities and are able to recognise and make sense of each other's actions and the movement of traffic along the line. The natural history of specific events, such as the management of a 'suspect parcel' or a 'person under a train', even the natural history of the operation of the traffic 'on this morning' and 'on this day', provides for the intelligibility of actions and their relevance for particular conduct by particular personnel within the line control room. In making sense of the actions of colleagues, the various information displays and the events at hand, the DIA and others orient to a body of practice which interweaves their particular actions and the ways in which those practices have configured and rendered intelligible the immediately prior events. Take, for example, a case in which a controller might ask a DIA to perform a particular action. However 'explicit' that request might be, it unavoidably relies upon the DIA's current understanding of the service to assemble the sense of the action. Consider the following instance in which a controller (Cii) requests the DIA to ask a driver of a train at Oxford Circus to continue his journey southbound.

Fragment 4.5   Transcript 1

>   *((Cii replaces one receiver and picks up another))*
>
>   (2.5)
>
> Cii: T̲ell him to go: (.) if you've got a clear sig ⌈nal
> DIA: ⌊Yeah
>
>   (6.4)   *((DIA resets the PA system))*

DIA: This is a <u>staff</u> announce:<u>men</u>:t↑ (0.2) to the train
operator (.) if you have a:: Green Signal:↑ you may
pro<u>ce</u>ed. (1.4) If you have a Green Signal you may
pro:ceed, Southbound.
(1.2)

DIA: Staff announcement to the train driver. If you have a
Green Signal you may proceed, (.) S<u>outh</u>bound.
((The train leaves Oxford Circus))

Until the request, Cii and the DIA have been engaged in distinct and apparently unrelated tasks. Cii has been attempting to contact a driver who has unaccountably 'sat down' at Oxford Circus for some minutes and caused a severe backlog of traffic on the southbound service. Meanwhile, the DIA prepares to make a public announcement concerning an unrelated difficulty emerging elsewhere in the service. On the failure of his third attempt to contact the driver, Cii abandons the radio phone and grabs the telephone in order to call the station manager at Oxford Circus and ask him to go down to the platform and tell the driver to go. As Cii looks for the station manager's number on the touch-screen telephone, he 'suddenly' turns to the CCTV monitor and asks the DIA to tell the recalcitrant driver to go.

Despite their involvement in distinct activities prior to the request, and the absence of any 'communication' about the difficulty at Oxford Circus, Cii assumes that the DIA knows who the 'him' is and has some understanding both of the problem and why the DIA is being asked to help to solve it. The design of the utterance presupposes a common orientation to a particular domain and problem, and assumes that the DIA is in a position to immediately and efficiently contact the driver. The controller's assumptions prove well founded. The DIA demands neither explanation nor any additional information, but rather accepts the request, resets the PA system and a few moments later delivers an announcement to Oxford Circus asking the driver to go 'if he has a Green Signal'. As the DIA accepts the request, Cii turns to deal with another, unrelated problem. After making the announcement, the DIA witnesses the train leaving Oxford Circus and then resets the public address system in preparation for a public announcement to tell passengers when their next train will arrive.

In part, the controller's request achieves its intelligibility and performative impact by virtue of its position within the local configuration of the DIA's actions. Immediately prior to the delivery of the request, as Cii searches the screen of the touch-screen telephone for the station manager's number, the DIA turns from the fixed line diagram to the station CCTV monitor (with an intermediary glance at the PA monitor). As he turns from the fixed line diagram to the station screen, a picture of the train at the southbound platform of Oxford Circus begins to emerge. Before the image has settled, Cii looks up and produces the request.

Fragment 4.5   Transcript 2

at
station screen

......————————————————————

Cii: --------, ---<u>T</u>ell him to go:–if you've (got) a clear signal
DIA: yeah

>>>>>>> ————————————————————

at   at
fixed   station
line   screen
display

5.10   5.11   5.12   5.13

at fixed   at station   Cii: <u>T</u>ell him to go: – if you've (got) ..
line display   screen

As Cii delivers his request, both he and the DIA are looking at the train standing in the platform. The DIA makes sense of the utterance with respect to his own and the speaker's orientation towards the image on the monitor; the southbound platform at Oxford Circus. The DIA can therefore make sense of the request and the referent 'him' in the light of his own and his colleague's orientation: the utterance and the looking reflexively establishing a scene in common.

Although the design of the utterance and the participant's visual orientation towards the screen provides a preliminary explanation for the success of the request, one or two questions remain unanswered. It is clear from the data that the image of the train at Oxford Circus station only begins to emerge a moment before the onset of Cii's utterance (less than one-fifth of a second), and it seems unlikely that the request is designed (at least from its onset) in the light of Cii seeing and recognising the train. Moreover, though it is possible that the DIA could make sense of the request by virtue of the speaker's orientation towards the monitor, it seems unlikely that he would be able to undertake the relevant course of action unless he had a sense of the difficulties at Oxford Circus that Cii was attempting to solve. The question remains, therefore, why (and how) can Cii presuppose that the DIA is not only aware of the problem at Oxford Circus, but also may be in a position to contact the driver and effectively solve the immediate difficulties at Oxford Circus? To answer this question it is worth considering some of the activity in the control room that occurred prior to the event.

In the few hours leading to the period from which fragment 4.5 is drawn, the personnel within the control room have had to deal with a station closure, a fire on a train, a mechanical failure and a missing driver. These problems have meant that two controllers have become involved in managing the traffic on the line. These problems have also meant that personnel in the control room, including the signal assistants, have lost the location of particular trains, and are trying to maintain an adequate service irrespective of the timetable and the scheduled running times.

The following fragment begins approximately fifteen seconds before Cii's request to the DIA. Cii is having a heated discussion with his colleague (Ci) concerning the failure of a signalman (located outside the line control room) to undertake various changes to the running times of the trains. During this discussion the telephone rings. Cii picks up the handset, but delays taking the call until an opportune moment arises in the discussion. On his colleague uttering 'Oh for fucks sake' (frame 5.4), Cii responds to the call.

Whilst Cii takes this call, a second phone rings (indicated by the arrow – frame 5.2). After replying to one of the signal assistants (Sii) with the identification of a train at Baker Street, the other controller (Ci) answers this second call (arrowed – transcript 3).

The first incoming call informs Cii of the difficulties at Oxford Circus. Cii then grabs the radio phone and tries three times to contact the driver. Whilst Cii is attempting to intervene, the DIA and the other signal assistant (Si) have been trying to identify the train at Baker Street. The DIA switches the CCTV monitor to Baker Street South and attempts to read the number from the front of the train as it enters the platform. The DIA utters 'all the two::s' and Si returns to his own desk, calling out to his fellow signal assistant 'two two two:↓' (frames 5.5 and 5.6).

Ci Cii	DIA	Si

5.1

.
.
.

Ci: How could he have done it
      if he's taken the only
      (one <u>round</u> it)
      (0.4)

5.2

Cii: said he (would not have) and
      then swapped them around
      behind (Beeb)
      (0.5)

Ci: Well (.) I just spoke to <u>Mi</u>ckey (.)
      <u>Kni</u>ght and I said (then) why
      didn't you do tha:t and he said

5.3

      he wouldn't
      (0.4)

Cii: He (interferes a lot)
      (0.6)

5.4

Ci: Oh f ⌐or fucks <u>sake</u>

Cii: ⌊Controller
      (1.5)

      Cii: Ye:s:
             (0.6)

	Ci	Cii	DIA	Si

Cii: Controller to the <u>train:</u> at Oxford Circus	**5.5**
(0.1) DIA: (pretty quick)	
on the S<u>ou</u>th:th Bound, >Driver	
all the two::s	
do you receive: over↑	
Si: (Ah right thanks Dick) (0.5)	

Cii: Controller to the train

Si: two two two:↓

5.7

at Oxford Circus Sou:th (0.5)

Sii: two two two.

Fragment 4.5   Transcript 3

```
                (1.5)
        Cii:  Ye:s:
                (0.6)
(Sii):  what's that at Baker Stree ⌈t↑ (Frank)
Ci:                                 ⌊Ye:s:
        (0.6)
Ci:   ain't got a fucking clu:e
        (2.2)
Ci:   ain't got a clue
        (0.4)
▶           Cii:  Okay ri:ght↑ (.) thank>you>very>much
                (0.1)
```

We have then at least two parallel and independent activities: Cii attempting to free the hold-up at Oxford Circus and the DIA, signal assistants and Ci, in various ways, concerned with the number of the train at Baker Street.

As the DIA utters 'all the two::s', he turns from the CCTV monitor (showing Baker Street) to the fixed line diagram. The alignment of gaze from the one representation to the other serves to mark not only the completion of the previous activity, but the onset of another, namely an assessment of a particular aspect of the operation of the service. In re-aligning his gaze, the DIA adopts a parallel orientation to the fixed line diagram to Cii, looking towards Oxford Circus just as the latter is uttering 'do you receive: over↑' (frame 5.5). As the DIA aligns his gaze towards the diagram, Cii momentarily adjusts his own orientation towards the area of mutual regard. The position of the DIA's alignment of gaze, at the point at which Cii voices the potential location of the 'problem', coupled with its orientation towards the domain in question, suggests that as the one activity is brought to completion, the DIA is already sensitive to the attempts by Cii to contact the driver and intervene in the operation of the service. Moreover, Cii's reorientation may suggest that he is also sensitive to the DIA's alignment towards his own attempts to contact the driver at Oxford Circus.

As Cii begins his second attempt to contact the driver, he turns from the diagram to his desk. The DIA simultaneously turns from the diagram towards the console (frame 5.7). As Cii produces the word 'Oxford' in 'Oxford Circus South', the DIA moves his hand forward toward the key controls of the PA system in readiness for a public announcement.

The juxtaposition of the DIA's actions with components within Cii's utterances which identify the locale of the problem, coupled with the ways in which his physical alignment and realignment parallels the actions of his co-participant, suggests and displays that the emergent activity of the DIA is convergent with the problem with which Cii is attempting to address. Moreover, moving his hand to the PA controls serves to confirm, retrospectively, that the initial alignment by the DIA towards the fixed line diagram is indeed a first action within an emergent trajectory of conduct, this trajectory being concerned with the delivery of an announcement to the passengers who may be suffering due to the delay at Oxford Circus. Through the use of particular tools at successive stages within Cii's attempts to deal with the problem, the DIA's actions become visible and intelligible as part of a routine and recurrent activity – the delivery of an announcement following an intervention by a controller. Cii's actions not only provide the resources to enable the DIA to examine the fixed line diagram and infer the reasons for the upcoming intervention, but allow him to prepare to undertake a series of public announcements as soon as the problem is solved.

By the beginning of Cii's third attempt to contact the driver, the DIA is setting the PA switches to enable him to deliver an announcement.

Ci Cii   DIA

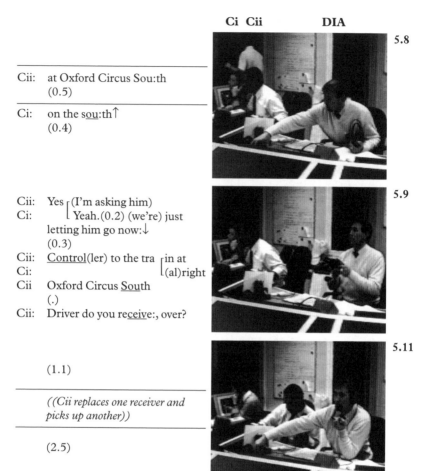

5.8

Cii:	at Oxford Circus Sou:th
	(0.5)
Ci:	on the s<u>ou</u>:th↑
	(0.4)

5.9

Cii:	Yes ⌜(I'm asking him)
Ci:	⌞ Yeah.(0.2) (we're) just
	letting him go now:↓
	(0.3)
Cii:	<u>Control</u>(ler) to the tra ⌜in at
Ci:	⌞(al)right
Cii	Oxford Circus <u>South</u>
	(.)
Cii:	Driver do you re<u>ceive</u>:, over?

5.11

(1.1)

((Cii replaces one receiver and picks up another))

(2.5)

As Cii abandons the radio and grabs the telephone to call the station manager, the DIA is resetting the CCTV in preparation to witness the train finally leaving the station at Oxford Circus. This would enable him to provide precise information concerning the arrival of the train to the long-suffering passengers at Piccadilly Circus and beyond. Whilst resetting the CCTV, the DIA glances at the fixed line diagram, as if to assess once more the severity of the problem generated by the driver at Oxford Circus (frame 5.10).

We can begin to see, therefore, how the production and intelligibility of the request 'Tell him to go: if you've (got) a clear signal' is not simply dependent on the participants' mutual alignment towards the object in question, namely the train standing at Oxford Circus. It emerges in the light of two interrelated activities. On the one hand, we find the DIA producing a trajectory of conduct which foreshadows a public announcement. On the other, we can see the ways in which the components of this activity are co-ordinated with Cii's attempts to intervene in the service; an activity which routinely engenders a sequentially appropriate activity from the DIA, namely a public announcement. The request itself is occasioned by Cii's sensitivity to the DIA's alignment towards the problem at Oxford Circus, and appears co-ordinated with the DIA beginning to deliver the announcement. Through the ongoing juxtaposition of his colleague's actions with his own attempts to contact the driver, Cii recognises that the DIA is preparing to make an announcement as soon as the problem has been solved, and exploits his colleague's awareness of the problem right at the point at which the DIA is ready to use the public address system. For the DIA to contact the driver, it requires him to reset the system to speak to Oxford Circus rather than the passengers at the next station, namely Piccadilly Circus.

There is evidence to suggest that Cii is sensitive not only to the DIA's alignment towards the problem at Oxford Circus, but also to the conduct of other colleagues within the control room. As Cii attempts to contact the driver, Ci takes the second incoming call. It is another colleague mentioning the problem on the southbound platform. Ci utters into the mouthpiece of the telephone 'on the sou:th↑' just as Cii completes his second attempt to contact the driver (frame 5.8). Overhearing 'on the sou:th↑', Cii turns away from the mouthpiece of the telephone and utters, 'Yes (I'm asking him)'. In overlap, Ci then informs the caller on the telephone 'Yeah (0.2) (we're) just letting him go now' (frame 5.9).

Whilst engaged in one activity, therefore, Cii is able to produce a timely contribution to an activity in which his colleague is engaged. It may even be the case that the utterance 'on the sou:th↑' not only is designed by Ci to confirm the locale of the difficulty being reported by the caller, but also is shaped through volume and intonation to elicit, but not demand, confirmation from Cii that he is indeed attempting to deal with the problem at Oxford Circus. In either case, Cii interjects an utterance in juxtaposition with Ci's utterance, which provides the resources through which both the caller and Ci are assured that the problem is indeed being dealt with.

For the controllers and the DIA, therefore, who until recently have been engaged in distinct and unrelated activities, the problem at Oxford Circus momentarily becomes the primary focus of their conduct, as they establish distinct, but interrelated, orientations towards the 'the problem at hand' and its management. Their various activities converge, as they systematically monitor and participate in each other's actions and produce a co-ordinated response to the difficulties at Oxford Circus. A few seconds later, the controllers address a range of other issues and only the DIA remains concerned with the problems generated by the delay at Oxford Circus.

Ci   Cii   DIA

5.12

(2.5)

Cii: <u>T</u>ell him to go: (.) if you've (got)
        a clear sig ⌜nal

DIA: ⌞Yeah
        (2.3)

5.13

5.14

DIA: This is a <u>s</u>taff announce<u>men:</u>t↑

        (0.2)
DIA: to the train operator (.) if you
        have a:: Green Signal:↑ you may
        pro<u>cee</u>d
        (0.4)

Cii's request to the DIA to tell the train to go, therefore, is embedded in a complex configuration of activities and mutual monitoring that provides for the intelligibility and impact of the utterance, and allows the participants to solve one of the more immediate problems at hand. In designing the request Cii presupposes that the image appearing on the monitor is the train that he is attempting to contact at Oxford Circus, and the DIA disambiguates the utterance with respect to Cii's orientation to the emergent scene on the CCTV monitor. The request, and Cii's accompanying orientation, both invoke and accomplish a (presupposed) common referent, and provide the resources through which the DIA can address the problem at hand and encourage the driver to continue his journey. It is positioned at a juncture within the developing course of an activity undertaken by the DIA in order to provide passengers with timely and relevant information. The DIA scans the fixed line diagram, sets the public address system to the relevant platforms, and selects Oxford Circus on the CCTV monitor to witness the train leave the station and provide precise information to passengers. Watching the train leave the station is the last move in a package, or trajectory of action, which fore-shadows the delivery of an announcement to passengers. (In particular, an announcement to those passengers waiting at Piccadilly Circus, the next station along the line.) Cii recognises the trajectory of conduct and exploits the DIA's apparent orientation to the 'problem' at Oxford Circus, and his readiness to make an announcement, in order to contact the driver and encourage him to continue his journey.

As fragments 4.2 and 4.3 suggest, many of the activities undertaken by the DIA are engendered by actions of the controller and in particular his interventions in the routine operation of the service. So, for example, in fragment 4.2, the controller holds a train at Charing Cross and the DIA provides information to warn the passengers of the delay. In fragment 4.3, as the controller intervenes to 'reverse at Piccadilly', the DIA informs the station manager and then delivers a series of public announcements. The participants appear to orient to the sequential relationship between particular activities, the DIA undertaking specific actions with respect to the interventions of the controller. In the case at hand (fragment 4.5), the DIA undertakes a series of actions which foreshadow a public announcement. These actions begin as the DIA completes one activity and whilst the controller is attempting to contact the train at Oxford Circus. The DIA's trajectory of conduct is not simply in immediate juxtaposition with the controller's attempt to call the driver; suggesting a sequential relationship between the two activities. Rather, various actions within the developing course of the trajectory that typically foreshadow a public announcement are co-ordinated with the controller's conduct and his successive attempts to contact the driver. The routine organisation of particular activities, the sequential relationships between the contributions of control room personnel, and the ability mutually to monitor each other's orientation towards particular sources of information, provide the foundation to the design of Cii's request and the DIA's ability to render it intelligible and deal with the emerging crisis at Oxford Circus.

Finally, it is interesting to consider briefly the activity of the DIA following his success in encouraging the driver at Oxford Circus to continue his journey southbound. Indeed, the DIA returns to a sequentially appropriate activity that he was ready to begin when the controller asked him to contact the driver. After he witnesses the train leaving Oxford Circus, he resets the PA system and delivers the following announcement to the passengers waiting at Piccadilly Circus and Charing Cross. It is worth noting that the anticipated times of arrival of the next train are precisely the journey times between the locations excluding the time it has taken to prepare to make the actual announcement.

Fragment 4.5   Transcript 4

DIA: (ev'ning) Ladies and Gentlemen↑ (0.2) this is your
        Baker<u>loo</u> Li:ne Information Serv<u>ice</u>.
        (0.2)
DIA: ( ) southbound trai:n
        (1.5)
DIA: should arri:ve at Piccadilly Circus within <u>one</u> minute
        (0.7)
DIA: and at Charing Cross in two and a half minutes.
        (0.5)
DIA: Thank you.

4.7   The co-ordination and mutual visibility of conduct

It is widely recognised amongst both staff and management in London Underground that it is difficult to provide trainee personnel, in particular line controllers, with formal instruction on how to work within the control rooms. Indeed, even such specialised and seemingly formal tasks as reforming the timetable are not explicitly taught, but rather left for trainees to learn *in situ*. Following a brief period of learning rules, regulations and technical procedures in the classroom, trainee controllers and information assistants are apprenticed to particular personnel for a series of successive three-week periods, where they attempt to learn the trade through observation and instruction in the light of managing actual problems in the operation of the service. It is an extremely difficult process, and more than 80 per cent of applicants for the position of controller fail to make the grade first time around.

The difficulty faced by trainee controllers, information assistants and signalmen is not simply learning to undertake a body of relatively complex and specialised tasks, but rather learning to accomplish those activities with respect to the real-time contributions and demands of personnel both within and outside the line control room. Following the classic essays of Hughes (1958, 1971), we might think of the trainee's problem as one of becoming familiar with an unexplicated and tacit organisational culture which might consist of skills, collective representations, defences, mandates, ideologies and the like. Whilst such features may well inform occupational performance within the line control rooms, and perhaps in other work environments, the difficulties faced by the trainees derive from the ways in which tasks are systematically co-ordinated in real-time with the actions and activities of colleagues. Indeed, it appears that individual tasks and activities are inseparable from, and thoroughly embedded in, ongoing concerted interaction with colleagues within the local milieu. Whilst the socio-interactional foundations to task-based activities within the line control room are paid tribute to by staff and management, the complex web of practices and reasoning upon which they rely are taken for granted and necessarily remain an unexplicated resource, 'seen but unnoticed'. The organisational culture is essentially social and interactional; tasks are accomplished in and through interaction with others, and their competent and skilled performance is inseparable from the tacit practices and reasoning which inform their production, intelligibility and co-ordination. The 'situated' organisation of line control is the interactional and contingent accomplishment of a body of routine tasks.

One aspect of this socio-interactional organisation is the ways in which personnel co-ordinate, sequentially, particular tasks and activities. It was noted earlier that personnel use, and orient to, conventional relations between particular activities; the conduct of one participant engendering sequentially appropriate activities from others. So, for example, a controller's intervention which delays the running time of a particular train leads to a series of public announcements undertaken by the DIA. Or, a controller turning a train short demands that the DIA informs relevant personnel including station managers. The DIA's activities are seen as related to and engendered by the controller's interventions; just as the controller's interventions project the relevance of a specific action or activity to be undertaken by the DIA. These procedures inform the ways in which personnel recognise the relevance or appropriateness of particular actions, as well as forming the foundation to their intelligibility or sense. They also feature in the ways in which individuals produce particular sequences or trajectories of action, and interrelate the 'components' of one activity with the activities and contributions of colleagues.

Collaborative activity within the line control room, however, does not solely rest upon the sequential relationships which pertain between particular activities. It is also dependent upon the ways in which personnel shape their participation in the activities of their colleagues, even whilst they may be engaged in distinct and unrelated tasks. For example, we can see the ways in which the DIA systematically monitors the activity of a controller to enable him to retrieve the details of particular changes which are being made to the running of the service. In many cases, more active participation may be required. So, in fragment 4.5, the controller does not simply 'monitor' the activity of his fellow controller, but makes an essential and timely contribution to the communication that his colleague is having on the telephone. The contribution is produced whilst the controller remains principally engaged in attempting to contact the driver at Baker Street. In other words, the production of a 'task' is sensitive to the emergent activities of colleagues within the local milieu.

The practices that personnel use and rely upon to participate simultaneously in more than one activity are not small additions to the formal procedures which 'underlie' their various occupational tasks. Rather, they are an essential feature of work in the line control room without which personnel would be unable to accomplish their individual tasks or co-ordinate their activities with each other. These indigenous practices and reasoning are the resources through which personnel competently and reliably maintain the operation of the service, for all practical purposes.

Whilst control room personnel are undoubtedly sensitive to prescribed ways of undertaking specific tasks, such as delivering a public announcement or altering the destination of a train, undertaking competent and reasonable work demands that seemingly 'individual' activities are produced with regard to concurrent actions of colleagues within the local milieu. This may involve no more than delaying a public announcement so as to avoid disrupting a delicate negotiation between a controller and a driver. Alternatively, it may involve co-ordinating the production of an activity with the concurrent actions of a colleague who is engaged elsewhere, so that, for example, a timely contribution can be interjected into a telephone conversation. Or it may necessitate producing actions in such a way that potentially private and specialised tasks, such as rewriting the timetable from 'within' a crisis, are rendered visible in particular ways to colleagues within the local milieu, enabling them to co-ordinate their own actions accordingly. The production of activities within the line control room, including relatively complex and specialised tasks, is co-ordinated with, and sensitive to, the concurrent actions of colleagues.

One way of conceptualising the social and interactional organisation of task-based activities is to draw on Goffman's (1981) discussion of a participation framework. Goffman suggests that any activity is dependent upon a particular production format which establishes, or attempts to establish, the ways in which 'those within the perceptual range of the event' will participate within the activity. In the materials at hand, we can begin to discern how the design of particular activities may be simultaneously sensitive to the potential demands of different 'recipients' both within and beyond the local milieu. So, for example, whilst speaking to a signalman on the telephone to ask whether he has corrected the running order of a couple of 'out-of-turn' trains, the controller may not only articulate certain segments of his talk with respect to his conversation with the signalman, but shape particular words or phrases so that they are overheard by, and implicate certain actions for, the DIA. Indeed, even a single utterance may be designed to engender different actions by different colleagues who may be positioned at different locations within the organisation. The production format of many activities within the line control room is subject to multiple demands and implicates different forms of co-participation from various personnel. The same activity can be systematically designed for different forms of co-participation, and can even momentarily merge different ecologies within the organisational milieu.

4.8   Technology and collaboration in action

The usefulness of the fixed line diagram, the computerised line displays, the CCTV monitors, and the various other tools designed to facilitate work within the line control room, relies upon practices and reasoning through which personnel produce their own actions and make sense of the conduct of their colleagues. In the light of these practices, control room personnel are continually and unavoidably, implicitly and explicitly, gathering and distributing information to each other concerning the current operation of the service. Such information informs the very intelligibility of various diagrams and representations they use for seeing and assessing the service, and infuses the ways in which they recognise certain events and are able to develop a co-ordinated response. The use of the technology to identify and manage the various problems which routinely emerge in the operation of the service is dependent upon the routine ways in which personnel produce and co-ordinate their actions with each other.

For example, the fixed line diagram displays the position of trains on the Bakerloo Line between Queens Park and the Elephant and Castle. Each train appears as a strip of between 2 and 6 lights depending on how many sections of track the train is covering at a particular moment (see Figure 4.6). At any time between 6.30 a.m. and 10.00 p.m. there are likely to be between 15 and 25 trains indicated on the board. The diagram provides staff within the control room, and, of course, visitors including management and even sociologists, with the ability to make, at a glance, an initial assessment of the current operation of the service.

An even distribution of trains (lights) along the board with relatively few gaps between them, on both the South and North lines, tends to indicate

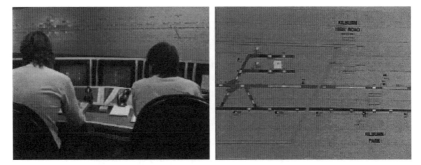

Figure 4.6 The fixed line diagram from the signalman's desk and a
detail showing the junctions around Kilburn.

that the service is running according to plan, i.e. the timetable. Yet, as any
controller knows, such an even distribution of vehicles along the line can
conceal important problems which may later lead to difficulties. The fixed
line diagram does not tell whether the trains are in or out of turn, or which
particular train is where. Neither does it provide information concerning
an upcoming shortage of drivers, vehicles which are causing difficulties,
stations which are closed 'due to a London Fire Brigade investigation', nor
reveal any of the complex body of timetable reformations which may have
already been undertaken and which may lead to difficulties later. In short,
the fixed line diagram and the information it provides is a critical resource
in control and crisis management, but only in the light of the natural
history of the operation of the service on any particular day. Without
knowledge of timetable reformations, out of turns, vehicle problems,
station closures, that is, the incidents which have occurred and the ways in
which they were managed, the technology is largely redundant. The socio-
interactional organisation of individual tasks and activities within the line
control room, and the ways in which personnel monitor and participate in
each other's conduct, provides for the possibility of using the tools and
technologies at hand.

In the light of practices which provide for mutual monitoring and co-
participation within the line control room, the technology provides the
controller and DIA with the ability to assess the current operation of
traffic, and undertake, if necessary, remedial action or provide information to staff and passengers. The 'public' availability of the technology
within the control room, whether it is a fixed line diagram, a CCTV
screen, a screen-based line diagram or an information display, provides a
critical resource in the collaboration between controller, DIA and signal
assistant. For example, personnel are able to assume that they have equivalent access to the different technological sources of information and

that, in principle, observations concerning the current operation of the service are mutually and commonly available. More importantly, perhaps, personnel can use the common sources of information as a reliable means of accounting for a broad range of actions and tasks undertaken by others. So, for example, in fragments 4.2 and 4.5 we noted how the DIA turned to the fixed line diagram as a source of explanation for the controller's intervention. Or, it was observed how the controller could produce a request which is embedded within, and constitutes, a mutually available scene on a CCTV monitor. The mutual availability of the various information displays allows personnel to presuppose that information available to one is available to all; a presupposition which is dependent upon the systematic ways in which individuals monitor and participate in each other's actions and activities.

Whilst the mutual availability of particular sources of information is utilised in making sense of each other's actions and co-ordinating them, it is the mutual visibility of the use of technology within individual activities which provides an important resource in the production of collaborative action. For example, a glance towards the fixed line diagram, a gesture towards the radio phone, or a scroll through a display of the points at a particular junction, can all provide resources through which a colleague can recognise the actions or activities of another. The use of a particular tool, even looking at a particular piece of text such as the timetable, can render the activity of a colleague visible; allowing others to co-ordinate their own actions with the apparent conduct of another.

Whilst the very use of tools such as the PA system, even before the onset of an announcement, can provide a relatively unambiguous sense of a colleague's conduct, the intelligibility of the use of a particular technology is embedded within the activity at hand. For example, switching a scene on the CCTV monitor may gain its particular sense by virtue of the immediately preceding actions, such as glancing at the fixed line diagram and grabbing the PA microphone and headset.

The intelligibility of the action (involving the use of some particular tool or technology), not only may be embedded within the developing course of the individual's conduct, but also may be located with respect to a colleague's activity. So, for example, in fragment 4.2, the intelligibility of the DIA's setting of the PA system, is accomplished by virtue not only of the actions position within a developing trajectory of conduct being undertaken by the DIA, but also the action's location with respect to the concurrent conduct of the controller. Or, for example, consider how in fragment 4.5 the controller presupposes that the DIA's orientation towards the CCTV concerns the driver at Oxford Circus. The location of the looking within the trajectory of the DIA's actions, coupled with the juxtaposition of the DIA's actions with the attempts to contact the driver, provide the resources through which the controller can assemble the sense of the look and produce the request to contact the driver.

The visibility of a colleague's use of a particular tool or source of information, even if it consists of no more than a momentary glance at a line diagram, is made sense of by virtue of the action's location not only within the colleague's emergent conduct, but also with respect to how that action, given its occurrence 'here and now', may be sensitive to actions being undertaken by others within the local environment. So, whilst on the one hand the action may 'naturally' emerge within a trajectory of a particular individual's conduct, it may also be simultaneously embedded in and co-ordinated with the activities of other individuals within the control room. For the 'relevant' sense of the action to be assembled, personnel have to be sensitive to the colleagues' concurrent participation in multiple activities within the local milieu. The use of the various tools and technologies is embedded in the accomplishment of simultaneous and overlapping activities, which themselves are dependent upon an indigenous socio-interactional organisation that provides for their production, intelligibility and co-ordination.

The ways in which an individual's use of a particular tool or technology may be monitored by a colleague and feature in the production of multiple activities, leads one to question, once again, the conventional wisdom in HCI which places the single user and their cognitive capabilities at the centre of the analytic domain. Even more innovative conceptions of the 'user', which aim to take into account the perceptions and attitudes of a range of participants who employ particular tools (e.g. Mumford, 1983), perhaps draw too sharp a distinction between a person handling a system and those others within the 'local' environment whose actions feature in the accomplishment of a particular task. For example, consider how the use of the CCTV monitor by the DIA occasioned a request by a colleague and provided the resources for both the design and impact of the utterance. Or how, in fragment 4.3, the DIA's use of the telephone to call the station manager, during the request for the train to turn short, allows the controller to recognise that his colleague is tracking the activity, and that he can confidently inform the driver that the 'DIA will make announcements for you'. So, whilst the 'direct' use of a particular system may indeed be undertaken by a particular individual within the line control room, the action may well be monitored by colleagues and feature in their production of activities. Noticing another's noticing of one's own conduct, and sensing that another's actions are sensitive to one's own actions and activities, informs the accomplishment of tool-mediated tasks in which an individual is engaged. It is not simply that work within the line control room is 'collaborative', it is rather that personnel, even within the accomplishment of apparently individual tasks, are sensitive to, and participating in, the activities of colleagues, and this participation is an intrinsic part of the organisation of the task. The use of the various tools and technologies in the line control room features in the accomplishment of these various activities and their co-ordination, and provides resources through which potentially 'private' actions are rendered visible within the local milieu. The various and complex ways in which the accomplishment of specialised tasks within the line control room, as in other working environments (Filippi and Theureau, 1993; Goodwin and Goodwin, 1996; Joseph, 1995; Suchman, 1993; Whalen, 1995) is embedded in, and inseparable from, interaction with the concurrent actions of colleagues, may lead us to question the usefulness of traditional approaches to the development of requirements for new technologies; approaches which place an individual user with a relatively circumscribed set of tasks at the forefront of the analytic agenda.

Whilst the socio-interactional organisation of task-based activities within the line control rooms might lead one to question the individualistic and psychologistic conceptions of conduct which underlie a substantial body of work in HCI and requirements analysis, it does not necessarily provide wholehearted support for recent initiatives in CSCW; in particular the growing body of conceptual and technical work in the area. With its emphasis on co-operation, and, in particular, technical support for 'group' and co-operative activity, CSCW runs the risk of entrenching the distinction between the individual and the collaborative, allowing us to preserve a demarcation between particular tasks and their co-ordination. Indeed, even well-meaning and sophisticated distinctions in recent literature in CSCW which emphasise, for example, 'articulation work', 'negotiation', 'mechanisms of interaction' and the like, run the danger of inadvertently separating the production of an activity from its co-ordination with the actions of others. As we see in the line control rooms, as in the environments we have discussed in previous chapters, the very production of an activity may be embedded and inseparable from its real-time co-ordination with the actions of others. In consequence, it becomes not only difficult empirically, but conceptually tenuous, to demarcate the individual from the collaborative. It is not simply, therefore, that the concept of the group which underpins an important number of technological innovations in CSCW is a crude characterisation of what happens in team work, but rather the very concept presupposes distinctions which are misleading and drives analytic attention away from the very organisations which provide for the routine and contingent accomplishment of workplace activities.

In the line control rooms, whilst different personnel have distinct responsibilities and areas of jurisdiction which are not undertaken by members of the other occupational categories, the competent accomplishment of their specialised tasks is dependent upon an indigenous organisation which systematically shapes and co-ordinates their activities with respect to the contributions of others. The controller and the DIA produce particular activities, even relatively complex tasks, with respect to the responsibilities and concurrent conduct of their colleague(s), tailoring their actions so that they preserve a mutually co-ordinated response to particular incidents and events. Moreover, whilst engaged in one activity, we find the controller and DIA monitoring each other's conduct and able to discriminate the local environment with regard to contingencies which may be relevant to either their own conduct or the actions of their colleagues. Work within the line control room does not simply necessitate that the participants distribute information and maintain a compatible orientation to the current scene. Rather, it requires that even the most apparently individual tasks are 'ongoingly' accomplished, moment by moment, with regard to the conduct and responsibilities of the co-participants. This may involve mutually focused interaction between control room personnel, but in a large part it requires the controller and DIA to engage in distinct tasks and activities, whilst simultaneously participating in the conduct of their colleague(s). The activities of personnel within the line control room continually flow between the private and the public, between the individual and the collaborative, so that any attempt to demarcate the co-operative from the individual, or still less delineate the formal properties of the group within the line control room, is unlikely to prove either insightful or conceptually fruitful.

5 The collaborative production of computer commands

> The division of labour, in its turn, implies interaction; for it consists not in the sheer difference of one man's kind of work from that of another, but in the fact that the different tasks and accomplishments are parts of a whole to whose product all, in some degree, contribute. And wholes, in the human social realm as in the rest of the biological and in the physical realm, have their essence in interaction. Work as social interaction is the central theme of sociological and social psychological study of work.
>
> Hughes (1958)

5.1 Introduction

In recent years, there has been a significant change in the nature of the technology which is used to support command and control in rail and rapid urban transport. Electromechanical displays, public announcement systems and mechanical signalling designed in the 1950s have been increasingly replaced by computer and telecommunication systems which can schedule trains automatically, set the appropriate signals and generate the relevant information for the travelling public. In the control room, rather than seeing the state of service through a set of lights on a fixed line diagram, augmented by screen displays as in the Bakerloo Line Control Room, the railway is viewed solely through visual display units and controlled through keyboards and mice. In this chapter, we wish to consider work and interaction in such a control room, one which is perhaps one of the most sophisticated, technologically, in the London area, if not the United Kingdom. The Docklands Light Railway (DLR) was built during the 1980s to enhance the infrastructure of a large redevelopment area in east London, north of the Thames. Substantial government funding through the Docklands Redevelopment Agency provided the opportunity to build a state-of-the-art railway and control system. Automatic, driverless trains are guided by a complex computer system which is overseen by two controllers based in a single, centralised control centre.

The use of automated technologies for dynamic processes and environments has long been an area of interest for those working in human factors and related disciplines such as cognitive ergonomics and human factors (e.g. Alty and Johannsen, 1989; Rasmussen, 1986). With respect to systems for process control, command and control and, more recently, C^3I technologies, researchers have been particularly concerned with the capabilities of individual users to operate such systems (e.g. Kolski and Millot, 1991). These technologies provide a domain in which users draw on a complex range of cognitive skills in using computers to oversee a dense network of real-time operations. In many cases, like railway networks, nuclear power plants and chemical processing, such systems are safety critical, a mistaken command potentially leading to a threat to human life (Bignell and Fortune, 1984; Perrow, 1984). In these circumstances, the design of the technology and its ability to support the real-time thinking and performance of personnel is critical, as we have unfortunately discovered in airline crashes, nuclear 'leaks' and collisions on railways. Aside from the growing interest in naturalistic studies of air traffic management (see, e.g., Harper et al., 1989, Vortac et al., 1994) there remains a relative paucity of literature concerned with the ways in which individuals use command and control systems in everyday, working environments. Instead, research has focused on the knowledge, intelligence and cognitive abilities of individual users, considering, for example, how decisions are made using incomplete information, how an individual's workload is managed when accomplishing multiple tasks, and the varying affordances of different types of displays (Lind, 1988; McLeod and Sherwood-Jones, 1992; Sundström, 1991). Typical analyses have characterised the individual's competencies in terms of different classes of knowledge required to operate and make sense of a system, and the interrelationships between those classes. Assessment of the models derived is frequently then made through experiments with users or simulations of situations. Where the activities of operators are examined *in situ*, this is typically of circumscribed activities, decomposing these into goals, operations and functions. Hence, the predominant forms of analysis neglect the organisational competencies of the participants, particularly with respect to the tacit skills and practices through which individuals co-ordinate their activities with colleagues in the setting.

In this chapter, we wish to examine occasions on which the controllers intervene in the automatic operation of the service either to cope with problems which arise or to deal with more routine requests, such as shunting a train around a depot. (For further details and background see Luff (1997).) These interventions involve one of the two controllers entering commands into the system, using a keyboard to enable a train to move according to a revised schedule. It is a task undertaken by a particular individual, alone, and yet we hope to demonstrate that this seemingly individual activity is systematically co-ordinated with the actions of colleagues, in particular the second controller. We also want to consider how personnel within the domain are able to retrieve a sense of each other's conduct by virtue of their colleagues' use of the system, and how the operation of the computer 'ongoingly' informs the conduct of others, including their conversations over the telephone. In one sense, therefore, the chapter is concerned with how the use of the computer is sensitive to, and relevant for, the concurrent actions of colleagues, both those within the control room and others distributed around the railway network.

In examining how the production of computer commands is sensitive to the actions of colleagues, the chapter touches on a number of more general issues. For example, despite the burgeoning critique of traditional models of organisations, and conceptual innovations such as 'new institutionalism', the idea of a division of labour, in which personnel have roles and responsibilities and undertake prescribed forms of conduct, still underpins a great deal of organisational theory (in contrast, see, e.g., Anderson et al., 1989). The DLR Control Room is interesting in this regard. The two controllers work alongside each other and orient to a relatively formal division of responsibility, dividing the network into separate regions. In the course of their activities, however, they continually configure, and reconfigure, who does what, when, and thereby shape an emerging division of labour. In the case at hand, it is not simply that an informal division of labour emerges to deal with problems in the application of a formal specification, but rather that the actual distribution of tasks and responsibilities is interactionally accomplished, step by step, moment by moment, within the production of various activities.

A second more general issue, which once again arises in this chapter, concerns the ways in which we consider the use of technology in the workplace. In various ways, we have been attempting to reposition how technologies feature in workplace activities, developing a way through the excessive individualism of HCI and cognitive science and the group-laden theories of (certain approaches in) CSCW. In this chapter, we interweave an analysis of an individual's use of a system, the actual entry of commands into the computer, with the 'users' real-time interaction with co-located and distributed colleagues. In this way, we hope to provide a further sense in which the operation of a complex system is embedded in, and embodies, socially organised practice and procedure. The system's use is made intelligible to others not simply by virtue of a 'community of practice', but rather the production of commands is a collaborative activity, which is both oriented to the conduct of others and in various ways permeated in real-time by and through their actions.

There is one further point of some methodological significance to those working in both CSCW and qualitative sociology. Over the past couple of decades, Conversation Analysis has generated a substantial body of research concerned with the social and interactional organisation of institutional talk in settings such as medical encounters, the media and courtrooms. Such studies have drawn on the sequential organisation of conversation to delineate the ways in which participants accomplish specialised activities which require, and are embodied in, particular forms of talk. The material addressed in this and previous chapters begins to demonstrate how the sequential organisation of workplace activities, be they vocal, visual or some combination of both, provides a critical resource for participants in co-ordinating their actions with each other and in recognising the conduct of others. Unlike conversation and the specialised forms of institution talk addressed in the literature, the organisation of work, in this and other settings we have addressed, does not necessarily involve 'mutually focused' interaction and its implications for topic coherence and the like. Rather, as in Reuters and the Bakerloo Line Control Rooms, personnel may be engaged in distinct and seemingly unrelated activities, some of which even involve conversations with individuals located outside the immediate domain. Yet, participants not only orient to each other's conduct, but make sense of the activities of others, and co-ordinate their own actions with each other, by orienting to the sequential organisation of particular activities, including the conversations of co-located and distant colleagues. Temporal features of context, and in particular the sequential organisation of activities, remain a critical resource in the co-ordination of these seemingly fragmented, technologically informed, workplace activities.

5.2   The setting: scheduling trains and dealing with problems on the line

Although the activities in DLR Control Room have many similarities to those in the Bakerloo Line Control Room, there are significant differences. Principal amongst these is the automated train system. Driverless trains are controlled automatically by an Automatic Train Supervision (ATS) computer system. The operation of the system is overseen by two controllers who sit alongside each other in the control room. Each controller has a monitor which provides them with information concerning the movement of traffic along the line and can use a keyboard, if necessary, to reschedule the path and timing of particular vehicles. It could be possible for each controller, in principle, to take responsibility for, issue commands to, and view, the same section or area of line. However, the controllers develop a 'working division of labour' in which

Figure 5.1 The DLR Control Room.

they distribute activities between each other. At first glance, the division of labour appears relatively straightforward. The controller on the left, jokingly called the 'God of the Line', is the principal controller (referred to as Ci). He or she operates the radio and if necessary is responsible for rescheduling traffic on the main sections of the line. The controller on the right is known as the 'secondary controller' (Cii) and ordinarily deals with problems that arise in the depot. Individuals take it in turns as to who is the principal and the secondary controller. Despite the apparent simplicity of the division of labour, as we will see, the actual distribution of responsibilities and activities is 'ongoingly' accomplished with regard to the circumstances and contingencies which arise in dealing with the numerous problems faced by the Docklands Light Railway.

Figure 5.1 gives a general view of the control room focusing on the controllers' desk. The general organisation of the technology available to the controllers is shown in Figure 5.2. Both controllers have a keyboard which can operate the ATS, with a display to it in front of each of them. The phone system is positioned on the left of the workstations, and in consequence it is the controller on the left (Ci) who tends to take and make calls.

Given the general distribution of activities between the controllers, it is normal for the two controllers to have different views of the line presented on the screens in front of them. Thus ATS1, the screen in front of Ci, often displays a schematic map of the line (Figure 5.3).

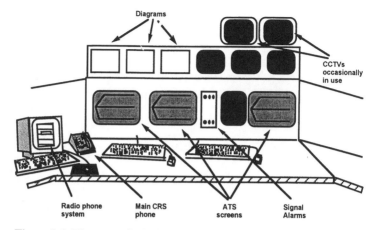

Figure 5.2 The controller's desk and technology.

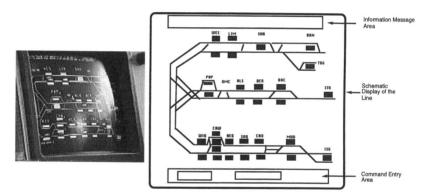

Figure 5.3 The ATS1 display and a schematic diagram of what it presents. The ATS diagram transforms the geography of the line. The middle line actually goes to the northeast, whilst the upper ones goes northwest into central London.

ATS2, the screen in front of Cii, often displays the shunting yard (or 'Operations and Maintenance Centre', OMC, see Figure 5.4). (Although it is common for the ATS1 and ATS2 screens to present the main line and the OMC respectively, they can be used to give other views, for example the points and signals in a particular area such as a station, a track where trains can cross over or a complex intersection. The displays, therefore, present a configurable view of the operation of the service, which can be altered to fit the particular circumstances that controllers face.)

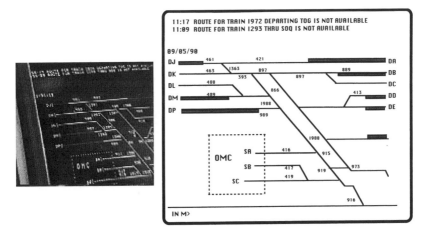

Figure 5.4 ATS2 display of the depot and, on the right, a sketch of what it typically presents.

The controllers' commands to the ATS are sent to the appropriate docking unit located on each platform of every station. To prompts such as 'TRAIN AT' or 'PLATFORM', which appear at the bottom of the screen, the controllers issue commands to the relevant unit. The timing of these commands is critical. In order to alter the route of a train, the controller has to enter the command either whilst the train is docked at the appropriate station or before it arrives. In consequence, it is usual for controllers to transmit changes to the schedule to particular stations way before the arrival of a particular train, though, of course, only following the departure of the train ahead.

Although the trains on the DLR do not have drivers, each has a train captain (or TC) who is responsible for dealing with queries from passengers, checking tickets and the like. When vehicles have to be controlled manually, TCs can operate the vehicle from a console at the front of the train. Unfortunately, despite the substantial investment in Automatic Train Supervision, it is necessary to operate trains manually more frequently than might be expected. For example, at the time of data collection, trains had considerable problems 'docking' at stations, and it was not unusual for the TC to have to shunt the train backwards or forwards to get into the required position at a platform. Such difficulties, as well as others when there are disputes or violence from passengers or when suspect packages are identified, not only delay the train in question, but often require a series of changes to the schedule of the traffic following the vehicle.

Commands to the ATS mainly consist of 'packets' of track and station identifiers. Sections of track are identified by three number combinations, stations by an abbreviation of their name using three letters, for example DER is Devons Road.

Consider the following example. In the transcripts the typing of function keys is indicated by '■', number keys by '⑨', and letter keys by 'A B C...'. 'Enter' is represented by '↲' and other unidentified keys by '❏'. Keys that are struck with some force are underlined and pauses between characters are indicated by '...' each '.' representing one-tenth of a second.

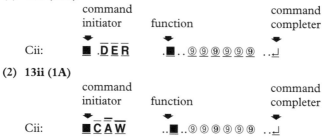

(1) **42ii (10A)**

	command initiator	function	command completer
Cii:	■ .D̲E̲R̲	.■..⑨⑨⑨⑨⑨⑨	..↲

(2) **13ii (1A)**

	command initiator	function	command completer
Cii:	■C̲A̲W̲	..■..⑨⑨⑨⑨⑨⑨	..↲

After typing the appropriate special function key to initiate the command, a station identifier is entered for Devons Road (D̲ E̲ R̲) in (1), and for Canary Wharf (C̲ A̲ W̲) in (2). This is the location of the docking unit where the command is to be directed. The location is completed by a function command identifying the direction of the train. Then numbers, identifying portions of track that specify the new routes are entered. So, for example, a controller might type '■ C̲ A̲ W̲ ■ 412 453 ↲' to alter the route of the next train entering Canary Wharf to track sections '412' followed by '453'.

The operation of the ATS system is designed to stand alone, to enable one controller to reschedule the time and route of trains. However, the distribution of access to the radio telephone, coupled with the necessity to undertake a series of rapid and interrelated changes to the schedule when problems emerge, requires controllers to systematically co-ordinate their use of the ATS system. In some circumstances, this may simply involve rescheduling a series of trains in the light of commands entered into the system by the principal controller, more often than not, however, it requires controllers to anticipate action and produce sequentially appropriate conduct prior to the completion of particular activities.

5.3   Transforming calls into commands

Since the principal controller ordinarily handles the radio telephone, it is not unusual for calls to be received which require the secondary controller to undertake particular actions or activities. For example, a call may occasion rescheduling traffic in the depot, and thereby require the secondary controller to enter a series of relevant commands into the ATS. Given the proximity of the two participants in the control room, and the presence of a loudspeaker which broadcasts the incoming talk at least within the vicinity of the desk, the secondary controller can overhear conversations between the principal controller and the party with whom he is speaking on the telephone. Consider the following fragment in which Ci takes a call from the depot.

Fragment 5.1   Transcript 1

Ci: four seven?
       (1.5)
E: four seven↓ (.) Dee Pee (you are moving around) in the
       depot tester over↑
       (1.5)
Ci: Dee Pee to depot tester↓ yep thats message received
       ma:te↓ (.) proceed on green aspects on the (clear) signal↓
       (0.6)
E: (thanks) for your help↑

Ci receives a call that a train is ready to be moved in the depot. In response he instructs the driver to proceed on a clear signal. The call requires a relevant command to be entered into the system. As Ci confirms the train movement from the location 'Dee Pee' to the 'depot tester', on the word 'yep', Cii begins to enter the command.

Fragment 5.1   Transcript 2

Ci: Dee Pee to depot tester↓ yep thats message received ma:te↓ (.) proceed
Cii: ■   ■   ⑨   ⑨   ⑨

The secondary controller therefore is able to initiate a relevant course of action prior to the completion of the call. His actions rely upon his ability not only to hear his colleague's confirmation of the train movement, but to have heard the previous utterance by the caller. The controller's confirmation 'Dee Pee to depot tester yep' serves to confirm the movement of the train to the caller, and simultaneously provide the resources through which his co-present colleague can undertake a sequentially appropriate action: setting the system so that the train is free to pass along the appropriate section of line.

The secondary controller's actions provide resources through which the principal controller can determine that the necessary actions enabling the train to pass along the line have been undertaken. The actual commands entered by the secondary controller may not be visible to the principal controller, yet the immediate juxtaposition of the onset of the actions with the repetition 'Dee Pee to depot tester' and confirmation 'yep' would appear to suggest that the one activity is sensitive to the other.

In contrast, in the following fragment there seems to be some delay before the secondary controller begins to address an issue which arises in a telephone call between a member of staff in the depot and the principal controller. The delay in the production of the sequentially appropriate conduct is treated by the principal controller as his colleague's failure to grasp the reason for the call. Cii starts typing sometime after the confirmation by the controller. Indeed, his typing follows the remote party's final turn in the conversation (arrowed).

Fragment 5.2   Transcript 1

> *((Ci is talking to the Control Room Manager, the phone
> begins to ring and Ci turns to the phone system to answer
> the call))*

Ci: two ni:ne
      (.)
E: (   )
      (1.2)
Ci: thats (a roger::) (fully at greens when I get them from you)
      over
      (1.5)
E: (   )
      (0.2)
▶   *((Cii starts typing))*
      ((Ci puts phone down))

The secondary controller begins to enter the relevant commands as the call comes to completion. The commands are relatively complex and involve a long sequence of numbers for a lengthy section of track. The secondary controller's actions appear to be sensitive both to the talk which has emerged in the call, and to the principal controller's confirmation of the request. They also appear sensitive to a series of gestures which serve to clarify just what needs to be done, where (see transcript 2).

Towards the completion of the silence following confirmation of the request, the principal controller begins to gesture. The gesture consists of two components. He begins by first pointing towards the top of the secondary controller's ATS monitor (image 2.1), and then points to the bottom right (image 2.2). As the pointing hand withdraws, the secondary controller begins to enter the long sequence of numbers.

Fragment 5.2   Transcript 2

2.1   Ci   Cii   2.2   Ci   Cii

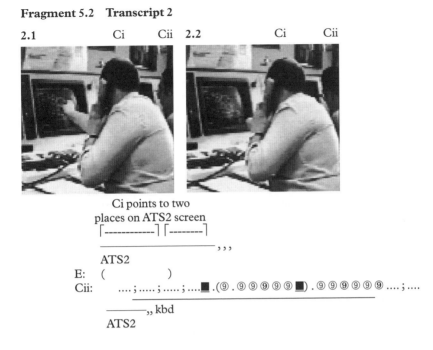

        Ci points to two
    places on ATS2 screen
    ⌐------------⌐ ⌐--------⌐
    ─────────────────────── ,,,
        ATS2
    E: (   )
    Cii: ....;.....;.....;....■.(⑨.⑨⑨⑨⑨⑨■).⑨⑨⑨⑨⑨....;....
         ───────── ,, kbd
    ATS2

The gesture appears to encourage the secondary controller to enter the relevant commands; the commands which are relevant to rescheduling the traffic requested by the caller (and confirmed by the controller). The gesture also, coupled with the utterance(s), provides the secondary controller with a sense of what needs to be done. The pointing hand shows 'what's going where', and thereby clarifies the relevant vehicle and the path of its movement on the screen. In the light of hearing and seeing his colleague's actions, the secondary controller is able to enter the appropriate commands, the sequentially appropriate activity.

The principal controller's gesture itself, appears to be produced with regard to the initial absence of the sequentially appropriate activity, namely the entry of a set of commands at the moment at which the requested action is confirmed by the principal controller. Finding the sequentially relevant actions absent at that moment, a gesture is produced which not only serves to clarify the proposed path of the vehicle, but simultaneously encourages the secondary controller to produce the appropriate actions. The absence of the commands, during or immediately following the principal controller's utterance, occasions the gesture, a gesture which serves to retrospectively clarify the talk which the secondary controller undoubtedly heard. In this way, the participants orient to a distribution of actions, a division of labour, which is instantiated and repaired during the very production of the activities which are attributed to particular individuals.

The secondary controller therefore enters commands into the system on the basis of requests and instructions he overhears. He listens to the telephone conversations of his colleagues, with regard to the ways in which the talk may implicate conduct in the control room and in particular the rescheduling of the signalling system. The confirmation of a request can also provide the secondary controller with the resources through which he can enter commands into the system, and thereby produce the very signalling arrangements which are implicated by the agreed course of action in the phone conversation. The use of the system in this way therefore involves the secondary controller in participating in the call, in as much as he listens to what is going on, and using the talk of others to organise the arrangement of commands that he enters into the computer. Moreover, the principal controller, whilst seemingly engaged in the telephone conversation, is sensitive to the responsibilities and actions of his colleague, organising his talk so that instructions are clear and audible within the immediate domain, and initiating clarification where it is noticed that the secondary controller fails to immediately initiate the relevant course of action. The use of the system, though operated by typing on their own keyboards displayed on the personal monitors in front of them, involves the controllers in close collaboration. Both individuals produce independent but interrelated activities and participate in each others' actions (if only to notice whether the other has produced the sequentially appropriate conduct). In this way, rescheduling of the traffic is managed efficiently and 'with dispatch' (see Sacks, 1992); the 'ad hoc' division of labour serving to generate the appropriate commands to the signals with little delay between the request and its entry into the system.

5.4   Discriminating calls' relevancies

Although the principal controller frequently controls traffic on the main line and the secondary controller the depot, they do not always work in this way. In the next fragment, for example, the controllers have their views the other way around: ATS1 has a view of the depot, and ATS2 the main line. As a call comes in, the secondary controller (Cii) starts typing (indicated by the arrow) a command to a station on the main line (Westferry).

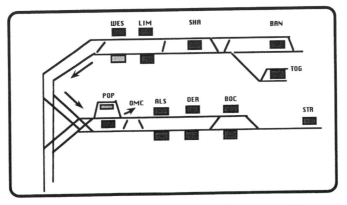

Figure 5.5 A sketch of the train movements considered in fragment 5.3. During the call, the train is stationary at Westferry (WES). It is on a route heading towards Stratford (STR) in the east. The caller is at Poplar (POP), between it and both Stratford and the depot (OMC).

Fragment 5.3   Transcript 1

    Ci: transit base receiving↓ from transit one five go ahead
         over↓
         (0.5)
    M: one ↑fi:ve↓ (try) and pick(ing) up at (route) one
▸   one (.) <u>six</u> at (0.2) Poplar <u>o</u>ver↑
         (0.7)
    Ci: much appreciated thanks Chas↑ (0.6) (nice to have <u>you</u>:)
         (1.3)

    ((Ci puts phone down))

Although the reason for the call is not completely clear, the initial turns of the call are distinctive, revealing the remote party to be 'Chas' or 'transit one five': the 'mobile' CRS at the time. Mobile controllers travel around the region covered by the DLR system and can intervene on the spot, wherever appropriate. To do this, they also have a radio and can listen in to the interactions between their colleagues in the control room and the train captains. In this case the 'mobile' volunteers to undertake some activity at Poplar to assist with the operation in the service. Cii's typing then at the next station Westferry, appears to be related to the call (see Figure 5.5).

Cii's typing commences as the mobile completes the 'reason for the call': 'pick(ing) up at (route) one one (.) <u>six</u> at (0.2) Poplar <u>o</u>ver↑'. Indeed, Cii's hands move towards the keyboard just after the mobile utters the location 'one one (.) <u>six</u>' and she starts typing '**W E** <u>S</u>', just after he gives the name of the station 'Poplar'.

Fragment 5.3   Transcript 2

M: pick(ing) up at (route) one one (.) <u>six</u> at–Poplar <u>over</u>↑----.--
Cii: ■.$\overline{\underline{W}}$ $\overline{\underline{E}}$ $\overline{\underline{S}}$...

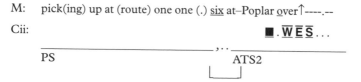

hands down to keyboard

Although the command typed in to the ATS and the ongoing call may only be co-ordinated in time, further examination reveals they may be more tightly interrelated, and that through her typing Cii displays a discernment, not only of the nature of the speaker and his circumstances, but also of a potential course of action to be taken.

Both the command and the call appear to relate to the same train, of which the train captain has, some time before, called in to report a problem. As well as this difficulty, the communication between the train captain and the controller has also been hampered by the train captain's radio only working intermittently. At the time of reporting the problem, even when the train captain has had to repeat several utterances, these repetitions have been barely audible. After this call, Ci throws his phone down in frustration and commences a course of action to 'stable' the vehicle in the depot (the OMC). The first action being for the train captain to get to Westferry and report from there.

Fragment 5.3   Transcript 3

Ci: on ar<u>r</u>ival Wes(t) Ferry report one three seven>set A: Tee
        Manual (clear to) Poplar (0.2) once at Poplar ( ) O eM
        Cee. <u>over</u>.

Prior to the mobile supervisor's call, this train can be seen entering Westferry and remaining there, and it appears to be the target of Cii's command. Indeed, just after Ci puts down the handset of the phone, the train identifier on the screen starts to move along the track eastward (to the left) towards Poplar. The timing of this, following its long stay at Westferry, the typing of a command directed at that station and the subsequent departure of the train are consistent with its eastward movement. Moreover, it is consistent with the earlier instructions of Ci to the train captain to move the train towards Westferry then through to Poplar to the OMC.

It appears that the call is also related to this train; the mobile's talk on the radio being heard as directly consequential to the participants in the control room. Indeed, his utterance provides resources for the controllers to revise the system and set the train at Westferry moving; his offer appearing to be to join the train at Poplar. Cii's command thus both sets the train in motion for its eventual movement out of service, as suggested by Ci, and also makes it possible for the mobile controller's offer to be accepted.

To do this, Cii has to attend to the details of the call. It is not just that talk on the radio is monitored for matters of particular concern by a principal controller, say the depot or the main line, and that once these are confirmed the secondary controller then enters the appropriate command into the system. Cii has to attend to who is making it, what actions they are requesting or taking, and to which trains and which locations these relate. Ciis have to discriminate between the remote parties on the radio and the range of possible co-interactants on the line, and make sense of, and act on, their contributions. They have to discriminate a call's relevance for their own activities: who the speaker is, their responsibilities, their location and any course of action proposed – all may provide resources to make sense of a call and enter a command into the system.

In fragment 5.3, the call can be heard to be distinctive through the particular organisation of the talk and the nature of the turns that are produced. It may be that the call sign and even the voice of the remote party can be recognised by the participants in the control room, but his contribution has to be heard as relevant to the circumstances at hand: the particular happenings on the line. In 5.3, an activity at Poplar is heard to relate to a train at Westferry. This requires the talk on the radio to be heard in relation to the current state of the service. Once the mobile states where he will be picked up, Cii can enter the command into the system to start to move the train at Westferry. The typing of the command is tied to the talk by a remote participant in the call.

Cii's use of the computer can thus be seen to be tied within a web of interactional activities happening in the control room and outside. The talk between the controller and the mobile CRS provides the resources with which to type the command. Cii has to discriminate the relevance of the call for her own activities. The speaker in the call, their location and responsibilities may all contribute to what next actions are relevant. These all are made sense of with respect to the current state of the service and the projected activities of her colleagues, as displayed on the screen and made apparent in the prior talk. Hence, the entry of commands into the system and the readings off the screen are irretrievably embedded within the local interactions within the domain.

These three fragments begin to raise issues concerning the use of computer systems not normally addressed within studies of human–computer interaction. HCI, with its focus on the individual subject and his or her cognitive processing, typically places as secondary the activities of others within analyses of computer use. In the material at hand, however, we can begin to discern how the very activity of entering commands, or retrieving information from the screen, is embedded in the 'local context', and in particular the emerging action and interaction of the various participants.

5.5   Concurrent participation in multiple activities

From the previous fragments, it might appear that the secondary controller's principal responsibility is to enter commands into the system in the light of telephone conversations. This is not the case. Like principal controllers, they have a range of responsibilities concerned with the traffic management and dealing with problems and emergencies, not least of which is providing personnel both in the control room and outside with information concerning the current state of service and changes which are being implemented. For example, secondary controllers work closely with control room assistants (CRAs) particularly when dealing with problems which have implications for crewing trains. In the following fragment, for example, the secondary controller is talking to a CRA concerning a train that is being held at Stratford. In the meantime, the principal controller is finishing a conversation with an engineer who is visiting the control room, and then takes a phone call from a train captain who needs to operate the train manually.

Fragment 5.4   Transcript 1

Ci   E

Cii   CRA

Ci: Train base (to)
train seven <u>one</u>: (0.1) go ahead
<u>over</u>

(0.1)

CRA: How long are you keeping that A: Tee
Pee train there↑
(0.2)
Cii: There is a train (leaving) (0.2) all the ones↑
(0.2)
CRA: (oh there is one↓)

TC: (Stratford
       West India Quay over)
       (0.4)
Ci: Select emergency shunt<proceed
     for<u>w</u>ard in that mode<dock at
     Poplar routeboard tw<u>o</u> zero seven↑
     (0.2)

(0.5)
CRA: ((*on phone*)):   (   ) leaving
       Stratford now↑

As the principal controller talks with the train captain on the phone, Cii replies to the CRA and then enters three commands into the ATS: the first is to Heron Quays station, the second and third to Devons Road. The commands to Devons Road are concerned with taking out of action and stabling the next train to arrive; the train which has left Stratford.

On completion of his phone call with the train captain, the principal controller turns to the secondary controller and says '°ehhm (0.2) I was going to <u>say</u>:<let the one (one one) <u>go</u>↑'. The utterance appears to refer to some aspect of the secondary controller's previous actions, in particular the commands that she entered into the system whilst he was talking on the phone. Following the utterance, Cii goes on to to enter a further command.

Fragment 5.4   Transcript 2

       (0.2)
Ci: (thats a rog) thank you↑ (0.2) (over)
       (1.7)
       ((*Ci puts phone down*))
       (2.3)
▸ Ci: °ehhm (0.2) I was <u>going</u> to <u>say</u>:<let the one (one one) <u>go</u>↑
       (0.2) (run through)

       ((*Cii enters command*))

To understand how the secondary controller makes sense of her colleague's utterance, we need a little background information.

When the principal controller's call with the train captain commences, there are only three trains on the line between Canary Wharf and Stratford. One train is about to leave Stratford going south (the subject of CRA's conversation with the secondary controller), one train is stuck at West India Quay going north (the subject of the call to Ci), and the third train is going north towards Poplar. Figure 5.6 is a sketch of the state of the main line diagram when the call commences.

Cii's first command to Heron Quays (HEQ) is addressed to the train that follows the vehicle currently at West India Quay (WIQ). The commands to Devons Road (DER) are for the train just leaving Stratford; the train which will be stabled after it arrives at Devons Road. It is this train

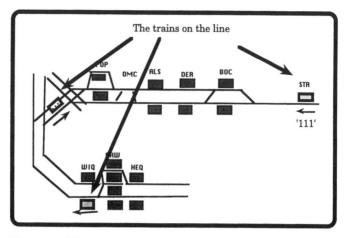

Figure 5.6 The trains between Canary Wharf (CAW) and Stratford (STR) at the beginning of the call in fragment 5.4.

which is being discussed by the CRA and the secondary controller. The CRA's query to the secondary controller is occasioned by a conversation he is having on the phone.

Fragment 5.4   Transcript 3

CRA ((*on phone*)):	hang on a minute ma:te↓
	(1.3)
CRA ((*to Cii*)):	(how long are you going to keep that) A:: Tee Pee train
	(out)
	(0.3)
Cii:	What?
	(0.1)
CRA:	how long are you keeping that A: Tee Pee train there↓
	(0.2)
Cii:	there is a train (leaving) (0.2) all the ones↑
	(0.2)
◆ CRA:	(oh there is one↓)
	(0.5)
CRA ((*on phone*)):	( ) leaving Stratford now↑

The secondary controller points to the train on the screen, showing the CRA that it is leaving Stratford and proceeding to Devons Road. It is this train, the 111 ('all the ones') that the principal controller later refers to when he says "°ehhm (0.2) I was going to say:<let the one (one one) go↑".

Fragment 5.4 Transcript 4

((Ci puts phone down))

(2.3)

Ci: °Ehhm (0.2) I was going to say:<let the one (one one) go↑ (0.2) (
run through) thirteen (0.2) (wi ┌th these delays)

Cii: └(which ones) thirteen

(0.1) (Oh there ┌it is)

Ci: └(here) (0.2) Let that one run (.) (I'd) put
it back into auto:↓

The principal controller's utterance occasions a change in the activities of the secondary controller. Rather than stabling the train 111 after it arrives at Devons Road, the principal controller decides to return the train to automatic '(I'd) put it back into auto:↓', that is to allow the vehicle to run its scheduled course. The principal controller's utterance appears to provide an account as to why the train should follow its original schedule, namely that he wants to try and retain thirteen vehicles on the system and thereby avoid reducing the service any more than it need be. The secondary controller agrees with the suggestion and immediately enters a new command for Devons Road.

Fragment 5.4 Transcript 5

■ . .. ; **D̲ E̲ R̲** . .

Ci: (here)--Let that one run (.) (I'd) put it back into auto:↓

In one sense, therefore, the fragment simply involves the controller rescheduling a vehicle and then, in the light of her colleague's recommendation, returning the train to its original automatic course. In this way, the principal controller is able to maintain some semblance of a normal service. Interactionally, the fragment is more complex and interesting. It reveals how the principal controller, despite his participation in other activities, remains sensitive to the actions of his colleague, and where necessary, intervenes in particular decisions. So, in the case at hand, we find the principal controller firstly talking with an engineer in the control room and then dealing with specific problems which arise with a train which requires shunting. During these activities, and in particular whilst he is providing instructions to the train captain over the phone, the principal controller is able not only to overhear his colleague's conversation with the CRA, but to make sense of the talk with regard to the commands that the secondary controller enters into the system. The principal controller recognises, by virtue of the commands that his colleague enters, the solution which is being put into place, and, on completing his own separate activity, is able to recommend an alternative course of action. It seems likely that the conversation between the CRA and secondary controller draws attention to the commands, so that, by remaining sensitive to the actions of his colleague, the principal controller is able to follow what is happening and initiate remedial action.

5.6   The collaborative production of a command

In the fragments discussed so far, we have seen how secondary controllers remain sensitive to conversations of their colleagues and, in the light of problems and instructions which arise within those calls, are able to enter commands into the system and provide sequentially appropriate activities. We have also seen how principal controllers orient to the actions of their colleagues, and, where necessary, are able to initiate remedial action in order to initiate organisationally relevant conduct, and even repair actions which have already occurred. This process of mutual monitoring and assessment of each other's conduct is rarely accomplished through direct, or mutually focused interaction, but rather works alongside and within distinct activities in which the participants are engaged. The use of the system, therefore, is dependent upon the participants' abilities to remain peripherally sensitive to each other's conduct and participate in concurrent activities.

In the following instance, we find the principal controller agreeing to a particular course of action in the light of activity undertaken on the computer by his colleague, the secondary controller. We join the action as a call is received asking whether it is possible to set the Automatic Train Protection (ATP) to manual at an upcoming station to engage in a shunting exercise. The caller is an instructor ('driver Ed' or 'driver education') putting a train captain through his paces, in this case, the train captain's ability to manually operate the vehicle. The train protection system prevents other vehicles entering the appropriate area of track near a train.

Fragment 5.5   Transcript 1

Ci: train base to train at five two::↑
    (3.3)
I: fi::ve two↓ (check) five two:↓ request permission to (.) change
    into A: Tee Pee (0.2) driver (0.3) (Ed) at Crosshar:bour: (0.4)
    over.
    (2.9)

As the instructor completes her request to the principal controller, the secondary controller begins to enter a command directed to Heron Quays (HEQ); a command which will change the train protection of the vehicle in question at Crossharbour. After entering the first packet, he pauses.

Fragment 5.5   Transcript 2

I: (Ed) at Crosshar:bour:---- over.-
Cii: ■....;$\overline{\text{H}}\,\overline{\text{E}}\,\overline{\text{Q}}$....;..

It is unclear why the secondary controller pauses following the completion of the first packet. However it may be the case that he is waiting to see how his colleague responds to the request, prior to completing the command. Curiously, the principal controller himself delays responding to the caller, and, when he does speak, he asks the instructor to stand by, that is, he delays a decision as to whether a change to the ATP can be made at Crossharbour. It may be that the principal controller is waiting to see what specific command is entered by his colleague, prior to confirming the request. He waits for nearly a second following the completion of the first packet of the command, and then replies.

Fragment 5.5   Transcript 3 (simplified)

        (2.9)
Ci: (I can see) if you could stand by and let me get back to you in a mo::
        (1.5)

As the principal controller commences his reply, his colleague begins to type, entering the section of track to which the command applies. The utterance which delays confirming the Instructor's request is co-produced with the entry of commands which change the operation of the vehicle at Crossharbour. As the secondary controller enters the details, his colleague watches the ATS monitor to discern what command is being entered (see transcript 4).

The secondary controller completes the command just following the completion of his colleague's request to the caller to 'stand by'. As the command is brought to completion, the principal controller turns back to the telephone, re-establishes contact with the instructor and confirms that she can change to manual when she arrives at Crossharbour. The affirmation of the request therefore is produced with regard to the actions of the secondary controller. In watching the ATS monitor, the principal controller is able to see not only that his colleague is producing an action which is responding to the instructor's request, but also the details of the solution found by the secondary controller to the problem of allowing the vehicle to be operated manually. For the principal controller, therefore, his colleague's actions provide him with the ability to confirm the request and recommend the instructor to follow a particular course of action, namely to set to manual operation at 'routeboard 143' and to proceed on the section of track from there 'until further notice'.

Fragment 5.5   Transcript 4

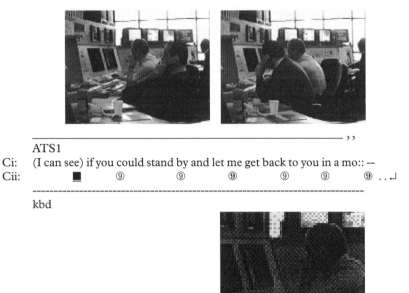

```
                                                                        ''
      ATS1
Ci:   (I can see) if you could stand by and let me get back to you in a mo:: --
Cii:     ■      ⑨        ⑨       ⑨        ⑨       ⑨       ⑨ . . ┘
      ------------------------------------------------------------------------
      kbd
```

Fragment 5.5   Transcript 5

```
       (1.5)
       ((radio ring, phone system beep))
       (2.3)
Ci:    fi:ve two, are you still receiving?
       (4.7)
TC:    () receiving over?
       (0.2)
Ci:    (that change is fine) thats affirmative when you arrive
       at Crossharbour (0.3) (routeboard) one four three (0.4) you
       may set A: Tee Pee manual (0.2) and proceed (on your
       section and clear) (0.2) until further notice↓
```

In this case, therefore, we can see how the principal controller orients to the completion of a sequentially appropriate activity by his colleague, prior to confirming a course of action for a vehicle and its driver. The secondary controller's activity, is itself rendered relevant by virtue of the incoming call and the instructor's request, and, of course, is produced with regard to the controller's sensitivity to a conversation in which he is not a participant. It may be the case that the secondary controller delays the production of the second packet of the command until he hears how the principal controller will respond to the request, and on hearing the onset of the reply assumes that there is no obvious objection to agreeing to the request. Indeed, it may well be the case that the controller's reply is designed not only to delay the response, but to display his deference to his colleague, and in particular to his solution in these circumstances to changing the train to manual.

The fragment provides a delightful illustration of the ways in which the use of the system is bound into talk, and how the participants, both present and remote, co-ordinate their activities with each other and the system's use. Not only does the call itself, or at least the request, occasion and provide the resources for a computer-based command, but the use of the system informs the very instructions that the caller receives. Moreover, on the one hand, we have the secondary controller overhearing the conversation of his colleague with the instructor, and transforming that call into sequentially appropriate (system-based) conduct, whilst, on the other, the principal controller 'reading' the ATS monitor in order to discern the solution being undertaken by his colleague. Underpinning this close and complex collaboration is the participants' orientation to sequentially appropriate conduct, that certain actions render relevant conduct which should occur, and should occur 'with dispatch'. The emergent division of labour is the product of these sequential relationships, procedures which interweave actions if particular activities are going to occur. In the case at hand, these relationships span and interconnect simultaneous activities which involve different participants, in different locations.

5.7   Intervention

As suggested at the beginning of the chapter, both controllers have the ability to enter commands into the system, and thereby to reschedule traffic when problems emerge. In many circumstances, however, it is the principal controller who deals with outside contacts, and the secondary controller who enters the relevant commands into the system. At times, this division of labour can lead to difficulties. For example, the secondary controller may have a lengthy series of commands to enter the system and have neither the time nor the inclination to deal with less immediate problems. Moreover, it is not always the case that the principal controller knows precisely what his colleague has to do, and may delay a particular course of action thinking his colleague is too busy to deal with the problem at hand. For our purposes it is interesting to note, however, that, despite the range of commitments that have to be managed during a crisis or emergency, the secondary controller remains sensitive to incoming calls and the actions that they may implicate.

Consider the following instance. It is a difficult time in the control room. A suspect package has been found which requires a suspension of the service, and also a train captain has lost his keys which means that his vehicle cannot be operated manually. We join the action as the principal controller informs an engineer that they are too busy to help move some vehicles around the depot.

Fragment 5.6   Transcript 1

```
Ci:   impossible to say ma:te. (.) As I say>we are investigating
      a suspect package at the moment (0.4) and also got a train
      captain who's lost his keys over.
      (1.6)
E:    (okay mate )
      (0.3)
Ci:   (that sort thing) mate (.) as soon as we ca::n.(.) (and
      actually) if you would like to get back to me in half an
      hour. just in ca:se  ⌈( )
♦ Cii:                     ⌊I'll do it now:.
      (0.4)
```

As the principal controller talks to the engineer on the telephone, his colleague is entering a series of commands into the system rescheduling trains on the main line between Canary Wharf and Heron Quays. As the principal controller utters 'as soon as we can', his colleague completes a command, clears his screen of warning messages and displays route numbers and route information on the monitor. The actions foreshadow an intervention. As the principal controller says 'just in case' to the caller, his colleague points to the screen and utters 'I'll do it now'.

Fragment 5.6   Transcript 2

```
Ci:  half an hour.  just in ca:se  (  )   (1.2)        Paul are you
Cii:                        I'll do it now - - - - - - -
     ■                                        ■ ⊔ ⊔....⊔ ⊔⌟
       ▲                        ▲                  ▲
     displays route          gestures to       commences
     numbers                 screen & kbd      command
```

The secondary controller intervenes in his colleagues' phone conversation just as it is drawing to completion. The intervention is accomplished through his switching the monitor to the 'relevant' domain, pointing towards the screen, and simultaneously saying he will undertake the necessary action. As with earlier instances, whilst the secondary controller is not a participant in the conversation between his colleagues, his actions are positioned and designed with regard to their talk, and in particular the principal controller's suggestion that the engineer should call back in half an hour. The secondary controller's actions achieve their impact by virtue of the ways in which they align towards the talk of his colleagues. The intervention is designed not only to display that the secondary controller is familiar with what the others are talking about, but also to show that he will immediately produce the appropriate next activity, entering the commands to enable the vehicle movement to take place. The utterance, 'I'll do it now', coupled with changing the screen on the ATS monitor, serves to foreshadow and mark the beginning of the next activity, namely entering the relevant commands. The intervention arises by virtue of the secondary controller's sensitivity to his colleague's awareness of his own current activities. Both the screen display and the preceding actions suggest that he is rescheduling trains on the main line rather than dealing with vehicles in the depot. The vocalised announcement, coupled with his visual conduct, is produced to show to the principal controller that he is now able to undertake actions relevant to the phone call. They stand in marked contrast to his conduct up until that moment within the emerging course of the phone call.

We can see, therefore, that, even though the secondary controller is engaged in actions unrelated to the conversation in which his colleagues are engaged, he remains sensitive to the talk, and is able to use the talk as a resource in his subsequent intervention. Moreover, the intervention not only is designed with regard to the emerging talk, and perhaps forestalling the call's closure, but is sensitive to his colleague's understanding of the secondary controller's activities during his conversation with the engineer. The fragment reveals the ways in which each participant is sensitive to the other's understanding of his conduct, even though they are engaged in distinct and unrelated activities.

The secondary controller's intervention does indeed forestall the call's closure. As he goes on to produce the command, which allows the engineer to move the vehicle in question, his colleague is faced with a problem. He has just turned down a request from a colleague, saying that it is unlikely that they will be able to deal with it for at least half an hour, only to discover, as the call is still open, that the relevant action can be undertaken immediately. The principal controller goes on to check whether the engineer is still on the line.

Fragment 5.6   Transcript 3

```
        (0.4)
    Ci:  Paul are you still receiving?
        (.)
    E:   (  )
        (.)
    Ci:  Paul are you still receiving ma:te?
        (1.2)
    E:   still receiving↓
        (0.2)
    Ci:  what was your request again? (0.2) four two seven to
         whe:re?
        (1.3)
    E:   (   four two nine four two eight) back to Dee Ell↑
        (0.3)
 ▶  Ci:  yeas its being done now ma:te (0.3) we had a li(t)ll (0.2)
         lull in whats happening↑ (now you will probably move)
        (0.2)
    E:   right cheers then
```

In the call the principal controller asks Paul, the engineer, once again for the details of the request. It is a curious enquiry, since his colleague has already begun to enter the relevant command and has completed the activity prior to Paul providing all the relevant details. Moreover, as his colleague enters the command, the principal controller is looking at the ATS2 monitor. It seems unlikely, therefore, that the principal controller's query is merely concerned with getting the details of the original request.

Of course, the production of the query and the response by the engineer serves to confirm the action taken by the secondary controller, for the engineer and for both the principal and the secondary controllers. By the time the query has been produced, the effects of the command are visible on the screen and the principal controller can see that it is indeed the appropriate action to take.

The query may, however, be sensitive to the concerns of the caller in other ways. It helps provide an account for the dramatic change of circumstances, from not being able to consider moving a train for half an hour, to doing it almost immediately. Indeed, Ci provides an account for this change of course to the caller: 'yeas, its being done mate, we've got a little lull in what's happening mate'. An utterance that, itself, displays that Ci has been following Cii's actions and their consequences. In this way, the remote caller is provided, at least in part, with a display of a coherent sequence of activities going on beyond the phone call to deal with his request. The query in the phone conversation is then produced by the principal controller both with regard to the concerns of the caller and in the light of the intervention and typing of his colleague.

Talking on the phone, therefore, has to be sensitive to both the co-conversationalists and the activities of co-located colleagues. In the case at hand, we can see how the actions of a colleague provide both a practical solution to the engineer's problem and an interactional difficulty for his interlocutor. The principal controller has to build the talk with regard to the actions of his colleague, and in particular the necessity to assemble an account for the change of circumstances. Similarly, in producing the activity requested by the caller, the secondary controller has not only to listen in on one of his colleague's conversations to assemble the sense of action required, but also to co-ordinate his intervention with the emerging sequentially organised talk. The intervention is delightfully positioned to avoid interrupting the participants' talk, whilst forestalling the call's closure. As an example of 'close monitoring', the secondary controller's conduct displays an orientation to both the structure of the call and the details of the engineer's request. Both the production of the intervention and the principal controller's subsequent enquiry and account, serve to preserve at least an impression to the caller that the two colleagues know what they are doing and that there is some consistency in the prioritising of their activities.

5.8   Discussion

The command and control system of the Docklands Light Railway, the ATS, schedules and organises the movement of traffic around the network, maintaining a principled and even service which is sensitive to the ebb and flow of predictable demand. The DLR, like any other rapid urban transport system, is subject to problems and difficulties ranging, as we have seen, from suspect packages through to the mechanical failure of vehicles. Almost all the problems which arise in the operation of the service require some rescheduling of the traffic on the lines. This is not done, nor in many cases could it be done, automatically. Rather, it is the responsibility of controllers not only to oversee the operation of the service, but to reschedule traffic when necessary by entering the appropriate commands into the ATS. The problems that arise in the operation of the service are largely unpredictable and the ways in which they should be managed are dependent upon the circumstances 'at hand'. So the time of day, whether, for example, the problem arises in a peak period, the location of the difficulty in the network, the distribution of traffic at the moment the difficulty arises, the nature of the problem, the availability of particular staff, even the weather, can all feature in the solution that the controller chooses to address. Problems therefore demand contingent solutions which are sensitive to the 'circumstances' in which the difficulties arise; the difficulties themselves helping to define just what those circumstances might be.

For the controllers who have to manage the network, it would seem sensible to divide the world they oversee into regions, and to allocate their responsibilities accordingly. When times are easy, there is little difficulty in handling problems which arise in the respective regions and entering the relevant commands into the ATS to reschedule the traffic. Nor is it the case that the geographical or network division of labour 'breaks down' when problems become more severe; controllers remain sensitive to the domains for which they might be seen as principally responsible. But the division of labour is subject to, or better permeated by, a more significant organisation: the sequential relations and trajectories that arise between particular activities. So, for example, the very confirmation of a request to change the route of a train requires a sequentially appropriate action, entering the relevant instruction into the command and control system. Either controller, if the information is available, can enter the relevant commands, and such entries are, or can be seen to be, occasioned by the confirmation of a requested course of action.

For controllers, therefore, the organisational relationship between particular actions and activities is an integral feature of the ways in which they produce and co-ordinate their conduct with each other (and deal with problems which arise in the operation of the service). Particular operations, for example stabling a vehicle, require particular actions by particular participants in a recognisable and routine order. So, for instance, hearing a request (and its confirmation) to move a train in a depot makes relevant particular actions: rescheduling a vehicle on the track in a specific way. If the subsequent action does not occur, then the vehicle is unable to progress, and can well generate difficulties for traffic which needs to use the relevant sections of the line. In the control centre, if the secondary controller does not issue the appropriate set of commands in the light of overhearing the request and its confirmation, then the principal controller can look for why the particular actions have not been undertaken. He can, for example, discover or assume that the secondary controller did not grasp what was happening and undertake remedial action, such as pointing to the monitor, in an attempt to have the other see what is needed and engender the relevant action. In one sense, therefore, the participants have developed, and orient to, a complex array of sequential relations and trajectories of conduct which arise in, and are preserved through, the produc-

tion and co-ordination of various actions and activities. The actions themselves may consist of entering commands into a computer system, giving
instructions over the telephone, even retrieving information from a screen,
but, most critically, particular actions serve to make relevant, or project,
subsequent conduct; conduct which if it fails to occur is organisationally
accountable. The division of labour, such as it is, consists, in large part,
not of an inflexible distribution of skills and responsibilities, but of an
array of practices and procedures which interweave particular actions and
activities, in various sequential relations.

We believe that the materials at hand have some bearing on how we
understand the 'interaction' between human beings and computers. The
system at hand, the ATS, is indeed designed to be operated by a single
individual, and, in almost all cases, it is one controller who enters commands into the computer. The entry of these commands, however, is sensitive to the actions of the controller's colleagues, and bears upon how
personnel make sense of each other's conduct and the activities in which
they engage. So, for example, we have seen the ways in which particular
commands are entered into the system, by virtue of the controllers' sensitivity to the telephone conversations of colleagues, or how, for instance,
one controller, by pointing to the screen, encourages a colleague to enter
the relevant command (and to see what that command should consist of).
Or, consider the ways in which colleagues can make sense of a controller's
actions by virtue of how he uses the keyboard and the information he
enters – the use of the computer itself, serving as a resource in the organisation of the activities of others, even what is said to a third party over the
telephone. The system, therefore, is relevant by virtue of the actions of a
range of participants, not only the individual entering the commands or
even looking at the screen, but those who will be affected by the changes
and whose work both informs, and is informed by, the system's use. In a
range of ways, therefore, commands entered into the system are co-produced, they require action by a number of individuals who in various
ways 'participate' in the use of the technology.

To understand how the system is used, and the sorts of competencies
which bear upon its operation, we might therefore need again to think
beyond the individual and his or her cognitive abilities. It is clear, for
example, that, in the DLR Control Room, the production of commands, the use of the system, is dependent upon the 'user's' analysis of
the actions of colleagues, both present and non-present. It is also apparent that the production of a command is co-ordinated with the real-time
articulation of the talk of co-participants, in particular of the fellow controller; the confirmation of request, for example, providing the sequentially appropriate position in which to enter computer commands. Even

then, the production of commands is sensitive to the continuing activities of co-participants; the commands being withheld, arrested, even transformed, in the light of concurrent activities. In the cases at hand, we can see the ways in which one controller designs his conduct to enable the co-participant to hear and see the 'relevant' actions and activities; the 'accomplished' visibility of the conduct serving as a resource for the timely production of associated action. In these, and related, ways, the entry of computer commands in the control room is a collaborative production; it relies on the two controllers co-ordinating their actions with each other (and related co-present and distributed parties) in order to accomplish, timely and sequentially appropriate activities which serve to maintain a safe and reliable service.

The production of computer commands in the DLR Control Room therefore relies upon competencies which lie far beyond the simple ability to enter information into the system. In the first place, it relies upon a working knowledge of the railway, the sorts of problems which emerge and the solutions which are used to deal with (even recognise) those difficulties. It requires a range of mundane competencies: the ability to listen in on part of phone calls, to piece together fragmented and distributed information, to use features of the local milieu, like changes on a computer screen, to render particular conduct intelligible, to assemble and maintain a natural history and the day's events, to use knowledge of the system to interpret the actions of others, and to design actions and activities so they are simultaneously visible, in particular ways to different participants. These mundane competencies are themselves put to the service of, or better embedded in, a range of organisational procedures and practices through which participants produce, co-ordinate and recognise their own conduct and the conduct of others. The use of the computer, therefore, is dependent on a complex array of abilities which enable the controllers to collaboratively produce relevant commands in particular circumstances and to co-ordinate their own actions with those of others, both those within the control room and colleagues outside.

6 'Interaction' with computers in architecture

Let him be educated, skilful with the pencil, instructed in geometry, know much history, have followed the philosophers with attention, understand music, have some knowledge of medicine, know the opinions of the jurists, and be acquainted with astronomy and the theory of the heavens.   Vitruvius (1960: 5–6, cited in Cuff, 1992: 84)

6.1 Introduction

One of the most noticeable developments in personal computers in recent years has been the widespread deployment and use of graphical user interfaces. Rather than typing commands and instructions, users are presented with a range of devices, such as windows, icons, menus and cursors, through which they operate the system. Particular activities on the computer, like word processing, organising electronic files, navigating around the system and switching tasks have been considerably transformed by the introduction of interfaces on which graphical objects are displayed and are manipulated around the screen. Although graphical interfaces appear to be easier to use, it is not clear what the reasons for this might be. Hence, these systems have been a focus of interest for researchers in HCI; research which has sought to explain the ways different kinds of interfaces are used in terms of the cognitive capabilities of the user and the semantic qualities of the system (e.g. Ankrah et al., 1990; Hutchins et al., 1986; Norman and Draper, 1986; Schneiderman, 1992). Of particular concern has been to develop an analysis of an individual's direct interaction with, or manipulation of, the system and how screen objects are perceived and understood. For the most part, these analyses follow the conventional approach within HCI and have tended to remain tied to the laboratory.

This chapter takes a different approach. Rather than examining the conduct of users through experiments, we explore the use of graphical user interface or 'direct manipulation' systems in the accomplishment of everyday work.

With their straightforward presentation of a drawing and capabilities to easily manipulate its components, recent Computer-Aided Design (CAD) packages provide typical examples of graphical user interfaces. Indeed, many require only minimal recourse to other ways of using the computer, often needing little to be typed and most actions being performed by selecting, moving and shaping objects on the screen with an electronic mouse. Computer-Aided Design is now widely used in a variety of diverse fields such as hardware development, product design and civil engineering, and perhaps, most familiarly, in architecture. Here, the Apple Macintosh has proved popular. This may in part be owing to Apple's imaginative marketing campaign which it is claimed appeals to the creative and slightly rebellious side of the individual (Jones, 1990), Nevertheless, it should be noted that from early on, particularly with the development of the Macintosh, Apple adopted the principle of 'direct manipulation' and developed a range of software which allows users to bypass the keyboard and interact 'directly' with the actual objects on the screen. Architectural practices, therefore, seem particularly appropriate settings not only to throw some light on the ways direct manipulation interfaces are utilised in work settings, but also to contribute to our understanding of the appeal of particular systems and how they might be enhanced.

In this chapter, we briefly consider one or two aspects of the ways in which architects use computers, in some cases in concert with other tools and artefacts, to make changes to particular plans and to co-ordinate their contributions with colleagues. The observations point to the contingent organisation of system use, even when individuals work alone, and how the technology provides a resource in the design and development of buildings. It also reveals, once again, how system use is embedded in the mundane and indigenous competencies of the 'users'; competencies which in various ways arise in, and are preserved through, the interaction of the participants. (For further details and related work see also Luff (1997) and Luff and Heath (1993).)

The potential of computers to support design has been the subject of a number of empirical studies over the past decade, particularly as design activities serve as examples of the forms of collaborative work which could be supported through advanced technologies. A range of insightful field studies of different forms of design (e.g. Bødker et al., 1987; Harper and Carter, 1994; Murray, 1993; Nardi, 1993; Rogers, 1992), including architecture, have been undertaken. In parallel with these, innovative systems have been developed which aim to support individuals working on a design in real-time, so that designers can collaboratively modify and transform the drawings they are working on, and also see each other whilst they are doing this (e.g. Tang, 1990; Tang and Leifer, 1988). Whilst providing a way of focusing on the collaborative practices of design, the ethnographic perspective has tended, understandably, to ignore the subject ordinarily addressed by researchers in HCI – the details of how tools and technologies are used to accomplish particular tasks and activities and how individuals co-ordinate their activities with others in real-world working environments. The very emergence of CSCW with its more sociological focus has tended to lead to a shift away from the interactional features of computer use, and left this interesting, and potentially rich, domain to those who might ordinarily be concerned with the experimental analysis of cognitive competence. It is interesting to note that the importance of more recent work by Hutchins (1995) and others is that they retain a commitment to interaction with tools and technologies, whilst driving analytic attention towards the circumstances of their use. In a similar way, in this chapter we wish to explore the individual and collaborative use of the system, and the 'interaction' which arises therein.

6.2   Technologies in architectural work

This chapter focuses on the use of a CAD system in a medium-sized provincial architectural practice in England. In this practice, there are about fifteen architects, town planners and graphic designers who use computers extensively throughout the process of design. So, for example, members of the practice use CAD systems to produce working drawings for contractors, to show clients what prospective buildings will look like and how they will fit into the landscape. In line with many architecture practices in the United Kingdom, they use Apple Macintoshes for their work; in this case, a CAD package called MiniCad (MiniCad is a trademark of Diehl Graphsoft Inc.). In MiniCad, menus and tool boxes (or tool palettes), which are permanently visible and can be selected using a mouse, provide a wide variety of ways of selecting different types of drawing operations. To carry out commands even more quickly, keyboard combinations (or key-chords, or key accelerators) are available for the most common functions. To give a general sense of the MiniCad application, Figure 6.1 shows the overall screen layout when it is opened.

Starting on the left-hand side of the screen, MiniCad's tool palettes provide ways for users to type text, draw rectangles, polygons, arcs and special, recurring symbols (such as double doors and desks) and also to constrain the placing of certain objects on the screen, for example constraining one line to be perpendicular to another or ensuring that two objects fit precisely together. The menus, along the top of the screen, provide more familiar Macintosh applications: to open, print, save and close files, to edit materials, and more specialised options for reshaping and joining objects together, combining several lines into a polygon, breaking up a polygon and changing surfaces for later three-dimensional manipulation. MiniCad allows the user to create drawings in layers rather like overlaying tracing paper. The architect can control the arrangement of the layers, and determine which drawings are visible and can be worked on.

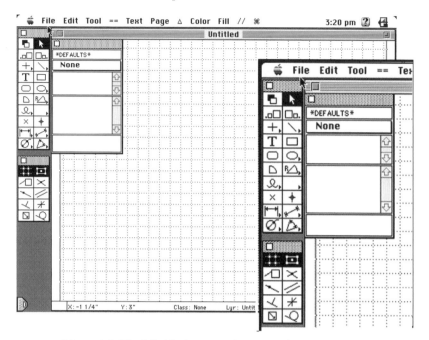

Figure 6.1 The MiniCad screen when opened. The details of the tools
on the top left of the screen are shown, enlarged, on the right.

In the following sections we will explore how these various resources
are used by the architects in their everyday tasks and activities.

6.3   The manipulation of objects

Novices are expected to complete what seem to be trivial undertakings, such as
working out the title block for all the drawings of a particular project. The task
that best explains entry-level architects' dislike for their tedious work and its lack
of status is doing bathroom details. In actuality, few people have ever had to do
bathroom details as their primary work. (Cuff (1992: 134))

Much of the architects' day-to-day activity is involved in making detailed
changes to the working drawings of the building. This requires the creation, shaping and movement of objects on the screen which need to be
positioned precisely on the drawing. MiniCad's capabilities provide invaluable resources for this work, making it possible, for example, to 'directly'
manipulate drawing objects like walls, windows and stairs using the
mouse.

In the following fragment, an architect is working on a drawing of a
toilet. He moves a wall that is immediately to the right of a set of urinals
further to the right (b).

Fragment 6.1

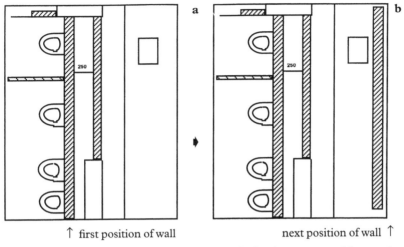

↑ first position of wall   next position of wall ↑

The architect then moves the wall, originally in the same position as the one just moved, to the right-hand side of the drawing (c).

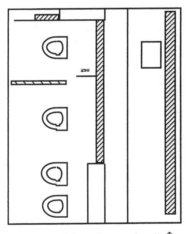

next position of second wall ↑

He then goes on to work in the space he has now made available to the right of the urinals, adding a thinner, shorter wall. Whilst he does this he keeps the walls he has just removed.

This fragment, extracted from an extended flow of activity, is typical of the kind of change architects make to working drawings. Demands from other parties, for example by a client or from surveyors, for alterations to the design of the building usually result in changes which have to be made to various plans, elevations and sections. These changes can also have knock-on consequences for other parts of the building. As these may be on other drawings made by other architects, it is critical that on a large project even small changes to a drawing made by a particular individual remain consistent.

In the following fragment, an architect is making changes to a staircase elsewhere in the building. He has just been moving around the plan, both panning across it and selecting various layers of the drawing, before he arrives at the relevant part of the staircase, where it meets a passageway at the base of the building (a). (An arrow is the usual way for architects to indicate the direction of the staircase. In the drawing, each stair is also numbered, the numbers being just visible in the data, from 1 to 15.)

Fragment 6.2

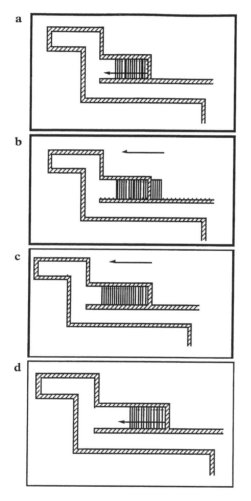

In finding the relevant place, the architect shapes a box (a Marquee (A Marquee is a dashed box which can be shaped by the user to mark out an area of interest on the screen.)) over the region of the staircase selecting a set of stairs. He copies and pastes the stairs into another drawing five layers below by using 'Command-C' and 'Command-V' keys. He then 'joins' the new portion of staircase onto the old one (Command-J).

After marking out an area of the staircase that contains all the numbers of the individual stairs, the architect selects each end of an arrow and then moves it upwards and rightwards (b). He then goes on to remove an indent in the wall below the staircase (not shown), move the wall along to the right, to the staircase's new end, and extend the wall alongside it (c). The architect then removes a portion of stairs at the left end of the staircase and makes several alterations to the numbers on the stairs. He then selects the right- and left-hand sides of the arrow and moves it into a new position on the stairs (d). Together these activities shift the staircase to the right.

As with the movement of the walls in the first example, the arrow in the drawing is moved into a space clear but related to the area in which the architect is to work. Moreover, in each case drawing objects, rather than being deleted, are preserved. In this way, they can be a resource for future activities. They can also be used for other purposes, for example, an object can be positioned to mark out a particular distance in the emerging drawing (cf. the positioning of the walls and arrows in the previous fragment). In other examples, we find the architects placing an object in an area of 'free space' and manipulating it there before replacing it in the original locations. Preserving objects and utilising the space available in these ways are recurrent features of the work in using the CAD package. Though seemingly trivial, they provide resources for the conduct of upcoming activities whilst leaving the precise nature of those activities open.

Just as the layout of papers and equipment on a desk may be used to perform various activities, the MiniCad system provides architects with the opportunity of creating arenas for different types of action. In the example at hand, we can see, for example, how the system offers the possibility of creating locations for manipulating objects independently of their surrounding detail. In some sense, therefore, we can see architects use the system to create domains for the accomplishment of particular activities; a sort of improvisation with the resources available.

As mentioned earlier, the nature of computer interfaces where objects are directly manipulated on the screens has been of considerable interest to researchers within HCI. It has been suggested that the ways in which an interface 'affords' the manipulation of objects, such as cutting and pasting staircases, is consequential to the relationship between a user's goal or intentions and his or her physical tasks (cf. Hutchins et al., 1986). For example, the manipulation of objects through a 'mouse' rather than the keyboard is thought to make the distance between goals and tasks shorter by avoiding the semantic translation necessary in more indirect typewritten commands. This may well be the case. However, we can also see that direct manipulation is also sensitive to the activities in which an individual is engaged and contingent on the constraints and practicalities at hand.

In fragment 6.2, for example, the architect's 'paste' is more than manipulating screen objects, it is an extension of a staircase. The architect has to make adjustments to the positioning of objects on the drawing, especially to related ones. It is carefully designed with regard to subsequent actions. Similarly, when the user moves the arrow on the staircase up and to the left it is out of the way of the staircase which the user goes on to manipulate. It also is vertically above the new location of the staircase, visible whilst he is working on the stairs and in a position where it can easily be moved back down. Its very presence on the screen can be seen to mark out future possible and necessary courses of activities. The more or less direct manipulation to objects, therefore, is embedded in the activity at hand: the production of drawings of specific features of the building.

Throughout the course of the day, the architects engage in making a series of such changes to the drawings that they are responsible for. Each can have knock-on consequences for other parts of the drawing and even for the drawings of others. The visual appearance – the size, shape and position of objects on the screen – is important for managing this work, but this is used within an unfolding course of the activities. An activity and the creation of the drawing on the screen, shapes the development and production of subsequent actions.

It is unclear how useful it is to conceive of the architects' conduct with regard to goals or plans. In some sense, many actions emerge in the light of preceding conduct and provide options and alternatives as to not only what should be done next, but how it might be accomplished. In looking at the ways in which the architects work, there seems to be a remarkable flexibility, a form of improvisation, unfolding temporally and sequentially. Trajectories of action emerge, but they are the outcome of locally managed, contingent conduct which may, more or less, be oriented towards some 'way of doing things', and, of course, used retrospectively to find and illustrate a particular order. The appearance of drawings on the screen is both the product and the resources in and through which the actions are accomplished. The movement of an object can make apparent not only the further actions to be undertaken, but the nature of those actions: adding the block of stairs reveals the ways the accompanying arrows and numbers need to be altered. Even the starting-point in fragment 6.2 suggests a certain improvised character; an unfolding nature to the activity. Rather than creating the additional stairs afresh, the architect 'borrows' the stairs from the layer above. Not only does this save work for the architect to perform, but helps ensure that the drawings on the various layers will match. The architect utilises the tools that are at hand, with what remains of previous 'constructions' and 'destructions' reflected perhaps in the discussion of the 'bricoleur' by Lévi-Strauss (1962).

> The 'bricoleur' is adept at performing a large number of diverse tasks; but, unlike the engineer, he does not subordinate each of them to the availability of raw materials and tools conceived for the purpose of the project. His universe of instruments is closed and the rules of his game are always to make do with 'whatever is at hand'; that is to say with a set of tools and materials which is always finite and is also heterogeneous because what it contains bears no relation to the current project, or indeed to any particular project, but is the contingent result of all the occasions there have been to renew or enrich the stock or to maintain it with the remains of previous constructions or destructions. (Lévi-Strauss (1962: 17))

6.4   Navigating the design: preserving coherence

Providing the ability to manipulate objects directly on the screen is not the only feature of graphical user interfaces which has been given as a reason for their success. By allowing different applications and files to be visibly available at the same time, it appears that graphical user interfaces make it easy for a user to navigate around a computer system, either between different kinds of functions or around a single file or document. Indeed, their capabilities to afford navigation are another focus of HCI research (Bush, 1945; Francik et al., 1991; Goldberg and Goodisman, 1981). Again, this capability is conventionally conceived in terms of how well an interface facilitates the search for a particular target to meet an individual's goals.

In working on the design of a large building with a CAD system, architects typically need to access a substantial number of drawings on their computer systems, each of which can be very complex. Moreover, the architects have to ensure that elements of the drawings, such as the position of columns, doors and windows, the number and direction of stairs and the orientation of rooms, are consistent. However, it is impossible to display an entire drawing on the screen. In consequence, they frequently move around the drawings to check whether the overall symmetry of the building is maintained. This involves navigating successive locations, levels or layers of the drawings. MiniCad provides several ways of navigating around a drawing: panning across a drawing, zooming in and out of an area of a drawing, and moving between layers of the drawing. The architects in the practice use each of these in the course of their work.

Panning allows the architect to move around a drawing that is too big to fit on the screen. It is possible to pan around the drawing either by using the panning tool on the drawing palette or by pressing the appropriate arrow key on the keyboard. This moves the view on the screen to a contiguous area of the plan.

Zooming in and out of a particular portion of a drawing allows the architect to focus in on a detail or to see a wider view of the current area of the plan. This is performed by selecting the Zoom In and Zoom Out tools in the drawing palette (on the second row). So, for example, to zoom in on a portion of the drawing, the Zoom In tool is selected with the mouse, the architect then specifies the area to focus on by shaping a Marquee over the appropriate area with the cursor and then releasing the mouse. Zooming out is accomplished by locating the Marquee over the area which will remain the centre of the wider view, after the Zoom Out tool has been selected. (Note that this is the opposite way of operation compared with similar functions on other Macintosh applications, where the selection on the menu applies to a previously selected object on the screen.)

Layers offer a way of providing different kinds of information on the same drawing. Each layer can be displayed or hidden, so that, for example, particular details, such as the plumbing, can be either available for manipulation or hidden from view. By changing the properties of a layer, or by explicitly moving between them, architects can work on different layers.

In the following instance, the architect uses all three ways of moving around the drawing (shown schematically in fragment 6.3).

After working on the title block in the bottom right-hand corner of a set of elevations (sketch a), the architect shuffles the drawing up twice (b–c), across to the left (d) and then types '⌘4' (e) to fit the drawing to the screen (the accelerator for '**Fit To Window**'). He then zooms out further using the 'Zoom Out' tool on the Drawing Tools palette, specifying the area the new image will focus on with a Marquee (f). By selecting the top window bar of the window and dragging it down to the bottom of the screen he effectively moves the set of elevations he has been working on out of view and reveals another elevation. He clicks on this elevation (g), zooms out (h), and goes to the menus to select particular layers of the drawings to display. The architect then goes on to alter the title block of this drawing.

The architect not only moves from one drawing to another in three different ways, he accomplishes this by moving the mouse, using a keyboard 'accelerator', the menus and the Zoom Out tool. Although it is

Fragment 6.3

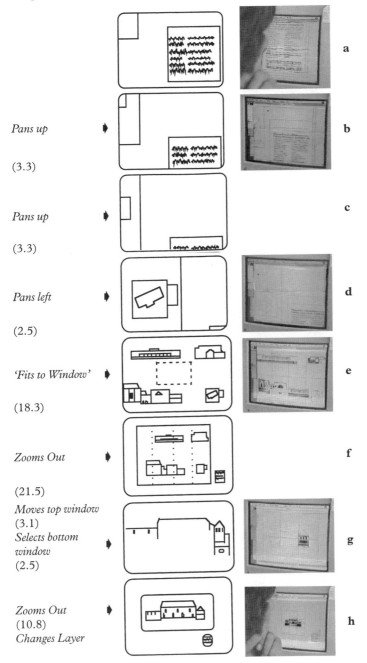

possible to consider these activities in terms of a path from one title block to another, zooming out of the first plan, jumping across to the other drawing and then zooming in on that, it would ignore the moment-by-moment development of the activity.

At the beginning of the fragment, very little of the main drawing is displayed, indeed only a few lines are visible on the bottom left of the screen. The architect pans up and left bringing into view a portion of the building. Once the details appear, the architect goes on to display most of the complete drawing. This takes some seconds to draw, as details of each elevation have to be presented. When completed, he then marks out the area which the 'zoomed out' picture will centre on: an area in the centre of the screen. Once he has specified this area, a much smaller image is presented with the title block. Only as the last bottom right component is being drawn does the architect move towards the window bar and on to the next elevation.

The architect, therefore, does not merely move from one component on one drawing to a similar component on another, but takes account of the images as they appear; the images provide the resources, for example, to confirm aspects of the drawings' completeness and correctness. Each activity then is embedded in the prior.

In the following instance, the architect has just finished altering some walls at the right-hand end of the service tunnel (shown schematically with fragment 6.4). By pressing the appropriate arrow keys, the architect pans left across the top of the tunnel five times, then down three times, adds some layers to the drawing, pans down again and then pans diagonally down to the right. At the end of the actions, the architect has a plan including the female staffroom in the main building displayed on the screen.

To provide access to the main building, a service tunnel runs underground which is roughly a 'T-shape' with a bend in the middle. At each end of the top of the 'T' there are staircases leading down to the tunnel. Starting at one of these, the architect pans across and down the plan following the service tunnel into the main building. He paces his activity with regard to the system's redrawing of the plan. As he nears the centre of the service tunnel, the architect reduces the pace at which he presses the relevant keys to allow him to review successive drawings. Progression down the tunnel slows down further once he passes the crook in the tunnel (arrowed). When he arrives at the main building, the architect adds layers to the drawing and then proceeds into the female staffroom.

There are a number of other ways in which the architect could move between the staircase at the right end of the tunnel and the female staffroom in the main building. For example, he could zoom out to a plan

Fragment 6.4

Pans left

(0.3)

Pans left
(0.4)
Pans left
(0.5)
Pans left
(1.2)
Pans left

(2.5)

Pans down

(3.3)

Pans down

(8.5)

Pans down
(5.3)
Selects layers
(0.7)
Pans down
(12.0)
Pans diagonally
down and to the
right

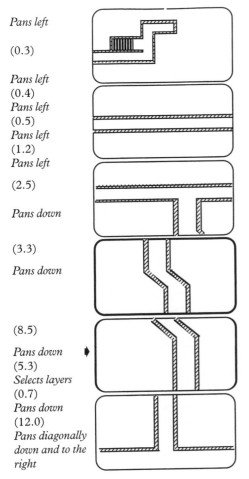

of the whole drawing, and then zoom in to the relevant area. As MiniCad takes longer to draw the details of a plan if it has to draw several layers each time, this would however require waiting tens of seconds to display the relevant drawings. In moving down the tunnel, the architect can co-ordinate this activity with the projected speed of the system. For moving around the drawing in this way, it is not necessary to have all the details presented. The details need only to be seen once the destination is neared. The organisation of the activity in fragment 6.4 can be seen to be shaped by a range of contingencies. The movement down the tunnel and the drawing of the details of the layers are shaped with respect not only to when items appear on the screen and the geography of the building, but also with the projected speed of the system.

Navigation around the plan can also be seen as contingent on aspects of architectural practice in general. The building the architects are working on has certain consistencies and symmetries. The architects can make use of these in their drawings, for instance, copying portions of a plan from one area to another. It also means that work on one localised area of a plan has important implications for changes that need to be made to other areas. For example, changes to an internal staircase on one level will involve similar, but not identical, changes to other staircases on that level. In the materials at hand, there are numerous instances of movements back and forth between spatially distant areas of the plan, moving along corridors, up and down stairs and across to other corners of the building.

Within HCI it is not uncommon to consider the use of a computer system in terms of a cycle of activity, where an individual establishes a goal, specifies a sequence of actions to accomplish that goal, executes one of these and then evaluates its results with respect to the overall goals, before repeating the cycle (Norman and Draper, 1986). Indeed, this 'interaction' has been considered in terms of a stream of symbols, a communicative dialogue, flowing back and forth between user and computer (cf. Card et al., 1983: 4). So, the activity of navigating around an interface would typically be conceived of in terms of a search for a particular goal or target, the results of successive attempts displayed on the screen being interpreted with respect to that overall goal (e.g. Young et al., 1990).

From materials considered here, speaking of the user, the architect, 'interacting' with the computer in this way would seem to draw attention away from how the use of the system is embedded in the architect's practical activity, in this case reviewing and inspecting successive drawings. The appearance of the successive drawings does not so much engender actions from the architect, but rather form part of an emerging sequence of actions through which he reviews successive drawings of the building.

6.5   Interweaving resources

Even relatively sophisticated computer systems are rarely used alone, as the sole resource through which work is accomplished. We have already seen, for example, how the use of various multimedia technologies in the line control rooms on London Underground relies, in part, on a paper-based timetable through which personnel mark up changes to the schedule. Similarly, in architectural practices, even those which have a wide-ranging commitment to advanced technologies, it is not unusual to see individuals use various more mundane tools including calculators, rulers and pen and paper. Indeed, even in the more advanced practices, paper remains a critical resource both in the production of particular designs and in co-ordinating plans with the contributions of others.

For example, we mentioned earlier that a critical aspect of the work of architects, especially when designing large and complex buildings, is co-ordinating the contributions of different architects in the practice. A number of individuals may be working on distinct elements of a particular area of a building, and the drawings and their modifications need to be carefully interrelated. In many of the larger projects, one way in which the architects maintain a record of a design is to annotate a paper version of the plans so that all those working on a particular portion can see, in principle, modifications or changes which need to be made. It is interesting to note, therefore, that the paper document provides a resource for identifying and co-ordinating contributions which is not facilitated by the computer. However, reconciling screen and paper versions of the 'same' section is by no means unproblematic, and architects spend much time attempting to preserve coherence between alternative, and sometimes conflicting, 'representations'.

As a way of illustrating some of these issues, and providing a glimpse of how individuals use various tools to co-ordinate their activities with each other, we wish to discuss the following fragments. These fragments are drawn from a lengthy and complicated sequence of activities in which two of the architects in the practice discuss changes to the direction of a staircase. An additional room has been added to the top floor of the building which means all the staircases leading up to it have to be turned round or 'flipped'. One of the architects, Richard, comes over to Pete, a colleague, and asks 'are you su:re you're flipping the right one arou:nd↓ Pe:te'. There ensues a long discussion about the various staircases and levels of the building, the different versions of the drawings and the changes that have been 'marked up' to do. We join the action as Pete, who is seated at his workstation, attempts to assure Richard that he is making the correct changes. Pete encourages Richard to turn from the paper plans, where there appears to be some confusion over annotations, to look at the screen version (see Fragment 6.5, transcript 4).

Pete begins to point towards the screen as he starts to utter 'You see'. The vocalisation, coupled with his gesture and preceding shift of gaze from the paper plan to the screen, is designed to encourage Richard to turn towards the image on the monitor. Pete retains the finger of the other hand on the paper plan so as to preserve the point of reference, with regard to the overall plan, a modified version of which can be found on the screen. Richard does not turn immediately towards the screen, and Pete escalates his attempts to have his colleague change his orientation: he

Fragment 6.5   Transcript 1

Pete (P)   Richard (R)

P: You see (0.3) um: (0.6) <u>there</u> (.) this is
    the out<u>side</u> level
    (1.0)
R: umm↓
    (1.3)
P: and it can start (0.7) (part of the
    drawing) we are on now (2.3)
    righ(t) (here we are) (1.4)
    you've done a section through (1.2)
    this guy here (.) right?
    (0.6)
R: yep
    (.)
P: thats the start of the section I had↓ (0.3)
    to: give myself (them levels) and he
    (has to start) back there (.) and go up↑ =
R: =oh yeah↓ thats the same one

pauses following, 'you see', produces 'um', and once again pauses. The perturbations not only serve to encourage a realignment towards the direction of the speaker's gaze – the screen – but delay the gist of the utterance 'this is the outside level' prior to securing appropriate alignment from the co-participant. On the demonstrative 'there', Richard turns from the paper plan to the screen.

P: you see (0.3) um: (0.6) <u>there</u> (.) this   is the out<u>side</u> level (1.0)

Pete's actions foreshadow a sequence through which he juxtaposes Richard different sections of the drawings on the computer with the paper plans on the table. His gestures begin by locating a common landmark, the 'outside level' on the computer screen.

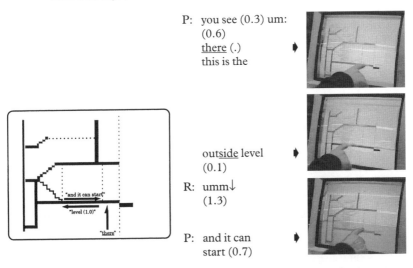

P: you see (0.3) um:
    (0.6)
    <u>there</u> (.)
    this is the

    out<u>side</u> level
    (0.1)
R: umm↓
    (1.3)

P: and it can
    start (0.7)

Pete continues his gesture, moving his hand first to the left and then to the right along the line for the outside level on the drawing. Richard then utters an 'umm↓'. Although this is rather a minimal response, Pete through his talk and visual conduct has at least secured an alignment from Richard, first to the computer screen and then to a particular component displayed on it. This has been accomplished through a delicate collection of interactional devices: the talk itself, pauses and perturbations within the talk and gestures designed with respect to the changing orientation of a co-participant. The computer screen is one resource through which the alignment of the co-participant is secured.

Having secured Richard's alignment towards the screen, and established 'the outside level' from which further references can be delineated, Pete utters 'it can start (0.7) (part of the drawing) we are on now' and goes on to to show Richard the section 'they' are 'on now'.

Fragment 6.5 Transcript 2

▶P: and it can start (0.7) (part of the
     drawing) we are on now

     (2.3)
     righ(t) (here we are)
     (1.4)
     you've done a section through
     (1.2)
     this guy here (.) right?
     (0.6)
R: yep
     (.)

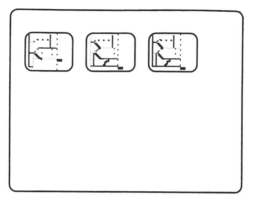

Figure 6.2 Sketch of the staircase sections (transcript 2, arrowed).

P: that's the start of the section I had↓
      (0.3) to: give myself (them levels)
      and he (has to start) back there (.)
      and go up↑=
R: =oh yeah↓ thats the same one

On the word 'start', he zooms out from the single section (using the key-chord '⌘4' – 'Fit To Window') to reveal three small images of sections in minute detail (see Figure 6.2). The computer requires some time to display these images. As they are being drawn, Richard temporarily turns away from the screen, back towards the paper and there is a pause in the talk for 2.3 seconds.

Pete's turn 'right here we are' marks the complete appearance of the respective images on the screen and Richard turns back towards the computer, moving forward to enable him to see the details of the plans. Just as Richard looks at the screen, Pete turns back to the paper plans and to the area at which his finger is pointing and utters 'this guy here (.) right?'; the utterance serving to display that the details on the screen correspond to the area marked out on the paper document. 'Right?' serves to encourage Richard to once again turn back to the paper plans and view the area in question with respect to the details on the screen; to treat the two representations as corresponding to the same location (see transcript 3).

Pete's actions receive a delayed and weak acknowledgement from Richard, namely 'yep'. The 'yep' provides the opportunity, perhaps encourages Pete, to elaborate on the section in question. Pete turns back to the screen and as he continues to speak uses the mouse to select the third image on the screen. On 'there', in 'he (has to start) back there', Pete raises his head upwards as if looking more carefully at part of the screen.

Fragment 6.5   Transcript 3

P: this guy here (.) right?   (0.6)   R: yep(.)

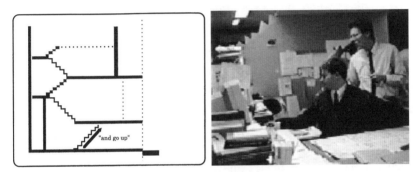

Figure 6.3 Sketch of second staircase section as Pete moves his cursor up the screen and utters 'and go up↑'.

The vocalisation, coupled with a marked shift in orientation, serves to encourage Richard to once again turn from the paper plan to the screen. As Richard begins to turn and look at the screen, seemingly out of sight of his co-participant, Pete produces 'and go up' simultaneously moving the cursor diagonally up the staircase (by moving the mouse). In this way, therefore, Pete points to the relevant section of the staircase and indicates the direction in which he is working (see Figure 6.3). He produces the 'gesture' having secured the realignment of his co-participant. The gesture is exquisitely designed. It is not only timed to co-occur with the arrival of Richard's gaze, but, by using the cursor, Pete is able to embed the point in the section to which it refers and show in detail the direction of his working. The cursor is put to the service of the interaction, providing a resource through which the participants can locate a common referent and pattern.

Richard's reorientation to the screen, looking over his colleague's shoulder at the monitor, allows Pete to use the cursor on the screen to point out quite precisely the relevant staircase and its direction. Richard's utterance 'oh yeah↓ thats the same one', produced immediately after Pete's gesture and latched onto Pete's 'and go up↑', displays an understanding of the location and the changes that Pete is making to the drawings. This simple cursor movement is delicately produced with respect to both Richard's immediate reorientation and the prior conduct on the plans and with the computer of both participants. Together with his talk, Pete provides Richard with the resources to make sense of the changes that he is making to the plans. In previous fragments, we saw how activities on the system, like the movement down a tunnel or between two drawings, were produced in the light of the practical concerns of the architects. In this fragment, we see how an activity on the computer by one architect where he moves from one section to another, via a set of thumbnail sketches, is delicately co-ordinated and, in some ways, produced for a colleague. The recognition of what they are looking at, and in consequence whether the changes they are making to the drawings are appropriate, is a collaborative accomplishment. Artefacts such as paper plans and computer systems are utilised for this, but the participants activities accomplished are made sense of through their talk and visual conduct.

On the one hand, the screen-based plan provides the resources through which the participants can inspect details, for example, the recent changes that Pete has made, which are unavailable on the paper document. On the other hand, the paper documents, because of their size and the annotations written on them, provide Pete and Richard with a way of identifying the general 'problems at hand'. There is a sense in which the participants are able to juxtapose the various representations of the building, in order to determine where they are and what they are talking about, and to delineate the changes each is making. Pete's hands, for example, his left-hand finger on a section of the paper plan, or the pointing gesture(s) at the screen, help preserve the continuing relevance of the two versions, the movement and talk uncovering 'just what' they have been talking about all along. In these ways, Richard is able to disambiguate the relevant section of the plans to determine what actions need to be undertaken, and Pete can find that Richard has recognised and agreed with his version of the events.

The ways in which the respective documents enhance each other in and through the participants actions, provide an interesting illustration of the documentary method of interpretation. Garfinkel (1967) suggests:

The method consists of treating actual appearance as 'the document of', as 'pointing to', as 'standing on behalf of' a presupposed underlying pattern. Not only is the underlying pattern derived from the documentary evidences, but the individual documentary evidences, in their turn, are interpreted on the basis of 'what is known' about the underlying pattern. Each is used to elaborate the other. (Garfinkel (1967: 78))

In the case at hand, we can see the ways in which the sense of plans is assembled by virtue of the juxtaposition and interrelationship of the screen and paper-based document. In this way, a coherent and satisfactory 'representation' is assembled; constituted in and through the interaction of the participants. It is not unusual to find tools and technologies helping each other out in this way. Computers rarely stand alone. All sorts of resources, ranging from pointing fingers, through to pens and papers, are deployed to undertake activities which are principally, or should be, accomplished through the more sophisticated technology, the computer. The simple inability to annotate screen-based documents, at least with the system at hand, or to bring forth overall plans of particular sections, undermines the architects' ability to represent and solve their problems with the computer alone. In working to make technologies work, 'users' utilise all sorts of devices in order to address the limitations of a technology dealing with the demands and contingencies of particular activities.

The activities in the architecture practice also raise an issue that has permeated discussion in previous chapters. Once again we find a technology which is designed to support the activities of particular individuals being used in some sense 'collaboratively'. The collaboration that it supports is not simply that plans undertaken by a particular individual inform the activities of another, but rather that participants refer to, and work with, on-screen drawings together, in interaction, in real-time. In the case at hand, we see the ways in which a particular participant invites a colleague to inspect a screen's contents; illustrating and elaborating the plans through talk and gesture. Moreover, the participants' interaction 'with' the system, which itself is ongoingly differentiated as Pete points and elaborates the details with regard to Richard's shifting alignment, simultaneously relies upon a corresponding version, embodied, and seen to be embodied, in the paper document. The screen-based plan is constituted in and through the interaction of the participants, interaction which itself preserves and presupposes the version in the paper document.

6.6   Discussion

In this chapter we have considered a few examples of the ways in which individuals use computers in the design of buildings. For the most part, the activities in which they engage are relatively mundane, certainly not the stuff that the layman associates with art and design. The examples involve the manipulation of objects, navigating through successive plans and identifying inconsistencies and problems. The drawings themselves are the material of design, not simply, if at all, a representation of a building out there in the world, but rather a complex array which can be seen with respect to each other, as forming a *Gestalt* which is assembled and appealed to in various ways in various circumstances. The individual's actions are produced with regard to sections and details in the plans, sections and details which become relevant in various ways with respect to the activities at hand. The activities themselves are both oriented to the plans, and literally constitute those plans, in the very course of their production. The architect is confronted by plans which feature in the activities in which he engages, and which themselves are the products or embodiment of those activities. The plan can serve prospectively to see and envisage activities which have to be done, and retrospectively to make sense of a hitherto unrelated set of actions in a particular fashion. In some sense, the plans embody goals, in as much as they have to be produced in certain ways with regard to particular characteristics, routines and constraints. For the architect, however, on any occasion of confronting and working on the drawings, what the plans mean, and the sorts of problems and issues they embody, are reflexively constituted within the developing course of particular activities. The system, and the 'interaction it affords', is one amongst various resources through which a disparate range of activities are accomplished; not simply drawing or designing, but discovering problems, pointing things out to colleagues, presenting designs, justifying suggestions and the rest of mundane architectural work.

Whilst principally designed to enhance the abilities of individual architects, the computer and other tools and technologies which litter the practice are put to the service of collaboration. Even from the brief fragments addressed in this chapter, we can see how design, even making small changes to plans, is relevant to the work of others within the practice. The growing complexity of building design, coupled with the emergence of new technologies, necessitates the distribution of activities and responsibilities with regard to the drawing of plans. Small changes in one drawing are relevant to others, and those others may well turn out to be the responsibility of a colleague. In consequence, the production of plans is essentially a collaborative exercise, involving a working division of labour and a persistent concern with how one's own work is sensitive to the conduct of others, and allows for the production of a coherent and consistent set of drawings. Given that a substantial body of work within the practice in question is accomplished in and through the use of the computer, it is not uncommon for the individuals' 'interaction' with the system to be 'mediated' through their interaction with others. So, for example, the computer becomes a resource in showing and discussing work, such as drawings of sections of buildings, and identifying problems and solutions. Occasions arise in which two or more architects gather around the screen and through their talk and visual conduct render aspects of drawings intelligible and in various ways consequential. The system's use relies upon the architects' mundane abilities to interact with others and make the computer serve the demands of the job; its ability to provide successive plans, scale the drawings, focus in and out, to point to things, is exploited by virtue of the participants' social interactional abilities.

It is possible for even the simplest activity on a computer, like the movement of a cursor up the screen or a shift between one screen image and another, to be co-ordinated through talk and visual conduct with the activity of another. Despite the increasing interest in the social and organisational issues surrounding the use of computer within HCI, such details of the use of computer artefacts within real-world settings still tend to be overlooked. However, it is the analysis of such details, the moment-to-moment, real-time production of computer-based activities that has been a critical part of the experimental work carried out within the field.

Needless to say, researchers in CSCW have been concerned with the collaborative use of both conventional artefacts and computer systems. Indeed, architecture and design have been domains of interest both as settings in which to explore collaborative activities and for potential applications of collaborative technologies. There has been particular interest in examining the informal interactions that surround design (e.g. Bly and Minneman, 1990; Murray, 1993; Rogers, 1992), particularly in the early phases. Such a focus has also pervaded the proposals for technologies to support design, particularly when developing systems aimed to support users who are physically remote from each other. Hence, design is often considered a useful application of the kinds of audio-visual infrastructures considered in the next chapter, where computer systems, video and audio technology are combined to provide a domain for collaborative work. Typical in such technologies is the inclusion of some shared drawing tool manipulated on the computer display and often supported by a video camera and monitor. Whereas the computer display is considered to support the design activity, the video connection is frequently seen as a resource for supporting the informal interaction between participants, where, for example, designers could see the visual conduct, particularly the gaze or the 'reaction' of their colleagues.

In examining the few cases above, it appears that the combination of these resources may not be so straightforward. In engaging in even such a mundane activity such as discussing a staircase, the participants delicately make use of their colleagues' orientation, talk and visual conduct. The artefacts at hand are seen in relation to another and with respect to the conduct of a co-participant. Hence, it would appear problematic to maintain a crude distinction in the design between one technology being used for the 'formal' work of manipulating a shared document and another being for 'informal' discussion or for monitoring a colleague. Indeed, in contrast to what might be considered a common activity on a CSCW system, the common viewing and manipulation of an object on the screen figures little in the work of the architects. Immersed in the talk and visual conduct of the participants, a cursor movement on the screen up the staircase is seen for a moment and recognised unproblematically. In this brief movement, an architect appears to identify the object in question and the problems he is facing for a colleague. However, in order to arrive at that common viewing, considerable work is engaged in by the participants. They collaborate through delicate interactional practices, including rather carefully designed gestures, subtle shifts in orientation, and the pacing and perturbations in their talk, whilst paying attention to similar features in the conduct of their co-participants. It may be that such practices suggest a different focus for developers of CSCW systems. Rather than concentrating on providing different kinds of capabilities for concurrently manipulating and viewing objects on the screen, developers of CSCW systems should consider supporting such features of talk and visual conduct. Designers of collaborative tools would then have to consider how apparently peripheral resources could be made available to a co-participant, and, perhaps more importantly, how these resources can remain integral to an emerging interactional context.

7   Reconfiguring the work space: media space and collaborative work

7.1   Introduction

Over the past decade or so some of the most interesting technical innovations have involved the integration of telecommunications and computing. The videotelephone and the videoconference suite are the rudimentary precursors to these innovations, innovations which attempt to reconfigure the work space, and provide a rich and flexible environment for work and collaboration amongst distributed personnel. These innovations attempt to go well beyond conventional file or document sharing. They attempt, in various ways, to build environments which provide individuals not only with (vocal and visual) access to each other, but to the variety of tools, artefacts and objects on which work ordinarily relies. One need, however, go no further than consider character of work and interaction found in the settings discussed earlier to envisage the difficulties in developing technologies to support the distribution of such activities, and, as yet, these technical innovations have largely failed to provide satisfactory domains for collaboration.

At the cutting edge of innovations to support real-time interaction and collaboration, at least a few years ago, were systems generally known as 'media spaces'. Media spaces consist of audio-visual and computing infrastructures which provide individuals with 'multimedia' real-time access to one other. For example, at PARC, Xerox Research Laboratories in Palo Alto, a video-window was established which provided scientists with audio-visual access to a common area in a related laboratory 600 miles away in Portland (Olson and Bly, 1991). A similar video-window facility was established at Bellcore (Fish et al., 1990). Elsewhere, at Rank Xerox Research Laboratories in Cambridge, and at the University of Toronto, audio-visual and computing infrastructures were developed which allow individuals to scan and search various offices, form links with colleagues based in other locations, and establish long-term connections, commonly known as 'office shares' (Gaver et al., 1992; Mantei et al., 1991). It is widely argued that research in media space, and more recent innovations in the areas of virtual environments and mixed reality systems, foreshadow the emergence of more generally available systems over the next five to ten years to support real-time collaborative working. Indeed, with the emergence of Integrated Services Digital Network (ISDN) and high bandwidth networks, telecommunications companies throughout the world are increasingly concerned with developing and supporting the 'virtual organisation'. Media space therefore both addresses the 'problem', how to support distributed working in the twenty-first century, and poses a 'solution', audible and visual access coupled with office resources, prior to the required telecommunications infrastructure being commonly available.

In this chapter, we wish to consider the use of an advanced media space by scientists and administrators at a well-regarded systems laboratory, namely Rank Xerox Research Centre in Cambridge, previously known as EuroPARC. The system was deployed to support communication and collaboration amongst members of the laboratory which was considered to be hampered by the general layout of the building. It was also felt that in systems research many of the best ideas and innovations often emerge in informal discussions and through chance contacts between personnel, and that it might be interesting to develop a technology which could support casual meetings, serendipitous encounters and a general aware-ness of the comings and goings of individuals in the laboratory. In a way, therefore, the media space was designed and deployed through an inspired commitment to render individuals, domains and activities 'visible' and provide a resource for sociability and co-operative work.

In exploring how individuals use the media space, we began to notice some curious features in their interaction with each other. In particular, we found that certain forms of conduct lose their impact when produced within the media space, and the relative impotency of the action intro-duces asymmetries into the interaction; asymmetries that, as far as we are aware, do not arise in other environments. These asymmetries undermine the use of the system for certain sorts of activity. In this chapter, we briefly examine the character of interaction in the media space, and go on to discuss two experimental systems we developed with our colleagues Bill Gaver and Abi Sellen which attempted to provide a more satisfactory environment for communication and collaboration (Gaver et al., 1993; Heath et al., 1995). In turn, we find that these experimental systems, whilst providing a more flexible and enriched workspace, themselves introduce some interesting problems; problems which we believe are crit-ical to developing technologies to support distributed collaborative work. In this way, therefore, the chapter is concerned with the design and evalu-ation of prototype and experimental systems. Before exploring the use of media space, it is perhaps worthwhile discussing why such technologies are important, and how they are serving to legitimise new approaches to contemporary work organisation

7.2 Organisational form and technical innovation

It is sometimes argued that the various technological developments which are emerging to support distributed working parallel the changing character of contemporary organisations (see, for example, Barnatt, 1995, 1997). In the ways in which 'matrix' organisation based on project teams increasingly replaced earlier bureaucratic models during the 1960s and 1970s, so a new mode of 'organic organisation' is beginning to emerge in the 1990s. It is based on a dynamic network, a slimmed-down organisation which buys in services and facilities by 'subcontracting' to external agencies. Organic or dynamic networks consist of loosely connected 'webs of agents and brokers' across industries, with a central core staff setting the strategic direction and providing the operational support necessary to sustain the network. With a range of facilities bought in, as required, the boundaries of the organisation become highly fluid and dynamic. The 'firm is really a system of firms – an open ended system of ideas and activities, rather than an entity with a clear structure and definable boundary' (Morgan, 1986). Or, in other words, such organisational forms provide 'flexible specialisation':

the individual forms comprising the network being specialised but the grouping as a whole being flexible with a potential mix of outputs and inputs that can be altered according to the mix of participants on any particular venture. (Starkey and Barnatt (1997))

It is envisaged that the increasing 'disaggregation' of contemporary organisations with its emphasis on temporary co-operative arrangements will place even greater demands on both information and communication technologies. For example, it is argued that information networks will have to make it possible for bodies of mutually accessible data to be available whilst organisations temporarily collaborate. Moreover, increased disaggregation coupled with globalisation will demand enhanced communication technologies allowing individuals located in different organisations not only to share and modify data, but also to work together, in real-time, on those data. So, for example, in the motor industry there is a growing interest in developing technologies to support co-operation between distributed design teams, involving individuals 'belonging' to different 'partner' organisations. Or, in the construction industry technologies are being developed which allow diverse organisations and professions involved in particular projects, which by their nature are typically 'short term', to access, modify and transform large-scale multimedia data sets and to use these data sets to co-ordinate their actions with one another. It is not surprising, therefore, that people speak increasingly of the 'virtual business' and 'virtual organisation', and that substantial government, intergovernmental and private resources are being devoted to designing and developing technologies to support distributed collaborative work. In a sense, therefore, it can be argued that the 'technical' is developing hand-in-hand with the 'social'; organisational change placing new and distinctive demands on communication and information technologies.

Alongside the growing technical interest in supporting distributed collaborative work, we have also witnessed a burgeoning number of studies within various disciplines concerned with interpersonal communication 'mediated' through new technologies. There is, for example, a substantial research literature concerned with the use of electronic mail and other forms of electronic interchange (e.g. Hiltz and Turoff, 1978 (1993); Sproull and Kiesler, 1991; and, on 'collaborative writing', Sharples, 1993). There is also a growing body of empirical studies, both experimental and naturalistic, concerned with aspects of the organisation of interaction in various forms of electronic or virtual environments, ranging from conventional connections through to computer-based systems which provide real-time audible and visual access augmented with document sharing facilities (Benford et al., 1995; Benford et al., 1996; Emmott, 1995; Finn et al., 1997; Heath and Luff, 1992c; O'Malley and Langton, 1994; Sellen, 1995). In various ways these studies examine the ways in which participants have to modify, change or even transform conventional communicative competencies when interacting through particular media rather than face to face. For example, O'Malley and Langton (1994) amongst others have been concerned with the ways in which gaze is oriented to when mediated though video rather than face to face and related research has touched on such issues as turn taking and turn allocation, repair, and speech patterns in video-mediated interaction (cf. McCarthy et al., 1991; Sellen, 1992). Such studies have begun to chart the communicative or interactional phenomena associated with the use of particular technologies.

These issues are by no means new within the social sciences. For example, in the 1950s Schutz (1970) remarked on the difficulties which may arise with communication through new technologies such as the telephone or television. He argued that such media introduce limited and asymmetrical access to the conduct of the participants in the interaction, and, in so doing, may undermine their ability to maintain a presupposition of a 'reciprocity of perspective', which, for Schutz, is central to the co-ordination of intelligible social action.

A B

Figure 7.1 Two offices using the audio-visual infrastructure at EuroPARC. In A, a small camera and monitor are to the left of the workstation and the microphone is omnidirectional, consisting of a small, flat metal plate on the wall. B gives more detail of the common relationship between camera and monitor positions.

It is further essential to the face-to-face situation that you and I have the same environment. First of all I ascribe to you an environment corresponding to my own. Here is the face-to-face situation, but only here does this pre-supposition prove correct, to the extent that I can assume with more or less certainty within the directly experienced social realm that the table I see is identical (and identical; in all its perspective variations) with the table you see, to the extent that I can assume this even if you are only my contemporary or my predecessor. (Schutz (1970: 192))

In this chapter, we hope to show that, as communication and information technologies become increasingly sophisticated and aim to interconnect individuals, their activities and the resources on which they rely in their respective environments, so we begin to confront some rather fundamental issues with regard to how people co-ordinate their conduct with each other.

7.3   Disembodied conduct

In common with several other system research laboratories, Rank Xerox established an audio-visual infrastructure at their site in Cambridge. This infrastructure allows scientists and administrative staff to establish visual and audible contact with each other, or to view public spaces such as common areas and meeting rooms. As EuroPARC's offices straddle three floors, it was felt that technology could facilitate informal communication and collaboration between organisational personnel. The media space consists of a camera, 14″ monitor, speaker and microphone in every office, with larger monitors in the public areas, interconnected and controlled through a computing infrastructure and a communications switching network. The video monitor, with camera placed on top or to one side, is typically positioned close to an individual's computer workstation (Figure 7.1). A flat PZM, omnidirectional microphone is used for sound and normally positioned on the desk by the workstation and operated by a foot pedal.

Over the past few years, the infrastructure has become increasingly sophisticated, and alternative configurations have been experimented with. A number of these developments have been designed to provide 'users' with more delicate ways of remaining aware of each other's activities within the local environment and in establishing connections with each other (see, for example, the use of a sophisticated interface on the computer system by Borning and Travers, 1991; and the use of sounds by Gaver et al., 1992). Despite these developments, however, the most prevalent use of the system is to maintain an open video connection between two physical domains, typically two offices. These 'office shares' are often preserved over long periods of time; sometimes over weeks or even over several months (cf. Dourish et al., 1996). They provide individuals based at different parts of a building with open visual access to each other. Audio connections, however, are normally switched off until one of the participants wishes to speak with the other.

As part of the introduction and development of the media space, we undertook audio-visual recording of connections between individual offices. To diminish the potential influence of recording on people's behaviour, and to enable us to gain an overall picture of how the system was used, we undertook 'blanket' recording of particular connections for up to two or three weeks at a time. These recordings were augmented by more conventional field observations and discussions with 'users' both alone and at 'lab' meetings. As part of the data collection process, and primarily for comparative purposes, we also collected audio-visual recordings of more conventional telecommunication systems, including Xerox Television (XTV), a videoconferencing link between Britain and the USA.

7.3.1   Observations and findings

Before discussing the more curious aspects of interaction in media space, it is perhaps worthwhile mentioning one or two of the ways in which the technology facilitates communication and collaboration amongst personnel in the laboratory. It should be noted that for certain members of the laboratory the media space provides an important resource for remaining aware of each other's activities, so that, for example, administrators can see when a colleague is talking to someone at reception or a visitor has entered the common area. It also allows scientists to be aware of happenings around the laboratory, for example, when meetings and talks are commencing. More particularly, however, the media space makes at least three important contributions to the ways in which personnel communicate and work with each other.

First, unlike a telephone or audio connection, the video connection at EuroPARC provides the opportunity for individuals to assess the availability of a colleague before initiating contact. More precisely, the video channel allows an individual not only to discern whether a colleague is actually in his or her office, but also to assess more delicately the state of his or her current commitments and whether it might be opportune to initiate contact. The infrastructure supports the possibility of glancing at a colleague before deciding whether to establish contact. In this way, video makes an important contribution not only to the awareness of others within a physically distributed work environment, but also to one's ability to respect the territorial rights and current commitments of one's colleagues (Dourish et al., 1996).

Secondly, once individuals have established contact with each other, video can provide participants with the ability to co-ordinate talk with a range of other activities in which they might be engaged. This aspect of video's contribution is particularly important to collaborative work where talk often necessitates discussion of, or reference to, paper and screen-based documents and use of various artefacts like pens, paper and keyboards. Visual access provides individuals with the ability to discern, to some extent, the ongoing organisation and demands of a colleague's activities, and thereby co-ordinate their interaction with the practical tasks at hand. Moreover, visual access provides individuals, to some extent, with the ability to point at and refer to objects within their respective environments. Such facilities have become increasingly important in recent years as designers have begun to develop shared real-time interfaces to computer applications (cf. Bly, 1988; Olson et al., 1990). Recent experiments have demonstrated that video can provide resources for participants to co-ordinate their screen-based activities with one another (Olson and Olson, 1991; Smith et al., 1989).

Thirdly, the video channel provides participants in multiparty conversations with the ability to recognise who is speaking and to 'track' the thread of a conversation. This is of particular importance where video-conferencing facilities support multiparty interactions and where each connection involves more than a single participant. In our analysis of multiparty audio-visual connections both at EuroPARC and through XTV, we noted how video plays an important part in the allocation and co-ordination of speaker turns amongst multiple distributed participants. The advantages of video in helping to identify and discriminate amongst speakers is also supported by experiments with various kinds of multiparty videoconferencing systems (Sellen, 1995).

Despite these contributions, however, our observations of video-mediated communication suggest that this kind of technological medium provides a communicative environment which markedly differs from physical co-presence. The aspects of communication and co-ordination are discussed at length elsewhere (Heath and Luff, 1991, 1992c), but it might be useful to summarise the key observations before considering the use of more sophisticated environments designed to support collaborative work.

7.3.2   Looking through technology

There is a significant body of research which has noted how looking at another person not only serves to provide the individual with certain information, but is socially significant: as a social action, it can serve to engender a response from the person who is being looked at (cf. Goodwin, 1981; Heath, 1986; Kendon, 1990). A look, like other forms of social action, can be interactionally significant, encouraging another to produce a particular action in response to the glance of another. The sequential relevance of a look, the ability of individuals to elicit particular actions from others by virtue of a glance, features within a broad range of activities within face-to-face interaction, not simply those involving the co-ordination of visual conduct, but in the very ways in which individuals produce and participate in each other's talk. For example, it has been observed how the ability of a look to engender action from another features in the ways in which individuals initiate interaction with each other and establish mutual involvement in some business or topic at hand (see Kendon, 1990, Heath, 1986). One interesting aspect of the ways in which gaze can serve to engender action, is that the individual who is the subject of the gaze of another may not necessarily be looking at the other, and yet may be sensitive to the shift of alignment of those who lie outside the direct of line of their regard. Peripheral awareness and sensitivity is central to the ways in which looking accomplishes social action and gains its sequential significance.

In media space, the look or the glance would appear, on occasions, to lose its interactional significance, its ability to elicit or engender action from a co-participant. It does not seem to achieve a comparable interactional significance. For example, in the following fragment, we find Maggie, the scientist, attempting to initiate contact with Jean.

Fragment 7.1

Maggie   10 seconds

Jean

To do this, Maggie turns towards Jean. Jean does not respond. Maggie then waves; still no response is forthcoming. She then stares at Jean for more than ten seconds. There is no response from Jean, or any indication that she is sensitive to Maggie's actions. Finally, Maggie dials Jean's number. Only when Jean replies to Maggie's greeting do the parties establish visual contact.

In fragment 7.1, therefore, Maggie assumes that by looking and waving at Jean she will be able to attract her attention. She presupposes the effectiveness of her actions; her ordinary ability to use glances and gestural activity, to engender sequentially relevant responses from Jean. Neither the initial glance, the gesture, nor even staring, achieve performative impact. Jean remains unmoved; she neither responds, nor looks further away, she does indeed appear insensitive to the actions being performed by her colleague. Maggie's actions pass unnoticed, and she has to use the telephone to initiate mutually focused interaction with her colleague. Whilst presupposing the effectiveness of the medium, it is as if the sequential import of the actions is undermined when they are 'performed' through video rather than face-to-face.

We find numerous instances in the data corpus where one participant will (attempt to) use a look and/or a wave to establish mutual engagement with a colleague. They assume, even after they have experienced many failures, that the resources on which they might ordinarily rely in co-presence to establish mutual engagement will be effective when performed in the media space. Time and again, however, we find that these delicate and often unobtrusive resources through which another's attention can be secured, fail when performed through video. Though participants assume that the technology will support delicate ways of moving from a state of incipient talk to mutual engagement, they discover that these forms of visual conduct are not necessarily supported by the technology. The following fragment, drawn from the same video-connection some time later, reflects the problems participants encounter when attempting to use the system to do the things they might ordinarily do.

Prior to the beginning of this fragment, Jean returns to her desk. As she sits down in her chair, she turns and acknowledges Maggie, in the way she might if she were re-establishing co-presence. Neither her reappearance in the scene, nor her initial glance serve to engender any response from her colleague. In consequence, she begins a series of gestures through which she attempts to gain Maggie's attention. She turns to her colleague, places her finger on her nose, and, rocking from side to side, waggles her hand at her colleague. This elaborate performance fails to attract notice and, continuing to look at her colleague, Jean places both thumbs in her ears, waggles her hands and utters 'Ooh::↑voooh↓ooh::↑voooh::.'

Finally, thrusting her face towards the monitor (the other), she abandons her attempt to initiate contact, uttering 'No, she won't look at hh me'.

Fragment 7.2

Jean puts thumb in ears and   Abandons
waggles fingers   Glances at camera attempt to contact

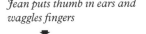

Jean: Ooh::↑voooh↓ooh::↑voooh::--------No. she wo nt look at °hh me ----------

Maggie looking at screen

It is interesting to note that the gestures used by Jean in her attempt to establish mutual contact, allow her to exaggerate her visual orientation towards Maggie. The waggling fingers balanced on the end of her nose that flicker across her line of regard, coupled with movements from side to side, exaggerate her bodily and visual alignment towards the other. Similarly, the hands to the side of the head, and the moving fingers, underscore her orientation towards her colleague, broadening the visual appearance of her head and its particular alignment. Despite her theatrical movements, Jean's attempts to gain her colleague's attention fail, and a few moments later she abandons her efforts to initiate contact.

As in fragment 7.1, an individual presupposes the effectiveness of their visual conduct through the media, assuming that a glance and then, more dramatically, a series of gestures, will 'naturally' engender a response from the potential co-participant. However, the glances and their accompanying gestures, the power of the look to ordinarily attract the attention of another, appear to be weakened when performed through video rather than face to face. In neither these, nor the many other instances we have examined, is there evidence to suggest that the potential co-participant is deliberately disattending the attempts to attract their attention. Rather, the looks and gestures of their colleagues simply pass unnoticed, as if their appearance on a screen, rather than in actual co-presence, diminishes their performative and interactional impact. It is as if the sequential significance of such actions is weakened by the medium. In consequence,

the relatively delicate ways in which individuals subtly move from disen-
gagement to engagement in face-to-face environments, especially when
they are in a 'state of incipient talk', appear to be rendered problematic in
video-mediated co-presence.

7.3.3   Talk and visual conduct

Looking at another may not only serve to initiate conversation, but plays
an important part in the production and co-ordination of talk within face-
to-face interaction. In conversation, speakers are sensitive to the gaze of
the person to whom they are talking and draw various inferences from the
visual alignment of their co-participant(s). As has been mentioned in
earlier chapters, it has been found that speakers have various devices to
encourage a co-participant to realign their orientation. These devices
include speech perturbations, such as pauses, the elongation of sounds
and various forms of self-editing and repair, all of which serve to delay the
delivery of an utterance whilst simultaneously encouraging other(s) to
participate in a particular fashion. They also include various forms of
body movements, such as gestures which are systematically designed to
encourage particular forms of co-participation (see e.g. Goodwin, 1981;
Heath, 1986; Kendon 1990). An important aspect of the ability to shape
the co-participation of others within the activity at hand is the gaze or
alignment of the speakers themselves which serve both to encourage
response and to set the parameters for the relevant co-orientation. The
speaker's gaze in many cases works with these various devices to establish
a reorientation from the co-participant and thereby establish heightened
involvement in the activity at hand.

The relative ineffectiveness of gaze and other forms of visual conduct in
the media space is not only consequential to the ways in which users are
able to establish mutual engagement. It can also generate 'difficulties' for
the articulation of talk and for the communication of information embodied in gestures and bodily movements. The following example is drawn
from an extensive collaboration between two scientists over a period of a
few weeks. We join the action as Ian initiates contact with Robert through
the open audio and video connection by enquiring what he should tell a
colleague (Marty) to do to deal with a problem that has been occurring
when transferring files to the United States.

Fragment 7.3   Transcript 1

   I: What I shall I tell Mar::ty↑ to do(hh).
      (1.2)
▶ R: Er:°m::
▶   (1.2)

▶ R: Let's see:: well first >first off I'd (0.2) what I did las: t night
       which seemed to (work) was send it tw::ice under different
       names:: <an then she did (a di::ff)
       (1.6)
R: en then she: could clean up the er::: (0.8) line noi:se. (...)
       (2.3)
R: °thhh
       (.3)
I: O:k ay
R: (Such a hack)

At the outset, it can be noticed that Robert delays his reply to Ian's
question firstly by pausing, then by producing 'Er:°m::', and then once
again by pausing. Even when he does begin to reply, the actual answer is
not immediately forthcoming, as if he is deliberately delaying the gist of
his response. The gist of the reply is delayed, pushed away from the beginning of the speaker's turn, by virtue of the preface 'Let's see:' and various
forms of speech perturbation, including a sound stretch ('see::'), a 0.2
second pause and consecutive restarts 'well first >first off I'd (0.2) what'.
The speaker's actions, and in particular his apparent difficulty in beginning his reply, may be systematically related to the conduct of the (potential) recipient, and in particular with Robert's inability to secure his
co-participant's gaze. A more detailed, illustrated transcript might be
helpful.

Fragment 7.3   Transcript 2

Ian

I: What I shall I tell
       Mar::ty↑ to do(hh).
                       ◄   (1.2)   ◄

R: Er:°m:: (1.2) Let's see:: well first>first off I'd (0.2) what I did

Robert

Ian's question is produced as the two colleagues are independently
engaged in individual screen-based activities. As he initiates contact by

asking the question, Ian momentarily glances at Robert and then turns back to his screen. By the time Robert reorients, he finds Ian looking at his screen apparently engaged in continuing to deal with some text. In the light of having a potential recipient who is apparently engaged in another activity, Robert uses an utterly conventional device for attempting to secure co-participant alignment; he delays the delivery of the reply and produces an object which projects more to follow but withholds the actual reply (cf. Goodwin, 1981; Heath, 1986).

Withholding the reply fails to engender any reorientation from Ian, and following 'Er:°m::', Robert begins to progressively shift his gaze towards Ian, as if attempting to encourage a reorientation whilst avoiding actually staring at his potential recipient. Both the withholding of the reply, and the subtle shifts in Robert's orientation, fail to encourage any display of recipiency from the co-participant. Robert begins the preface 'Let's see::' and looks directly towards his colleague. The alignment of gaze towards the co-participant, the preface, the sound stretch, the pause and the restarts are all devices which are regularly used to secure recipient alignment at the beginning of a turn. The pause appears to engender a response from Ian, and, following his realignment of gaze from the screen to his colleague, the speaker begins the gist of his reply.

It is apparent, therefore, that in fragment 7.3 the respondent has various difficulties in securing the relevant form of co-participation from the potential recipient, ironically the party who initiated the interaction in the first place. The potential recipient displays little orientation to the speaker's successive attempts to secure his gaze. It is possible that the difficulties faced by the speaker in attempting to secure a realignment from the recipient derive from the relative ineffectiveness of his visual conduct and, in particular, the apparent inability of the co-participant to notice the successive shifts in orientation undertaken by the speaker. In video-mediated interaction, the relative scale and presentation of a speaker's more delicate shifts in orientation and gaze may pass unnoticed and thereby undermine the performative impact of conventional devices to elicit gaze.

In passing, a further point should be mentioned. To provide individuals with the ability to vary their position whilst speaking with colleagues through the media space, we deliberately used omnidirectional microphones to provide audio connections. These microphones are designed to conceal relative changes in the direction of a sound within a circumscribed domain. In consequence, they mask changes in the sound level of a speaker's voice. These changes may allow a participant to discern whether a colleague is changing physical orientation, for example when another is turning towards them. In the media space, changes in the direction of sound are not necessarily available. Thus, the relative ineffectiveness of a speaker's shift of gaze to engender response during the course of utterance, may derive not only from the accessibility of their visual conduct, but also from the absence of changes in tone and loudness of the voice.

7.3.4   Gestural insignificance

One of the more persuasive arguments for enhancing audio with visual access in telecommunications is that it provides individuals with the ability to see each other and communicate non-verbally, as well as through talk. In part, the argument derives from the relative importance that both lay and professional observers of social life have attributed to the role of gesture and other forms of bodily conduct in human communication, whilst curiously down-playing the significance of talk. Indeed, perhaps it was because of the assumption that the visual channel was critical to complex forms of human communication that the telecommunication industries had so much confidence in the potential market for videotelephony and videoconferencing. It is perhaps worth adding that, despite the continuing commitment to the role of the visual channel in supporting interpersonal communication, especially a simulated face-to-face view of the other, the market, particularly for the videotelephone, has not emerged in the way predicted. Moreover, research undertaken by the telecommunication industries has to some extent failed to unearth why the visual may be important. So, for example, in a large-scale experiment undertaken by France Telecom in Biarritz some years ago, it was found that domestic users of video-phones often preferred to use the technology to look at themselves whilst talking with friends rather than at their co-participant (de Fornel, personal communication).

As we noted earlier, media space does provide individuals with the ability to see each other and to some extent co-ordinate their actions with visible aspects of their colleagues' conduct. It also helps individuals to identify who is speaking and to be able to see aspects of their conduct such as gestures, shifts in gaze and changes in their bodily orientation. It has also been argued (Olson and Olson, 1991; Smith et al., 1989) that participants in video-mediated environments are able to co-ordinate more subtle elements of their bodily comportment, reciprocating shifts in postural orientation and responding to particular facial expressions. The technology undoubtedly provides individuals with access to visual elements of the conduct of co-participants and with the possibility of co-ordinating their own conduct with the bodily comportment and movements of those with whom they are interacting. It should also be added that, in video-mediated environments, both in media spaces and in more conventional videoconferencing, participants appear to use gestures and other forms of bodily conduct as they might in face-to-face interaction, to organise, for example, the form of co-participation they require from a potential recipient during the accomplishment of a particular activity.

Whereas bodily conduct is largely visible to the co-participant, its seeming availability on screen does not appear to guarantee its interactional significance. Indeed, as with looking and gaze, we find numerous instances of individuals using the media space, where particular gestures or shifts in bodily orientation fail to achieve the import that they might if undertaken face to face. For example, as mentioned earlier, an utterly conventional sequence in face-to-face interaction consists of bodily actions such as gestures serving to elicit the gaze of a co-participant; the utterance itself being delayed through various forms of perturbation prior to the speaker gaining the appropriate orientation from the other. In video-mediated interaction, we find speakers producing gestures and other forms of bodily movement which appear to be designed to engender a realignment in orientation from the person to whom they are speaking. However, despite the movement appearing on screen before the other, it fails to engender the appropriate course of action from the co-participant. For example, in the following fragment we find a lengthy description of an interface in which the speaker (Robert) appears to encourage his recipient (Ian) to participate.

Fragment 7.4   Transcript 1

R: there's: two degrees of freedom you can move it in X an Y:::. (0.3)
    if there are mo:re than two degrees of freedom you can select
    which variables were to be manipulated: (0.5) which (will)
    remain fixed (0.3) and then manipulated at (.) two:: (.) <three
    variables by the control: icon.
    (1.2)
R: er:: is: this correct
    (1.0)
I: Well:: (.) not quite.

The description itself is accompanied by a series of iconic or illustrative gestures through which Robert suggests the operation of the interface. These include a side-to-side gesture occurring over 'X an Y:::.', followed by an open palm movement from side to side with 'were to be manipulated:'. Robert moves his palm down and flat as he utters 'remain fixed' and moves his second and third fingers down as he says 'two:: (.) <three variables'. These gestures illustrate the ways in which the variables might

be manipulated. Robert has the gaze of the recipient during much of this extract but only turns towards his co-participant during the final part of the description.

Fragment 7.4   Transcript 2

R: control: icon. (1.2) er:: is: this correct

                        ⬆   (1.0)   ⬆

I: Well::(.) not quite.

On the one hand, the speaker's gestures appear to be designed to provide a visual portrayal of the objects and actions mentioned in the talk (see Birdwhistell, 1970; Bull, 1983; Ekman and Friessen, 1969; Schegloff, 1984). There is little evidence, however, either in this fragment or in numerous other instances of iconic gestures in video-mediated interaction, that the illustrative component successfully provides the co-participant with relevant or sequentially significant information. On the other hand, the gestures also appear to be designed to encourage Ian to participate more actively in the description. They fail, however, to transform the way in which he is participating in the talk; indeed, he provides little indication, despite various opportunities and encouragements, that he is actually following the emergent description. Consequently, the speaker, who has been unable to encourage the recipient to indicate whether he agrees, disagrees or fails to follow the description, is then faced with having explicitly to elicit confirmation and clarification.

The relative inability of the speaker's visual conduct to effect some response from the recipient during the production of turns at talk is found elsewhere, amongst different users within the data corpus. Even relatively basic sequences that recur within face-to-face interaction, for example

when a speaker uses a movement to elicit the gaze of a recipient and co-
ordinates the production of an utterance with the receipt of gaze, tend to
be absent from the materials at hand. Speakers continue to gesture and
produce a range of bodily behaviour during the delivery of talk in video-
mediated communication. Yet visual conduct largely fails to achieve its
performative impact or sequential significance.

In such circumstances, we not infrequently find the speaker upgrading
their attempt to secure the appropriate alignment from the other, sometimes producing more dramatic gestures, but once again it is not unusual
to find that the actions fail to elicit a response. As with looking and gaze,
there is little evidence in such cases to suggest that the co-participant is
'ignoring' the actions of the other, that he is aware of what is happening
and withholding a response; rather, whilst seemingly visible, the bodily
conduct of the speaker fails to achieve sequential and interactional
significance.

The relative inability of bodily conduct to engender action from a co-
participant, or achieve sequential relevance, is not limited to a small range
of visual actions. Rather, the medium seems to undermine the production
of a relatively unpredictable, though wide array of actions accomplished
through bodily activity. For example, it is often argued that an important
element of communication consists of the ways in which participants use
gestures and the like to illustrate particular phenomena; the verbal
description achieving its significance by virtue of the accompanying
bodily actions. Whilst empirically it can be difficult to demarcate the
sequential significance of the visual components of such activities, our
analysis suggests that, in media space, there is evidence to suggest that
illustrative gestures like various other forms of bodily comportment fail to
achieve sequential and interactional significance. Similarly, in the analysis
of cases in which they do appear to fail, and that the speaker orients to
their failure, there is little evidence to suggest that the co-participant is
disregarding the actions of the other; rather they simply pass unnoticed. It
is interesting to add that, in cases where speakers do escalate their actions
in an attempt to secure a particular response, if the activity is responded
to, it is not infrequently misconstrued; the exaggerated conduct undermining the very character of the action.

7.3.5   Communicative asymmetries and incongruent environments

Video-mediated co-presence reveals asymmetries in interpersonal relations which, as far as we are aware, are found neither within face-to-face
interaction nor in other technologically mediated forms of communication, such as telephone calls. Despite providing participants with the

opportunity of monitoring the visual conduct of the other, and gearing the production of an activity to the behaviour of the potential recipient, the technology systematically interferes with the sequential impact or interactional significance of non-vocal action and activity. The speaker, or more generally the interactant, has visual access to his or her co-participant, so whilst he or she is speaking, can monitor how the recipient behaves and can remain sensitive to their behaviour. But, the resources upon which a speaker ordinarily relies to shape the ways in which a co-participant listens and attends to the talk appear to be disrupted by the technology. Even simple gestures to encourage the other to realign their gaze towards the speaker lose their performative impact. Speakers attempt to co-ordinate their activities, such as talking, with the visual behaviour of the person to whom they are speaking, and yet they are unable to affect the other, to shape their involvement within the activity itself. In video-mediated interaction, the speaker both has visual access and remains sensitive to the other and yet is rendered communicatively impotent. The technology undermines the local, sequential significance of a range of visual conduct, and introduces a curious imbalance into the interaction between speaker and hearers.

These seemingly insignificant aspects of communication in media space can generate some interesting 'social' problems. Take, for example, privacy; one of the ways in which individuals ordinarily preserve some semblance of privacy derives from their ability to remain sensitive to the actions of others outside the direct line of their regard. My ability to know that you may be looking at me, even though I am not looking at you, sets a constraint on your looking as well as my own. By undermining our ability to know when someone is looking at us, by removing the communicative impact of gaze, video-mediated environments allow individuals to look and stare, however inadvertently, without risk of detection. In the data, we found numerous instances of individuals watching others in a way that is unprecedented as far as we are aware in conventional co-present environments. Indeed, within EuroPARC, various technological solutions were explored that might address such problems. For example, Gaver (1991a) implemented a series of sounds, such as a 'creaking door', which would warn the unwitting recipient that a colleague had just glanced at him or her. However, as one might imagine, these more formal solutions failed to achieve either the flexibility or sensitivity of the practices whereby individuals ordinarily preserve each other's privacy when in co-presence.

The character of social interaction we find in media space may derive from an incongruity between the locale in which an action is produced and the environment in which it is received. It might be useful to consider, on the one hand, how the technology might transform the visibility or availability of actions of the other participant, and, on the other, the difficulties it may generate for the production of an action or activity.

As suggested earlier, much of the work performed through gesture and more generally through body movement is accomplished on the periphery of the visual field. It is critical that it is not attended to in its own right, but is rather viewed on the margins of the perceptual and attentional field 'seen but unnoticed'. In the case of video-mediated communication, the recipient's access to the other's gesture or bodily activity is their appearance on a screen. The gesture is either viewed directly, within the totality of the screen's contents, when the recipient looks directly at the screen, or, if the recipient is looking away, constitutes one element of the screen's image within the immediate office environment. In the first case, seeing the image as a whole destroys the relative weighting of a particular action with regard to the rest of the 'speaker's appearance'. In the second, it is found that recipients are largely unable to differentiate the contents of the screen image on the periphery of their visual field. Only occasionally are relatively gross movements, such as the other standing or blocking the screen, noticed and 'noticeable'. In consequence, much of the delicacy which features in the design and performance of certain forms of bodily activity is lost to the recipient.

These difficulties become more severe when one considers that the camera and monitor distort the appearance of any bodily movement. They transform the spatial and temporal features of a movement and remove the conduct from its surrounding environment. So, the graduated progression of a gesture, designed, for example, to elicit the gaze of a recipient, its movement towards the periphery of the other's visual field, or from side to side or backwards and forwards, is inevitably transformed when it appears on screen rather than in co-presence. The object received is not the object produced.

The way in which the technology transforms our ability to peripherally monitor the conduct of the other, and changes in the movement's appearance, might also explain why gaze or looking is sometimes ineffectual when performed through video rather than in co-presence. Unless the recipient is looking directly at the screen, it is unlikely whether he or she is able to discern relatively small changes of head and eye movement. This may well explain why on certain occasions speech perturbations which are commonly used to elicit the gaze of another fail to encourage a recipient to reorient when performed through video. The technology can render a look ineffective by virtue of the recipient's inability to peripherally discriminate small changes in bodily orientation of the other on the screen.

It is also worthwhile to consider the way in which an action is produced and the problems faced by, for example, a speaker in communicating through video. It was suggested earlier that gesture and other forms of bodily activity are systematically designed with respect to the local environment and the emergent conduct within the interaction. In video co-presence, mediated through audio-visual technology, the camera and monitor inevitably delimit and distort your access to the co-participant. Your view of the other is from a particular angle and severely circumscribes access not only to the other and their bodily conduct but to the local environment in which it is produced. In consequence, your ability to design a bodily movement such as a gesture which is sensitive to orientation to the other and their relationship to their own environment is problematic. Moreover, the limited access to the other also means that you are relatively unaware of changes within their local environment with which your visual conduct may well be competing; for example, changes to the contents of their screen or their workstation, or even people entering the room.

These problems become more severe when one recognises that in contrast to co-presence an individual is unable to adjust their position in order to secure a more appropriate view of the other. More importantly, perhaps, in media space you are not only unable to alter your own view of the other's domain, but cannot see how your conduct appears within the other's local environment. So, for example, if a gesture is unsuccessful, in say eliciting the gaze of the co-participant, a speaker is unable to discern how the movement might be redesigned in order to attract the notice of the recipient. It is hardly surprising, therefore, that in reviewing the data corpus one finds numerous instances of upgraded and exaggerated gestures and body movements, as speakers attempt to achieve some impact on the way that others are participating in the activity, literally, at hand.

The technology therefore provides physically distributed individuals with incongruent environments for interaction. What I see is not what you see, and I am unable to see how you see me and the actions in which I engage. Despite this incongruity, individuals presuppose the effectiveness of their conduct and assume that their frame of reference is 'parallel' with their co-participant's. They presuppose, for the practicalities at hand and their mutually co-ordinated activity, that their image of the other is congruent with the other's image of them. As suggested earlier, this presupposition of a common frame of reference, a reciprocity of perspectives, is a foundation of socially organised conduct.

Now it is a basic axiom of any interpretation of the common world and its objects that these various co-existing systems of co-ordinates can be transformed one into the other; I take it for granted, and I assume my fellow-man does the same, that I and my fellow-man would have typically the same experiences of the common world if we changed places, thus transforming my Here into his, and his – now to me a There – into mine. (Schutz (1962: 315–16))

In video-mediated presence, however, camera and monitor inevitably transform the environments of conduct, so that the bodily activity that one participant produces is rather different from the object received by the co-participant. The presupposition that one environment is commensurate with the other undermines the production and receipt of visual conduct and provides some explanation as to why gesture and other forms of bodily activity may be ineffectual when mediated through video rather than undertaken within a face-to-face, co-present social environment.

7.4   Enriching the work space

In providing distributed individuals with access to each other, media space and other telecommunication technologies have largely been concerned with supporting face-to-face communication. So, for example videotelephones and videoconferencing facilities provide individuals with a head-and-shoulders view of the person(s) with whom they are interacting. Even with more sophisticated computer-based systems, users are conventionally given a window which allows them to view, face on, their co-participants. Media-space technologies share this orientation. As we have noted at EuroPARC, individuals are provided with a camera and monitor and these are commonly positioned to enable personnel to see each other's face. There are, of course, some important exceptions. These tend to be restricted to prototypes in research laboratories. For example, a number of researchers have begun to provide users with a shared work space as well as an audio-visual link through which they can collaboratively work on text or diagrams (Bly, 1988; Scrivener et al., 1992). However, even in these more innovative cases, the audio-visual infrastructure is primarily designed to provide a face-to-face view rather than to allow participants to view each other with regard to their local environments, or to show and discuss objects, such as documents which are located within the respective settings.

It is not at all clear why the designers of such systems have been preoccupied with developing support for a distributed 'face-to-face' interaction, although it can be argued that the technology has been shaped implicitly with regard to a certain model of interaction which places a particular emphasis on visual communication. In particular, non-verbal behaviour has been understood with regard to bodily expressions of an individual often being divorced from their immediate environment (see e.g. Argyle and Dean, 1965). If, however, we are concerned with developing a technology which can support collaborative work between individuals who are physically distributed, that is, sited in distinct environments, then it may be necessary to consider how local resources can be brought to bear in the interaction between users. More generally, it would seem reasonable to suggest that we might learn some important lessons from how individuals collaborate in more conventional co-present environments when considering how we might design and develop advanced technologies for distributed work. This is not to suggest that media space, virtual environments, mixed realities and the like should try to simulate co-present settings. Even if this were considered desirable, such ambitions are way beyond the capabilities of current technologies, including those being developed over the next decade or so. Rather, a more thorough understanding of collaborative work in more conventional environments may provide some innovative ideas and minimal requirements for novel systems as well as point to some of the pitfalls which might arise in the development of useful technologies.

Putting to one side the communicative asymmetries discussed above for the time being, the limitations of media spaces become increasingly clear when one contrasts the technical support people receive in those environments with how they work within conventional settings. If we consider the richness and complexity of how individuals work together in the settings we have discussed so far, one can begin to see how media spaces severely impoverish the ways in which users are able to collaborate with each other.

It is perhaps worth reconsidering one or two examples. In Reuters, for example, we find journalists who have to co-ordinate the production of news stories with each other, talking with regard to the screen-based activities of their colleagues, and using various resources to render material visible without overwhelming colleagues with irrelevant detail and information. In London Underground and Docklands Light Railway control rooms, individuals make sense of each other's conduct with respect to the ways in which individuals glance at monitors, screens and diagrams, make notes on timetables, talk on telephones and, in a whole host of ways, use tools and artefacts based within the local milieu. Personnel within the control rooms draw on the local environment to make sense of each other's actions, and design their own activities so that they are visible and accountable to others within the local milieu. Moreover, much of the 'interaction' between personnel within the control rooms, not unlike Reuters, does not consist of direct, mutually focused, conversations, but, rather, highly variable participation in each other's activities, which more or less are ongoingly co-ordinated with the contributions of others. For example, we find personnel participating simultaneously in more than a single activity, so that even a single turn at talk may be designed to engender action from different participants located within different organisational domains; the utterance momentarily featuring (and being sensitive to) various activities arising at different stages in distinct ecologies. The studies reveal, therefore, the ways in which co-present collaborative work relies upon a complex body of interactional practices through which personnel remain aware of, and participate in, each other's actions and activities. Indeed, in such settings, it becomes increasingly difficult to demarcate individual activities from 'collaborative'; personnel mutually sustaining multiple activities which ebb and flow within various forms of co-participation and production. It is difficult to envisage how any of these aspects of workplace activity could be successfully undertaken in media space as it is currently configured.

Workplace studies therefore reveal aspects of collaborative work which may help us further understand the current limitations of media spaces and related telecommunications technologies. They may also provide a framework with which to reconsider how we might more successfully support distributed collaborative work and begin to deploy technologies which converge with the growing disaggregation of organisational activities. For the present purposes, the following observations and conclusions are probably the more critical.

(i) Both 'focused' and 'unfocused' collaborative work may often involve, not only face-to-face interaction, but an alignment towards a common focal domain within the local physical environment. The focal domain may consist of a paper or screen-based document such as a plan, a story or a record, or it may consist of a larger object which is located beyond the individual's reach. The individuals may not have equivalent access to the object or artefact. They co-ordinate their actions, not necessarily by looking directly at each other, but, rather, through a 'peripheral sensitivity' which allows them to focus on the object in question whilst remaining aware of the actions of their co-participant. As we have observed, in many working environments, including those which primarily involve focused interaction between the participants, such as in a general practice consultation and at times in the discussion of architectural plans, the local ecology is not arranged to provide a direct face-to-face orientation, but, rather, where individuals position themselves side-by-side in, as Kendon (1990) has noted, an 'F' formation.

(ii) In working with each other, individuals are continuously and unobtrusively adjusting their access and alignment towards each other and the emerging features of the local environment. They continually shape their orientation to each other and the objects and artefacts at hand, with regard to the ongoing demands of the activity/activities in which they are engaged. In this way, individuals establish and sustain differential forms of co-participation in the activities 'at hand'. The situational and emergent character of collaborative activities necessitates variable and flexible access. In multiparty environments, in which a number of individuals are working on distinct but related activities, settings such as newsrooms, control centres, dealing rooms, architectural practices and the like, the situation is made more complex, since the physical alignment of participants is often sensitive to the ongoing demands of various activities in which they are, more or less, involved.

(iii) Despite strict demarcation of tasks and a formal division of labour, in many settings work involves continual and seamless shifts between individual and collaborative activities. So, whilst it may be feasible to formally distinguish roles and responsibilities, individuals contribute to, and participate in, each other's activities. Participation may involve no more than remaining sensitive to conversations, or aspects of those conversations, which a colleague has both with those within the local domain and those based in other settings. It may, however, consist of talking through documents, making corrections or together solving a technical problem which has emerged within the domain. In more complex situations, individuals, as we have suggested, may design particular actions and activities so that they are sensitive to, or contribute to, simultaneous concurrent activities in which colleagues may be engaged (and who may be similarly sensitive to the conduct of others). Work is produced and co-ordinated through the ability of personnel to simultaneously participate in multiple activities, rendering the distinction between individual and collaborative work both empirically and conceptually problematic.

(iv) Many of the actions and activities which are undertaken within the contemporary workplaces are accomplished through the use of tools and artefacts. These may consist of pen and paper, information systems and telephones. The use of these tools and artefacts is not only relevant to the accomplishment of individual activities, but provides an important resource to participants in making sense of each other's conduct and in the co-ordination of action. For example, an individual's glance at a computer screen in a control room can serve to notify others within the local domain of a problem which might be emerging. Or, by entering information using a keyboard, not only can a body of data be preserved for use by colleagues on a later occasion, but also the activity (or elements of the activity) can be made visible to colleagues. The use of particular tools and artefacts by individuals is an important resource to others within the domain, providing a sense of the activities in which they are engaged. This ongoing sense of a changing domain of activity is critical for the coordination of action between participants.

(v) Access to the local environment or local ecology of the setting, not only provides resources (tools, artefacts and objects) to enable activities to be properly accomplished, but is a critical resource for the coordination of action. The physical arrangement of the setting, the stable location of individuals, sources of information, tools and artefacts, provides the participants with reliable resources through which they can make sense of spatial reconfigurations, shifts in orientation, gestures, manipulation of objects, talk; that is, the activities in which they engage both individually and collectively. Activities are embedded in, and embed, features of the local physical environment. Removing bodily activity and talk from the ecology in which it is produced undermines the ability of individuals to produce activities, and to draw the relevant sense and inference of the activities of others.

Despite the growing sophistication of technologies to support collaboration and the increasing interest in developing shared work spaces (Benford et al., 1996; Bly et al., 1992; Greenberg et al., 1995; Ichigawa et al., 1995), it is unlikely that current innovations in media space, virtual environments and mixed realities, are able to provide the forms of access that even relatively simple collaborative activities require. Whilst not suggesting that in the designs of new technologies we should attempt to reproduce a co-present setting, it would seem reasonable that in supporting distributed collaborative work we need to rethink the sorts of support with which we provide users. In particular, we could turn our attention away from interpersonal communication and the addition of further connections between individuals, to providing resources to enable individuals to accomplish and co-ordinate activities with each other.

In the light of observations derived from workplace studies, it is interesting to note that the location of camera and monitor in the respective user environments has been largely treated as unproblematic in the design of most media spaces. Indeed, despite the emphasis on peripheral awareness and sensitivity, it has been assumed that a head-and-shoulders view of the other would provide the relevant information. The forms of access that the user requires once they have established contact have been given less emphasis, so that, for example, the idea that another might be engaged in a task focused on an object, like making notes on a paper pad, did not feature as important for the design. In part, this relative lack of concern with task-focused collaboration may have derived from the decision to support informal sociability where it does not seem relevant to provide access to the working domain and the wider environment of the person with whom one is conversing. It appears, then, that the concern with providing support for sociability and (mediated) face-to-face communication throughout a variety of media spaces, and embodied in the 'head-and-shoulders' view they provide, may help to explain why such sophisticated technological environments have largely failed to support individuals' access to each other's activities and working domains.

7.4.1   Reconfiguring media space

To explore some of these issues, and to consider how we might use our empirical findings to inform the design of media spaces, we decided to reconfigure the technology in order to provide participants with more flexible and varied access to each other's activities and the local environment. With our colleagues Abigail Sellen and William Gaver at Rank Xerox Research Centre, Cambridge (formerly EuroPARC), we constructed two relatively simple systems which provided individuals, based in different offices within the same building, with the ability to see and talk to each other, share and show documents and other sorts of object and artefact, and to see each other's local milieu. We then ran a series of small exercises in which subjects had to undertake various tasks in collaboration in the modified media spaces. The purpose of these was to explore some of the interactional consequences of providing users with variable accessibility: to find out what the possible advantages and disadvantages of different design solutions might be. These experiments were video-recorded, and we also interviewed the subjects about the experiences using the systems.

To develop a virtual environment to support collaborative work in this way it is necessary to explore ways of providing users not only with alternative views of each other, their work space and their local environment, but with ways of flexibly and even 'seamlessly' varying their access to the other. Building a media space that fulfils these requirements is not straightforward. It is difficult to provide individuals with flexible access to each other and their respective settings, and in doing so one can exacerbate problems which haunt even the most basic media space, namely the perspectival incongruities of the different participants. Nevertheless, we believe that it is only by building and evaluating technologies 'in use', no matter how simple, that the benefits and problems of alternative configurations can be uncovered.

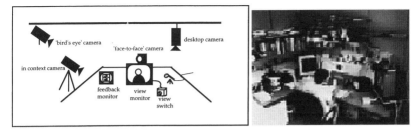

Figure 7.2 Configuration of the MTV-I system using multiple cameras, a switch and a single monitor for each participant.

7.4.2   Preliminary designs: multiple target video (MTV-I and MTV-II)

In the first exercise (MTV-I) we provided participants with the ability to select one of four views of the remote participant and his environment. This was accomplished by placing four cameras in each office. The views consisted of: (i) a conventional face-to-face view; (ii) a 'desktop' camera to enable the remote participant to see objects on their colleague's work surface; (iii) a wider 'in-context' view providing an image of the co-participant in relation to their immediate environment, principally the desk; and (iv) a 'bird's-eye' view giving access to most of a colleague's office environment (Figure 7.2).

Participants were given a single monitor, and using a simply rotary switch could select one amongst the four views. We also provided a small feedback monitor which allowed the user to see which view his co-participant had selected. The idea, therefore, was that individuals, in the course of working together, could select the view that was most appropriate to the actions or activity in which they were engaged. So, for example, they might begin with a face-to-face view and then decide to view each other's wider domain or look at an object together.

A number of pairs of subjects were asked to perform two experimental tasks. In the first, participants attempted to draw the other's office. In the second, they were asked to carry out a collaborative design exercise where they had asymmetrical resources. One participant was a given a model of a room, rather like a doll's house, containing various pieces of furniture, the other pen and paper with which to sketch various design solutions. The idea was that the subjects were to work together in laying out the furniture in the room. The results of these experiments are described more fully in Gaver et al. (1993). They reveal how, given the choice, participants mainly switched between the in-context, desk-top and bird's-eye views, and only rarely used the face-to-face setting. It was also interesting to note that, when working together on the documents (the drawings) or with the model, the subjects did not select the desk-top view which provided detailed access to the objects, but rather used the in-context or bird's-eye views which allowed them to see each other in relation to the drawing or the room. It was also found that subjects became relatively agile in using the system and would change views quite rapidly in order to maintain the most appropriate access with respect to the momentary demands of the activity. Given the nature of tasks, however, it is hardly surprising that the participants tended to select views which included the objects rather than simply the face-to-face orientation. Nevertheless, it is worth noting that the participants tended to maintain views which allowed them to see both the object and the other, even though at times this undermined viewing the particular details of the drawing or the room.

MTV-I did not altogether prove satisfactory. Switching between the views involved participants having to momentarily abandon the activity in which they were engaged to establish the appropriate orientation; there was no seamless transition in which users could subtly shift their alignment towards each other and the respective domains. Moreover, despite providing monitors which allowed users to see the view that the co-participant had selected, there was some uncertainty as to what the other could see and what they were actually looking at. Indeed, it was not unusual for individuals to assume that the co-participant was looking at, or able to see, an object under discussion, only to discover in the course of the talk that it was unseen or inaccessible in the way they had assumed. The necessity, therefore, to select particular views, and the inability of the participants to know what was accessible at some particular moment, generated various difficulties for the participants in co-ordinating their activities with each other.

In the light of these difficulties, we decided to reconfigure MTV-I. It seemed sensible to develop a system which provided a more stable and comprehensive environment to users which did not entail individuals selecting between alternative views of the other and their physical environment. So as to not overwhelm users, we also decided to remove one of the views we had provided in MTV-I; the one which was relatively underused, namely the bird's-eye view.

In the second experiment (MTV-II), we attempted to address some of these difficulties by providing a more stable configuration which allowed access to both the other and the workspace. Rather than providing access to the various views via a switch, each participant was provided with several monitors, so that all the views from the cameras were simultaneously available. The monitors provided three views: (i) a face-to-face view, (ii) a 'desktop' view and (iii) an 'in-context' view; the latter giving access to the periphery of the colleague's environment (see Figure 7.3).

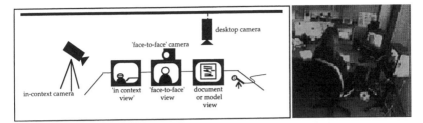

Figure 7.3 The configuration of the MTV-II system using multiple cameras and multiple monitors for each participant.

The three monitors were arranged in each room in a similar fashion with the face-to-face monitor and camera positioned in the middle. In this way, we were able to preserve some consistency between the two environments, so that, for example, when one party turned from the in-context view to face-to-face, the co-participant would see the reorientation in the same way. As both participants had access to all views simultaneously there was no need for a feedback monitor. The tasks the subjects were asked to perform were the same as those used in MTV-I.

We examined the extent to which participants used the different views. The findings were not dissimilar from those with MTV-I. Participants tended to use the desk-top and in-context views more than the face-to-face orientation. However, they did tend to shift between the views far more frequently than with MTV-I and appeared to face fewer problems in knowing where the co-participant was looking, or what views were accessible to the other. Despite the seeming ease in moving between the various views, the system did generate problems for users, especially when they attempted to refer to objects and artefacts in each other's respective domains.

Consider the following fragment in which Kathy attempts to point to the position in which David should place the speakers in the room. The model containing the furniture is located on David's desk and is visible to Kathy on both her desk-top and in-context monitors.

Fragment 7.5   Transcript 1

D: So: (.) the speakers need to go (0.5) s:(ome) s:<u>ome</u>where: like tha::(t)=

K: =yeah I would suggest the one on top of the fireplace actually comes down to this:::
    (0.7)

K: the corner.
    (.)

K: Actually you can't see where I'm pointing can you °hhh

To show David where he should place the speakers, Kathy points at the corner of the model room as it is shown on her desk-top monitor. As she says 'suggest the one on top' her finger points at the model, dropping down to the corner of the screen as if indicating that the speaker should be removed from the fireplace and placed on the floor. She continues to point at the screen throughout the utterance, recycling the pointing, emphasising the gesture with the word 'this' and 'the corner'. She only begins to withdraw the gesture as she begins to utter 'Actually you can't see where I'm pointing'.

Fragment 7.5   Transcript 2

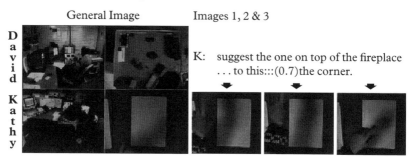

General Image   Images 1, 2 & 3

K: suggest the one on top of the fireplace
      . . . to this::: (0.7) the corner.

The co-participant, David, can see the gesture, although he appears unable to discern where Kathy is pointing. The gesture appears on two of his monitors, and the model at which it is pointing is placed before him on his desk. For David, the difficulty is that, whilst he can both hear and see Kathy, and knows presumably that Kathy is referring to the model, he cannot see the gesture with regard to the object at which it is directed. His view of the model, as it sits before him, is not simply different from Kathy's, but rather dislocated from his view of the co-participant. In other words, David is not simply unable to see the world in the way in which Kathy sees the world, but, more importantly perhaps, cannot reassemble his view of the model with his view of Kathy and the gesture. The fragmentation of the views undermines David's ability to assemble the reference and referent.

This fragment also reveals a second, perhaps more interesting, 'problem' which arises, in our experience, within various forms of virtual environments including the original media space at EuroPARC. Kathy is able to see David, she knows that the model is located on his desk, and she is aware of the views that he has of her. Despite this, she points to the model as it is displayed on her monitor. She presupposes that David can see her pointing to a location in the model; a model which is actually sitting on his desk. Moreover, in the face of receiving no acknowledgement from David, she recycles the gesture, continuing to assume that it and its referent are mutually visible. It is perhaps only as she begins to describe rather than show where he should position the monitor, uttering 'the corner', that she begins to realise that David cannot retrieve the actions. For some reason, therefore, users appear to assume that, if they can see it, the co-participant can see it in the same way; they presuppose a 'reciprocity of perspective'. They design actions which presuppose that the other can see what they can see, in 'roughly' the way that they can see it. They assume that not only can they be seen, but their co-participant is able to use their visual and bodily orientation to determine the character and location of features and objects within their respective environments.

It is perhaps worth considering a second example which further illustrates the difficulties that individuals faced when using the system.

In the following fragment, Emma is attempting to draw Julie's office. As she sketches, she asks Julie various questions concerning the room and the various bits and pieces it contains. We join the action as they discuss a pillar which runs up the wall on one side of the office.

Fragment 7.6   Transcript 1

J: What sort of pillar?
     (0.2)
E: No it's just a p<u>illa</u>r that (yer) you know (seems) like ar (0.3) ar (0.3)
     arm (.) <u>shaft</u>
     (0.2)
     tha ⌈t's going up through the building.
J: ⌊like that one right in front of you?
     (1.9)

J: Here (.) on your ri:ght, (.) by the window.
E: No that's ts ts sort of jus.jus.jus no (.) it's bigger than that.
J: Couldn't you move the camera?

As she attempts to describe the pillar, Emma turns and points to the object in question. Julie looks from one monitor to the other in an attempt to find the object and then points to what she believes is a similar pillar and utters 'like that one right in front of you?'

As she utters 'like that one right in front of you?' Julie points to what she believes may be like the pillar referred to by Emma. She points at the object on the in-context monitor. Emma is looking at the face-to-face view. Although the gesture points towards the monitor, it appears on Emma's face-to-face view, as if Julie is pointing to her right. Emma turns and looks for the pillar not directly in front of her as the description suggests, but follows the point to her right. She fails to find the object and then looks up and down in front of her.

Fragment 7.6   Transcript 2

J: like that one right in front of you? (1.9)Here (.) on your right, (.) by the
window.

E: It's going up through the building.

Seeing that Emma is unable to find the object to which she is referring, Julie once again attempts to help her co-participant find where the object is by both describing where it is, and pointing to it 'Here (.) on your ri:ght, (.) by the window.' Again she follows the direction of the pointing gesture, but is unable to discover both where the gesture is pointing or what the word 'right' means. Julie tags on the description 'by the window' and after a moments further search finds the object to which her co-participant is referring. It turns out to be nothing like the object in question, namely the pillar.

A simple reference to a feature within one of the offices therefore generates severe difficulties for the participants. They are unable to establish mutual orientation with ease and the production of a 'world in common' becomes an issue in its own right, undermining their ability to focus on and continue the activity in which they are engaged. Emma, for example, is unable to provide Julie with an adequate description of where the object in question is and what it looks like; adequate in the sense that her co-participant is able to find the object and know that the object she has found is indeed the pillar in question. Emma's difficulties are also reflected in the way in which she is unable to disambiguate Julie's gestures and descriptions. Aside from the way in which camera and monitor distort the direction of the gesture, Emma is unable to (re)connect Julie's gaze and pointing with her own physical environment, and yet she attempts to use her co-participant's bodily conduct to discriminate the local scene. Even Julie's descriptions fail to provide Emma with the appropriate resources with which to find the object in question; an object which it should be said takes up a large part of one corner of the room. The difficulties do not arise solely from Emma's inability to reconstruct Julie's actions with regard to her immediate physical environment. Julie is unable to produce a reference for an object that she can see on the monitor that Emma can use to locate the object in her own immediate environment. Julie presupposes that, in describing the object and pointing to the monitor, Emma can retrieve and discover the referent. However, Julie's access to her co-participant fails to provide the resources through which she can build an appropriate description, visually and vocally. In particular, she is unable to place herself in the standpoint of her co-participant, to render the object visible with regard to Emma's orientation to the scene. Moreover, Julie is unable to see the way in which she herself is seen by the other, so that it proves difficult to transform the way in which she points to the object, with regard to the other's point of view. In a sense, therefore, the problem derives not simply from what an individual can see, and cannot see, but rather from the individual's inability to be able to infer what the other has access to and the ways in which they see what the individual sees. Such phenomena give an interesting flavour to the idea that 'taking the role of the other' is central to the production and presumably the intelligibility of social order (cf. Blumer, 1962; Mead, 1934).

Whilst providing users with enhanced access to each other and their respective environments, both MTV-I and MTV-II were not therefore without their problems. The systems did provide users with the ability to share objects such as documents and, notwithstanding the difficulties, refer to features of each other's physical environment. They provided users with the ability to engage in various object-focused, collaborative activities, which, in a conventional media space, would be impossible. They also allowed individuals to refer to and use tools and artefacts, such as pencils and paper, which are an essential part of conventional office work but are largely neglected in advanced virtual environments. They also provided individuals with the possibility of seeing the other with regard to the focal area of the activities in which they were engaged; that is the 'in-context' view provides access to both the participant and the participant's use of various tools, artefacts and objects. In a sense, therefore, the MTV exercises might be considered as interesting steps towards taking the conventional working environment seriously in design, and in particular in utilising video and computing technology, in Weiser's (1991) terms, to 'augment' rather than replace 'reality'.

However, both MTV-I and MTV-II generated difficulties for users. The difficulties are interesting in that they reflect issues which arise with a range of advanced electronic environments in which distributed individuals are provided with the ability to interact with each other in real-time. They also reveal the ways in which advanced electronic environments can threaten the presuppositions through which individuals co-ordinate their actions with each other and thereby undermine the production and intelligibility of social action and activities. MTV-I and MTV-II exacerbate the problems that we find with conventional media space. In the course of particular activities, users discover that their co-participant cannot see what they see, in the way in which they believe they can see it. They presuppose congruent access to each other, only to discover that they, or aspects of their respective environments, cannot be discerned in the way in which they assumed it was available, at this moment in time. The disjunction between what is assumed accessible and what is available, not only undermines how the participants view each other and features of their respective domains, but renders the production of particular actions and activities problematic. So, for example, a relatively trivial action such as pointing to a particular section of a drawing or a line of text can become a matter of some concern, an issue in its own right, as the participants attempt to establish mutual orientation. More subtle actions, such as the ways in which individuals can use features of the local environment to momentarily make sense of a shift in a co-participant's gaze, or when a slight shift of bodily alignment can display a temporary commitment to a particular object on a desk, are largely 'invisible' in the media space.

The difficulty in producing particular actions, and the invisibility of a whole range of practical conduct, does not derive from the limited accessibility that the participants have to each other and their respective environments. They are able to see each other, from various angles, and able to see the local milieu in various levels of detail, from inspecting a document to viewing the overall scene. The difficulties appear to derive from the presupposition that the other sees the domain in the way in which you see it, and from the fragmentation and distortion of the images themselves. So, for example, if you are looking at the document monitor and your co-participant is pointing to a particular section, you might see the gesture, but the gesture will be literally 'dislocated' from the gaze and orientation of the speaker. Or, for example, you can see the other 'in-context' but from the image on a monitor it can be difficult to determine the alignment of the participant's gaze and even bodily orientation with regard to particular aspects of the local ecology. Curiously, however, such systems appear to mislead the participants, encouraging them to assume they have access to each other and their respective environments, only to discover in the course of interaction that their co-participant is unable to disambiguate their conduct.

There are, of course, different technological options for tackling the difficulties found in media space which might also, to some extent, address the problems found in the MTV exercises. For example, in trying to give variable and more flexible access to another domain, one could envisage a system which provided an individual with a less fragmented audio-visual environment. So, instead of the switched images of MTV-I or the separate views of MTV-II, an individual could be given one view of another which could be changed dynamically in the course of his or her activities. Such a solution has been attempted using eye (or, more accurately, head) tracking technology to monitor where a user is looking and then pan, tilt and zoom the camera in the other's domain to change view appropriately (Gaver et al., 1995). A 'roving camera' is one way of providing more continuous access into another's domain and for this access to be provided automatically. In so doing, such a solution could ameliorate the problems associated with both the fragmented views found in MTV-II and the obtrusive use of the technology found in MTV-I. However, there is a danger that a design which involves the automatic control of a single view of another's domain, would once again neglect the ways in which visual conduct is interactionally organised. The focus of such developments is on the capabilities which can be provided to an individual to view another's domain, and ignores how that can be embedded within ongoing collaborative activities. The delicate monitoring of another whilst initiating talk, a glance towards an object when engaging in a particular activity or a general look around another's remote domain are produced in concert with the contributions of a co-participant. Even if a technology can be devised that mimics a looking into another's domain, it is unclear how this activity can be made apparent to the remote party whilst not being intrusive to the activity at hand. Moreover, although a more sophisticated camera technology could be devised that is not so obtrusive to the activities of the participants, such a solution would exacerbate certain asymmetries within the interaction, for both participants are interacting within an unstable environment which is continually changing for themselves and for their co-interactants.

Given the difficulties with both conventional audio-visual environments and more sophisticated alternatives, it is not surprising that some researchers have looked to other types of computational infrastructure to support real-time interaction and collaboration. Of particular interest has been the possibility of developing collaborative virtual environments (CVEs) where representations, or 'embodiments', of participants are manipulated within 'virtual meeting rooms' and other spaces (Benford and Fahlén, 1993). In early versions of these systems, the embodiments can be moved on the screen to alter their orientation and thus their view of others within the virtual world. By such mechanisms, it is hoped that some resources utilised within social interaction can be simulated, for example for initiating or taking turns of talk (Bowers et al., 1995). Obviously such technologies, and the resources they offer, are relatively crude. At present, the representations of embodiments, the environment and, perhaps most importantly, objects in the environment, lack resolution and explicit mechanisms are required to manipulate the embodiments within an interaction. Hence, it is difficult to access the details of an artefact-based activity and problematic to manipulate the technology for interaction, whilst simultaneously trying to perform an activity through it. Therefore, in common with media spaces, initial trials of CVEs tend to focus more on their ability to facilitate informal interaction than on supporting collaborative work.

The various strengths and weaknesses of audio-visual environments and CVEs, particularly their differing capabilities of presenting detail and of being integrated with other computational facilities, have inevitably led to the exploration of combining the two technologies. One obvious route for such a development is that of mixed-reality systems where video images are included within virtual environments. Again, here the first experiments have been by simulating face-to-face interaction, with video images of participants being superimposed on embodiments within a virtual environment (Nakanishi et al., 1996).

A more intriguing possibility derives from initiatives concerning 'augmented reality' (cf. Weiser, 1991). In these, video and audio facilities are part of a more general attempt to enhance everyday activities and practices with computational support. These systems are seen as technological developments that can maintain and make use of, or at least do not undermine, the skills and practices of their users. Therefore, in some experimental systems, images are projected upon real-world artefacts to support some activity at hand, for example surgery. In others, video images are manipulable, as in object-oriented video where particular images, or parts of images, can be enhanced, moved around the work space and juxtaposed with other images and artefacts (Tani et al., 1992). The focus of these initiatives has moved from how they can support (certain versions of) face-to-face interaction, to their ability to enrich collaborative activities or tasks. It is interesting to note that, in shifting away from an emphasis on using audio-visual and computing technologies to simulate real-world actions, activities and interactions and towards enhancing or augmenting them, some novel and innovative technologies have begun to emerge. As yet, it is unclear, despite the explicit focus on real-world environments, how augmented reality systems would support collaborative activities, but it may be the case that analysis of the use of artefacts in real-world interaction would be a useful resource for the development of such technical innovations.

7.5   Summary

Those involved in developing innovative communication services seem convinced that systems which provide individuals with unprecedented access to each other will facilitate organisational change. In one sense, they are probably correct. New communication services will support the geographical fragmentation of particular segments of organisations and allow tasks (and personnel) to be distributed in ways that were unimaginable even a decade ago. Media spaces, or at least the imaginative combination of computing, video and telecommunications will undoubtedly foreshadow some of the more exciting technical developments and provide enriched support to both co-present and distributed collaborative work. However, current 'off-the-shelf' and experimental systems go little way in providing environments in which individuals can undertake even the more mundane organisational activities in collaboration with one other. Whilst markets will undoubtedly be found for videotelephones and videoconferencing, as well as more sophisticated forms of connectivity, we have to go some way before we successfully develop technologies which can support even the more straightforward forms of collaborative activity we find in almost all organisational environments.

The limitations of media spaces do not simply derive from the asymmetries which they introduce into interpersonal communication, though these asymmetries certainly undermine one of the basic arguments for telecommunication services; namely that they provide distributed access to non-verbal as well as verbal behaviour. Rather, the shortcomings of audio-visual connectivity, including the development of more sophisticated media spaces, derive in part through the commitment to support interpersonal communication rather than collaborative work. This emphasis has inevitably led to giving primacy to 'face-to-face' views, and in consequence disregarding how individuals, when working together, not infrequently co-ordinate their actions through objects and artefacts. If we consider any of the settings discussed earlier, then a critical part of the ways in which participants communicate with each other, and work together, is accomplished with reference to documents, images, diagrams, plans, even parts of their bodies. Media space technologies disembody action from its local material environment, and provide individuals with limited and distorted access both to each other and to the objects and artefacts on which their conduct relies. Moreover, the broad range of interesting developments which are increasingly being designed to support distributed collaborative working, ranging from shared editors (Olson et al., 1990), through to such innovations as Clearface (Ishii and Arita, 1991) and DigitalDesk (Wellner, 1992), does not adequately address the problem of providing a mutually accessible and flexible work space. These developments provide access to the textual contributions of others, even a sense of the other's gestures, and yet they do not allow individuals to see each other, either directly or peripherally with respect to the activities in which the participants are engaged. As Buxton (personal communication) has suggested, even the most sophisticated developments inevitably 'separate person space and work space' and thereby rupture an activity from its relevant milieu.

So, whilst some designers may be reluctant to take the ordinary, day-to-day character of workplace activities seriously when building novel technologies, the social organisation of collaborative activities can provide an important challenge to, and constraint on, the development of complex systems. Indeed, even a cursory glance at the ways in which individuals ordinarily co-ordinate their conduct with each other, when, for example, discussing a plan or updating a timetable, sets an enormous challenge to designers, posing a range of demands that even the most advanced technical innovations cannot adequately support at the present time. As the observations discussed here suggest, once we begin to recognise how practical action is embedded in, and inseparable from, the objects and artefacts, the environment in which it occurs, then the attempt to support distributed, collaborative activities becomes increasingly complex. It is no longer simply a matter of giving access to the head and shoulders of the other, or the data on which they are working, rather we need to consider how we can provide individuals with the ability to see others in their activities, to discern the ways in which they are participating in, and accomplishing the activities at hand. Rather than rely upon the emergence of *ad hoc* informal culture to manage the shortcomings of technology, we need to explore ways in which we can provide personnel with the resources with which to collaborate and participate, where necessary, in each other's activities, whilst unobtrusively preserving the individuals' sensitivity to their own and their colleague's environment. If we can begin to address these issues and build a technology which can support task-based collaboration, then we might well be surprised with the impact of advanced telecommunication services on work and organisational life.

8   Organisational interaction and technological design

> Everyone agrees that institutions should be the central object of sociological study, then promptly defines them in such a way that the most interesting and significant kinds of human collective enterprises are left out of account. The term *institution*, in short, suffers from an overdose of respectability, if not of hypocrisy: perhaps from overmuch definition and classification.
>
> Hughes (1971: 52)

> Instead of pushing aside the older ethnographic work in sociology, I would treat it as the only work worth criticising in sociology; where criticising is giving some dignity to something. So, for example, the relevance of the works of the Chicago sociologists is that they do contain a lot of information about this and that. And this-and-that is what the world is made up of.
>
> Sacks (1964 (1992): 27)

8.1   Introduction

The diverse substantive and conceptual concerns of workplace studies are reflected in their increasing significance to contemporary research and practice in a broad range of disciplines and fields. It has been suggested, for example, that naturalistic studies of technology in use, and more generally organisational conduct, are having a growing influence on cognitive science, and leading to a recognition of the importance of situated practice for human thinking. We also find that certain developments in both AI and HCI have arisen, in part, through the realisation that the contingent and, in particular, socially organised circumstances of human conduct bear upon information processing and representation. Whilst workplace studies will undoubtedly continue to flourish and find a home in CSCW, it is perhaps worthwhile here to take the opportunity to briefly explore the relevance of these studies to two rather different concerns. Firstly, we wish to begin by discussing how the studies reported here and cognate work might contribute to the long-standing concern in sociology with work and organisations. In particular, we wish to suggest that the social and interactional organisation of workplace activities should be placed at the forefront of the analytic agenda, and, by so doing, provide a vehicle for considering key conceptual issues and substantive concerns. Secondly, we wish to discuss briefly the vexed problem of design, and the ways in which workplace studies might feature in the development and deployment of new technologies. Rather than offer a 'method' or a procedure, we wish to discuss one or two examples drawn from earlier chapters and raise some practical issues concerning video-based analysis and the design of complex systems.

8.2   Interaction and organisational conduct

Some of the finest studies of work and organisations emerged in Chicago following the Second World War. Due in no small way to the lectures and essays of E. C. Hughes, a substantial body of naturalistic studies of work and occupations emerged which began to chart the routines and realities involved in everyday organisational life. Hughes, his colleagues and students powerfully demonstrated, through numerous empirical studies, the ways in which work is thoroughly dependent upon, and inseparable from, a tacit and emergent culture which is fashioned and refashioned in the light of the problems that people face in the routine accomplishment of their day-to-day work (see, e.g. Becker et al., 1961; Davis, 1963; Goffman, 1961; Hughes, 1958, 1971; Roth, 1963; Strauss et al., 1964). For Hughes, social interaction lies at the heart of organisational life. It is through social interaction that organisations emerge and are sustained; it is as a consequence of social interaction that people develop routines, strategies, practices and procedures, and it is by virtue of social interaction that clients receive, and perceive, goods and services in ways defined by the organisations and its occupation(s). For example, Hughes suggests that the aim of his own and his colleagues' studies is:

to discover patterns of interaction and mechanisms of control, the things over which people in a line of work seek to gain control, the sanctions which they have or would like to have at their disposal, and the bargains which were made – consciously or unconsciously – among a group of workers and between them and other kinds of people in the drama of their work. (Hughes (1971: 240))

The substantial body of research, the conceptual and methodological framework developed by Hughes, has had a long-lasting and powerful influence on not only the sociology of work and organisations, but also research in such areas as criminal justice, health and illness, and even new technology.

In workplace studies, we find a reflowering of the sociology of work. They consist of a burgeoning body of naturalistic research concerned with work and organisations. Like the post-war Chicago School, these studies are naturalistic, consisting of 'ethnographies' of organisational conduct and the occupational life. They are concerned with the routines and practices which inform the practical accomplishment of workplace activities and, like their forerunners, recognise that social institutions and organisations arise in, and are preserved through, social interaction. In workplace studies, however, there is a more focused interest in the mundane practicalities of organisational conduct, in particular the ways in which participants themselves accomplish and co-ordinate their activities. Indeed, perhaps because of their interest in tools and technologies, or more likely the underlying influence of ethnomethodology and conversation analysis, a range of workplace studies reveals a wide-ranging concern with the collaborative production of organisational conduct, particularly how particular actions and activities are interactionally accomplished. This revitalisation of the sociology of work is not just a simple development of the studies of Hughes and his colleagues, but rather involves a profound analytic shift; a change which has allowed a more considered and systematic concern with organisational interaction, the domain that Hughes himself helped place at the heart of the sociological agenda.

With their analytic focus and their growing empirical contribution, workplace studies may prove of relevance to developments in contemporary organisational theory and research. For example, despite the wide-ranging recognition that globalisation and market changes are generating new organisational forms, forms which require flexible co-operation both within and between 'firms', there is, as yet, little analysis on the ways in which these different collaborative arrangements emerge, coalesce and subside in particular circumstances. Whilst workplace studies are principally concerned with forms of co-operation within particular organisations, and in many cases specific departments within those organisations, one can begin to see how a deeper understanding of organisational interaction and communication will contribute to these more 'overarching' sociological concerns. The relevance of recent studies of work and interaction to organisational theory in this way has been elegantly articulated by DiMaggio and Powell (1991) in their ambitious attempt to chart a distinctive course through the increasingly relativistic debates found within (post)modern organisational theory (see also Acroyd, 1992; Reed and Hughes, 1992). Unfortunately, however, the 'new institutionalism' provides few examples of the ways in which we can begin to readdress key concepts and ideas within organisational theory and, as Silverman (1997) suggests, their programmatic recommendations remain somewhat problematic.

DiMaggio and Powell's synthesis, like *Theory of Organisations*, contains no clear guidelines for the organisational researcher, other than a pot-pourri of concepts with, at best, an unknown relation to the contingencies of data collection and analysis. Moreover, its theoretical character may, unfortunately, help to preserve a field in which 'pure theory' rules. (Silverman (1997: 181))

Workplace studies do not form guidelines, but may provide demonstrations of the ways in which we can begin to side-step the growing relativism in organisational theory and drive analytic attention towards the practical accomplishment of workplace conduct. They might also provide a foundation with which to readdress some of the more important issues and concepts which have hitherto underpinned organisational theory.

Consider, for example, the long-standing concern, from Durkheim and Weber onwards, with the division of labour and its associated roles, rules and responsibilities. Notwithstanding the recognition that divisions of labour are themselves dependent on 'informal' arrangements and local culture, the idea that order in the workplace is dependent upon pre-allocated roles and rules permeates a great deal of organisational theory and research. Workplace studies, such as those by Anderson et al. (1989), Bowers and Button (1995) and Suchman and Wynn (1984) have built upon the foundations laid by Garfinkel (1967) and others (e.g. Wieder, 1972; Zimmerman, 1970), and have powerfully demonstrated how formal prescriptions, including rules allocating tasks and responsibilities, are locally constituted within the course of workplace activities. These formal prescriptions themselves rely upon a body of practice and reasoning for their application and intelligibility within particular circumstances. Similarly, we can see how the studies discussed here throw a little light on the practicalities of divisions of labour, and the ways in which participants themselves ongoingly allocate tasks and responsibilities. Take, for example, the line control rooms on London Underground. They involve a relatively strict division of labour in which particular personnel have particular responsibilities, engage in specific activities and are accountable to others for the work in which they engage. Moreover, in hindsight, personnel can discover that they each did what they should have done, given the circumstances and practicalities at hand. In the course of their work, however, it becomes increasingly difficult to demonstrate how the division of labour is oriented to by participants themselves. Rather, personnel rely upon, and use, a body of practice and reasoning which allows them to recognise and co-ordinate their action and activities with each other, and with regard to the contingencies and circumstances at hand. As we have seen, much of this practice provides a vehicle for the sequential organisation of particular actions, allowing the participants to collaboratively produce, recognise and co-ordinate trajectories of action and activity which provide for the accountable management of certain events and problems. The division of labour is not simply flexible or contingent, but, at best, is embodied in a body of indigenous practice and reasoning which provides for the accountable production and co-ordination of activities within the domain. In a sense, therefore, the division of labour is largely irrelevant to the ways in which participants organise their conduct, and, at best, might be invoked retrospectively to account, where necessary, for why someone did something when.

The idea of a division of labour presupposes specialised forms of task or activity which are undertaken by a specific category/categories of personnel. Until recently, task has been conceived either cognitively, as deriving from specialised bodies of information and reasoning which enable the implementation of particular skills and actions, both cognitive and motor, or as the product of the internalisation of socially organised competencies, dispositions and expectations. The studies discussed here, and related research, provide a rather different sense of task, and perhaps point to the ways in which making a sharp distinction between the individual and collaborative may not be fruitful. Take, for example, the control room of the Docklands Light Railway, and the ways in which the two controllers co-ordinate their activities with each other. In one way, we can see that they do indeed engage in distinct activities, the one controller rescheduling the signalling, whilst the other takes calls and makes decisions, but it soon becomes clear that these distinct tasks are thoroughly interdependent and 'interproduced'. In the course of taking a call, a controller can shape his talk to encourage and enable a colleague to enter the relevant instructions, or he can recommend a course of action to a train captain, in the light of seeing his colleague reschedule the traffic on a particular section of the line. In these and other instances, tasks are not simply produced in the light of each other, one following the next in some seemingly sequential order, but, rather, the very accomplishment of an activity is sensitive to the concurrent actions of a colleague. In this way, the activity or task itself, the responsibility of a particular participant in the setting, is produced and shaped with regard to the emerging activity of the co-participant, and vice versa. The competent production of the task relies upon the individual's socially organised abilities to see, hear and recognise the activity of others and to co-ordinate, moment by moment, his action with that of his colleague. The task is accomplished in, and inseparable from, the interaction between the two controllers and, not unusually, the party at the other end of the radio.

As the materials from London Underground, the Docklands and Reuters suggest, the interactional accomplishment of complex tasks does not solely rely on the ability of one individual to remain sensitive to the conduct of another. Rather, in each of these settings we find that personnel, in the very production of a task, design the activity with regard to its potential relevance for the actions of colleagues, even though these colleagues may not be directly involved in the activity itself. So, for example, we noticed how journalists in Reuters will give voice to textual stories on which they are working, and in this way provide colleagues with the opportunity, should they so wish, to pick up on the news being dealt with on different desks. Or consider how line controllers on London Underground will emphasise a particular word or phrase in conversation over the radio with a driver; thereby encouraging the DIA to produce sequentially appropriate activities, like calling a station manager and initiating a series of public announcements. In these and numerous other cases, the accomplishment of a seemingly individual and specialised task, like writing a story about mineral prices, or reforming the train service, is dependent upon the individual's sensitivity to the organisational interests and actions of others. The task's competent production relies upon the individual's ability to shape the activity, in the course of its articulation, with respect to the practical concerns and commitments of others, even though those 'others' may not even be aware of what their colleague is doing. In these sorts of environment, being a 'competent journalist', or a 'good line controller', means being able to shape the activities in which you are engaged with regard to others; to have their interests, their commitments and their activities, both now and in the future, 'in mind' (cf. Sacks, 1992).

The growing body of research concerned with the interactional organisation of workplace activities complements certain developments within organisational theory. Alongside the emergence of the new institutionalism, we have witnessed a growing interest in the role of language in organisations and the ways in which institutional forms are constructed through talk. In this regard, Morgan's (1986) treatise on the significance of metaphor in organisational theory is of particular importance. Whilst it may have helped to encourage the relativism which now permeates organisational theory, it has also encouraged a growing interest in the ways in which both researchers and participants use language, including models and metaphors, to make sense of workplace activities (see e.g. Keenoy et al., 1997). Moreover, it is increasingly recognised that research on 'talk at work', including social psychology, discourse analysis and conversation analysis, which has arisen in a number of fields over the past couple of decades, may well be of relevance to understanding organisations and the detailed investigation of workplace activities. In this regard, we hope that workplace studies may provide further demonstration of the ways in which an empirical concern with language and interaction can provide a vehicle for side-stepping the relativism which seems to accompany social constructionism in many of its guises. In particular, these studies can begin to show how we can deal with the visual, material and vocal aspects of workplace activities and demonstrate how organisational forms derive from, and are preserved in and through, social interaction.

It is also hoped that the studies discussed here contribute to the growing body of empirical studies within ethnomethodology and conversation analysis concerned with institutional forms of interaction and in particular talk at work. These studies and related research have their roots in conversation analytic studies, and, with their emphasis on sequence and interactional organisation, continue a long-standing tradition in ethnomethodology. But in various ways they are very different, not simply by virtue of the sorts of substantive domains they investigate, but rather as a consequence of the sorts of activities with which they are concerned. In the first place, like earlier video-based research on social interaction, these studies are concerned with the visual and the material, as well as the vocal features of organisational conduct, and in particular the ways in which tools and technologies feature in practical action and activity. Secondly, they are not principally concerned with 'mutually focused interaction', but rather with the collaborative production of simultaneous and sequential activities which may involve very different forms of participation from individuals who have variable access to each other's conduct. Thirdly, the sorts of setting which have formed the focus of workplace studies have demanded that recorded data be accompanied by substantial field work to enable researchers to have a sense of what is happening, of who is doing what, and how it might be organised. It is not as yet clear how such field observations can be satisfactorily incorporated into, and legitimised within, the analysis, and yet it is widely recognised that a concern with the interactional accomplishment of workplace activities should not undermine the ability to detail aspects of the indigenous character of organisational activities.

The research discussed here, like other workplace studies, is attempting to provide a distinctive approach to understanding the use of technologies in everyday organisational environments. In contrast to more traditional work in HCI and cognitive science, the studies have begun to demonstrate how the use of computers, like other tools and technologies, is sensitive to, and embedded in, the circumstances in which they are deployed. Notwithstanding the cognitive competencies and the like which are brought to bear in 'interacting' with computers, the use of technology relies upon the individual's abilities to produce relevant and recognisable actions and activities with regard to practical contingencies which arise within the course of their work. Indeed, the relevant, acceptable and appropriate use of new technologies in organisations is dependent upon the socially accountable and recognisable ways of accomplishing particular activities, whether they consist of reforming trains on London Underground, writing notes in the medical record, or drawing plans in an architecture practice. The shortcomings of more conventional work in HCI and cognate fields, is not simply their reliance on an overdeterministic and cognitive conception of human conduct, but that they render epiphenomenal the socially organised and situationally sensitive practices and procedures which underlie the competent use of technologies for the accomplishment of tasks in practical organisational environments. Workplace studies are returning technology to action, and beginning to show how the use of particular systems is dependent upon the social and organisational competencies upon which participants rely to produce accountable actions and interaction within particular settings.

The foregoing studies have, for example, implications for how we conceive of 'users' when designing or deploying new technologies. In chapter two, for example, we raised a number of issues with regard to the way in which the 'user', in that case the medical practitioner, was implicitly regarded in the design of the computerised record system. It was found that, far from being 'rule followers' doctors defeased various rules and procedures for documenting information with regard to the circumstances at hand, and in particular the ways in which any 'competent' user would read the records. The computer system not only corrupted the indigenous rules and practices employed by the practitioners themselves, but ignored the practical knowledge and reasoning on which doctors rely in competently reading and writing medical records. In developing a conception of the user which is sensitive to the skills and competencies on which doctors rely when reading and writing medical documents, we need to take into account their abilities to reason with rules and procedures, the practical knowledge which they utilise and their orientation to the reader of the documents. The records are written with regard to a competent, skilled and reasoning reader, and the ordinary practical circumstances in which the information is used.

The CAD system used by the architects in chapter six is a typical example of a 'single user' application on a 'personal' workstation. It provides a great range of sophisticated tools and functionality for an architect to manipulate plans and drawings. It can also, however, be a resource for collaborative work, with its 'use' being produced through the delicate co-ordination of activities by co-participants. An apparently simple point to the screen being itself a collaborative accomplishment within an emerging course of action. Or, consider the use of the computerised signalling system on Docklands Light Railway. It consists of a relatively conventional command and control system through which an individual submits a series of instructions to reschedule the running times and direction of particular vehicles. The competent use of the system, however, involves much more than the simple ability to enter the appropriate instructions and draw the relevant inferences. In the first place, the ability to undertake a relevant course of action is dependent upon the controller's analysis of the current circumstances and anticipation of the 'knock-on' consequences of particular decisions. In the second place, the timing of an intervention, the submission of sets of coded instructions, has to be systematically co-ordinated with the actions of others, both those within the immediate domain and those who stand outside, such as train captains. Thirdly, whatever the details of instructions entered into the system, it is critical that particular colleagues are aware of the course of action undertaken by the controller. The practical and accountable use of the system, therefore, rests upon a complex array of organisational practice, contingent reasoning and interactional competency through which an individual is able to undertake relevant action and activity in concert with others. The system's competent use cannot be separated from the socially organised activities in and through which it is rendered relevant.

The settings also reveal the ways in which the use of tools and technologies features in a broad range of activities that appear, at first glance, to lie beyond the system's 'jurisdiction' or domain of relevancies. For example, we noted earlier how members of various settings use various devices to enable them to render particular activities visible within the local milieu, and how, in consequence, those activities can turn out to be relevant for individuals who may not otherwise have taken them into account. Whether it is the editorial system at Reuters, the paper timetable in the London Underground or a plan in an architect's office, the use of the system is momentarily rendered (potentially) relevant for others within 'perceptual range' of the event, and their response, or lack of it, features in their continued use of the technology. The 'user' is, indeed, the individual entering or reading information from the system, but the system's use is delicately sensitive to, and co-ordinated in real-time with, others who may turn out to have little involvement in the activity at hand. Similarly, whilst another's glance at a screen, a paper document or fixed line diagram may well be embedded in some individualised concern with what they are dealing with at the time, in the sort of collaborative working environments considered here, such glances can indeed provide resources to others with which to see the activities of colleagues. For example, a line controller's look at the fixed line diagram can provide others, such as the DIA and signal assistants, with a sense not only of what they are looking at, but, whatever it is, that it may be problematic. The controller's glance can occasion practical enquiries by others directed to discovering just what it is 'which caught his attention'. The use of tools and technologies in such domains, therefore, is deeply relevant to how individuals make sense of each other's actions and co-ordinate their respective activities. In some sense, the 'user', even of a system which is positioned directly in front of a particular individual and is seemingly unavailable to others, includes all those within the domain for whom an individual's use of the technology is relevant. For both practical and intellectual reasons, there has perhaps been a little too much circumspection when conceptualising the 'user'.

With the emergence of CSCW, we have witnessed a growing body of social and technical research which has increasingly directed attention towards the social and organisational character of technology. As the name implies, an important element of research in CSCW has been to develop technologies to support co-operative work, and ideas have been drawn from various domains within the social sciences. In consequence, the notion of group, as in 'groupware' and 'groupwork', has a significant influence on both system design and models of social action in CSCW, and perhaps has led to the danger that the 'psychological' and 'individual' user found in HCI will run in parallel with, or even be replaced by, the 'social' and 'collective' user found in CSCW. We hope, however, that the foregoing chapters suggest ways in which shifting analytic attention from the individual to the group in this way will have little benefit for either social science or those with a more practical concern in the design of technology. In each of the settings, we can see ways in which personnel are continually 'shifting' from the 'individual' to the 'collaborative', even during the production of particular actions and activities. Indeed, wherever a particular (technologically informed) activity emerges, one can see the ways in which it is systematically co-ordinated with the real-time contributions of others, even those 'others' who may have no more than a passing interest in particular actions of a colleague. Tasks and activities, even though they may be the principal responsibility of particular individuals, in specific locations, are ongoingly accomplished with regard to the co-participation of 'others'. The distinction, therefore, between the 'individual' and the 'collaborative' is somewhat ambiguous.

In addressing the interactional foundations of workplace activities, perhaps we can also begin to provide a distinctive contribution to understanding technology in organisations; a contribution which side-steps the 'technicism' associated with a range of earlier research (Grint and Woolgar, 1997). In particular, the studies discussed here provide a range of observations and findings concerning the ways in which tools and technologies feature in practical organisational conduct. It is clear that, like other formalisms, the technologies within the various domains do not exert an overarching 'influence' on organisational conduct, but rather feature in, and are ongoingly constituted within, the action and interaction of the participants themselves. In various ways, the essays presented here are preoccupied with explicating the practice and reasoning in and through which individuals produce and co-ordinate their actions and activities with each other, and with demonstrating how various tools, technologies and the like, are used within the practical accomplishment of the participants' work. In this way, it is not that technology *per se* is placed at the forefront of the agenda, rather the principal concern of these and related studies is the social and interactional organisation of practical conduct within the workplace; information systems, paper documents, diagrams and the like are relevant in as much as they are used and oriented to by the participants themselves in the production and recognition of their actions and activities. The 'technical and material' environment is reflexively constituted from within the concerted accomplishment of everyday workplace activities.

The studies discussed here, therefore, may have some bearing on the growing body of research concerned with the social construction of technology (e.g. Bijker et al., 1990; Mackenzie, 1996; Mackenzie and Wajcman, 1985). Whilst not principally concerned with technology in the workplace, such work has provided a rich and varied array of ideas and observations concerning how technologies and other sorts of artefact gain a particular meaning(s) and determination within an historical and cultural milieu. Putting to one side the programmatic debates which surround such work (Button, 1993; Pinch and Bijker, 1984), it is interesting to consider how workplace studies can provide a rather different understanding of the intelligibility and significance of technologies (and other sorts of object and artefact). In turning attention towards the practical and indigenous use of tools and technologies, we can see how their 'significance' or 'meaning' is locally and temporally constituted from within the actions and activities in which they arise. Whilst it is tempting to presuppose that the significance or meaning of a tool or artefact remains stable, if only for the transient episode of the activity, there is little empirical or theoretical ground for assuming that their sense is independent of the ways in which they are 'ongoingly' constituted from within social action and activity. In the materials discussed here, and throughout a range of everyday working environments, technologies are used by individuals in their dealings with others, and their sense and intelligibility is accomplished then and there, within the developing course of social interaction. To presuppose that the meanings of technology are established, bounded, circumscribed and the like, renders epiphenomenal the complex array of socially organised practice and competency which informs the moment-by-moment production and intelligibility of (technologically informed) workplace activities.

In this respect, it is worth remarking on 'interactionist' or 'symbolic interactionist' studies of work and occupational life and their extraordinary contribution to our understanding of everyday organisational activities. Despite their interest in the practical and the mundane, and their commitment to exploring the interactional foundations of workplace activities, the concerted accomplishment of workplace activities, and the human agency on which it relies, disappears from the analytic agenda. In part, the very absence of the interactional foundation of workplace activities derives from their concern with shared meanings and definitions; a concern which is reflected in some contemporary research concerned with the social construction of technology. The studies discussed here, and related research, are a small attempt to pursue some of the programmatic concerns of Hughes and his colleagues, and in particular to address the ways in which complex tasks and activities are accomplished in and through the interaction of the participants.

8.3   The analysis of workplace activities and the design of technology

Workplace studies help refocus analytic attention on the organisation of action and activities, rather than on cognitive abilities of the individual, and to examine the socially organised resources on which individuals rely in production, recognition and co-ordination of *in situ* organisational conduct. Such concerns demand that we look beyond a particular artefact and user, and consider how activities are ongoingly accomplished in collaboration with others. Moreover, they demand that we consider how a range of material and technical resources may feature in the use of a particular system; that in organisational environments activities rely upon a complex array of tools and artefacts. In directing attention towards the situated and interactional accomplishment of organisational activities, workplace studies are providing a body of findings and conceptual consideration which are of some relevance to the design, development and deployment of systems to support work.

There remains, however, some debate as to how observations generated through field studies and video-based analysis can 'methodically' inform system design, and provide a more reliable foundation for the development and deployment of new technologies. As Schmidt (forthcoming) has powerfully argued, whilst workplace studies increasingly may form part of short-term design projects, in the longer term their contribution may well be more profound, providing a corpus of findings and conceptual (re)specifications which can inform the development of innovative and novel systems to enhance co-operation and collaboration. We hope that the studies discussed in the previous chapters, like other workplace studies, do indeed cast a rather different light on the organisation of work, and the ways in which tools and technologies feature in practical, organisational conduct. They serve, perhaps, to question the cogency of some of the theoretical assumptions which have informed our understanding of both technology and its design, and point to ways in which we can begin to consider organisational conduct and, in particular, the socially organised character of technology in action.

Workplace studies, and, in particular perhaps, video-based studies of organisational interaction, are not simply concerned with placing the 'social' on the technical agenda. Rather, they are part of a burgeoning body of research which is concerned with readdressing organisational conduct with regard to ways in which participants themselves accomplish and co-ordinate their day-to-day actions and activities. Such studies, as we have suggested, provide a body of empirical findings and analytic insights through which we can begin to reconsider, for example, such concepts as the division of labour, task, user, information and collaboration; concepts which not only inform our understanding of organisational conduct, but which have had an important bearing on the design of technology.

It is likely to be in the area of CSCW that workplace studies will continue to have their most profound impact on the design and development of novel technologies. We have already discussed, for example, how studies of work and interaction have featured in the design and assessment of systems to support collaborative work, both co-present and distributed, and it is widely recognised that concepts such as 'awareness' and 'peripheral participation', which derived from research on organisational interaction, have had a wide-ranging impact on the development of novel technologies. We can also see how workplace studies are leading to a reconsideration of the very ideas of 'co-operation' and 'collaboration' and serving to question more traditional distinctions such as the synchronous and asynchronous, the distributed and co-located, and the distinct and shared workspace. They are also leading to a more general reconsideration of the necessary underlying computational support for collaborative activities. So, for example, Dourish (1992) and Jirotka (forthcoming) have explored more novel ways of representing data and discussed their implications for flexible computer architectures. Elsewhere, there have been significant advances in developing platforms and infrastructures which allow for different ways of collaboratively accessing information

(Bentley et al., 1994; Munson and Dewan, 1994; Patterson et al., 1990). Of particular importance has been the extension of 'object-oriented' paradigms developed within computer science, allowing for a range of capabilities to be supported, including the simple exchange of objects, the sharing of objects and providing different views of the same object (Bentley and Dourish, 1995; Rodden et al., 1992).

Aside from the more general implications of workplace studies for our understanding of organisational conduct and the design of technology, there has been a growing interest in exploring how they can directly inform the development of specific systems for particular applications. As we suggested earlier, the drive to discover new and more reliable methods to inform the design of complex systems, derives from both the recognition that technologies often fail to support the activities they designed to serve, and the recognition that systems will become increasingly concerned with supporting collaborative and organisational, rather than individual, conduct. One discipline in which such issues are of particular relevance is 'requirements engineering'; a field principally concerned with methods used in the early stages of developing computer systems. It is argued that many of the most serious and costly problems and failures derive from these initial stages (see e.g. Boehm, 1976; Jackson, 1995; Landauer, 1995; Norman, 1988, 1993; and Page, et al., 1993). In trying to develop more rigorous and systematic approaches to determining the requirements for systems, there has been a growing interest in placing the social and the environment of the system's eventual use at the forefront of the agenda. This has led to an interest in not only workplace studies, but various other 'social' oriented approaches (Goguen, 1993; Jirotka and Goguen 1994; McDermid, 1994; Sommerville et al., 1993). For example, drawing on Enid Mumford's socio-technical system's approach to organisational behaviour, Dobson et al. (1994) have developed a method entitled ORDIT (Organisational Requirements Definition for Information Technology). The method provides designers with the ability to examine and formalise the structure of the organisation and the various roles and responsibilities of the users who will be affected by the particular system. Or consider, for example, Espejo's (1980) attempts to introduce cybernetics into requirements engineering, or Flood and Jackson (1991) with critical social theory.

Many of these attempts draw upon conventional methods within behavioural and social sciences with which to advance our understanding of user-needs. So, for example, Holbrook (1990) recommends the use of 'scenarios', Loucopoulos and Karakostas (1995) the use of structured and semi-structured interviews, and Macaulay (1994) and Mumford (1983) the 'participation' of users in the design process. These arguments parallel suggestions in related fields for new and distinctive approaches to system design (see e.g. recommendations by Bjerknes et al., 1987; Carroll, 1990; Ehn, 1988; Kirwan and Ainsworth, 1992). In taking the social seriously, therefore, requirements engineering has not surprisingly begun to consider a whole range of analytic and methodological approaches found within the social sciences.

In the present context, however, it is the 'turn to the naturalistic' in requirements engineering which is of most interest. Goguen (1994) and Sommerville et al. (1993), amongst others, have argued that requirements engineering with its emphasis on user-needs could well benefit from an approach which places the tacit and indigenous organisation of human conduct at the forefront of the analytic agenda (Goguen, 1994; Potts and Newstetter, 1997; Sommerville et al., 1993). These suggestions parallel arguments found in CSCW and the idea that workplace studies may well serve to inform the design and evaluation of more novel technologies (see e.g. Ackerman, 1996; Bellotti and Sellen, 1993; Berlin and Jeffries, 1992; Moran et al., 1996; Murray, 1993; Schwab et al., 1992; Watts et al., 1996). Moreover, in a very different way, the interest in using workplace studies for design has been further enhanced by a widely discussed article by Seeley Brown (the research director of Xerox PARC) and Duguid, in which they stress the importance of communities of practice, genres and peripheral participation to understanding technology (Brown and Duguid, 1994).

Despite the interest in, even enthusiasm for, workplace studies, the ways in which they can or should inform design remain a vexed question (Plowman at al., 1995). There is even some debate as to what form of naturalistic approach or ethnography might be the most suitable orientation for technological design. For example, Nardi (1996) has argued that activity theory with its 'closeness in spirit' to distributed cognition provides the ideal resource with which to understand tools, technologies and workplace activities, and explore how a design can be sensitive to both technical and organisational considerations. Whilst, in a rather different vein, Hughes et al. (1992) have argued that conventional ethnography might be reshaped with regard to the practical constraints of industrial development projects, and that, for example, sociological researchers will have to work in concert with system designers, a collaboration which will transform the way in which the 'field' is both investigated and analysed. One of the critical underlying difficulties, of course, is that ethnography is not simply a 'method'; but rather involves an analytic orientation, and these analytic commitments generate very different forms of ethnography and 'findings' (cf. Button and King, 1992; Anderson, 1994). In CSCW alone, we find the proponents of distributed cognition, activity theory, symbolic interactionism, actor–network theory, ethnomethodology and conversation analysis, all, in various ways, suggesting that their particular approach may be relevant to the design, development and deployment of new technologies. This must be a little puzzling for those who build complex systems.

Rather than attempt to delineate a particular method – in one sense this is embodied in the earlier chapters – we thought it might be helpful here to discuss briefly the design implications of one or two of the studies, and the ways in which they have been developed as part of more technically focused projects. The previous chapter provides an example of the ways in which the analysis of work and interaction in the media space informed the design, development and evaluation of prototype systems to support distributed collaborative activities. In turn, studies of the original media space, and MTV-I and -II are currently informing the design of collaborative virtual environments, and providing a framework with which to consider the organisation for interaction and collaboration when accomplished in virtual worlds. The design and development of these systems is informed by both an understanding of the use of prototype technologies, and the broad range of observations and findings concerning work and interaction in more conventional environments. In the following sections we wish to discuss the ways in which our studies of London Underground, medical consultations and related work concerned with the construction industry, inform the assessment, design and development of particular systems.

8.3.2   London Underground: collaboration and control

The original research with London Underground was principally concerned with design. We were interested in undertaking a study of complex multimedia environments to consider the ways in which personnel used such technologies to co-ordinate their conduct with each other, make sense of the actions of others, and manage problems and difficulties. In part, the interest in such environments was driven by an interest, arising at Xerox PARC and EuroPARC, in technical innovations which would support distributing co-located activities. The findings of the original study have indeed influenced the design and development of these advanced systems, but they have also formed part of a number of more immediate design and development projects. In the first instance, at the time of undertaking the research, London Underground were involved in the design of new line control rooms and had commissioned a major company to undertake a requirements analysis and develop specifications. One of the recommendations for the design of the new control rooms was to provide each member of staff with a separate, individually configurable workstation, which would be positioned separately, with all line information being accessible on individual monitors. The electromechanical fixed line diagram, which was generally treated as archaic, could then be removed; the information in question retrieved, in various ways, by individual staff from their own monitors.

In one sense, the designers were correct; individual workstations and monitors do allow staff to gain traffic or line information in relevant detail and form. For example, as in the ATS system in the Docklands Light Railway Control Room examined in chapter five, such systems provide overviews of the line and more detailed section diagrams which then display the state of signals and the like. As the study demonstrated, however, the importance of the fixed line diagram does not simply derive from the information it provides, in terms, for example, of an overview of traffic on the line. Rather the scale and location of the diagram provides control room staff with the ability to point to and mutually reference aspects of the diagram; a shared work space which can be seen by, and referred to, individuals located at different parts of a large area. Secondly, the fixed line diagram allows individuals to see others looking at, or 'using', the display; it renders their 'looking' visible to others, and provides personnel with the ability to discern aspects of the actions or activities in which their colleague is engaged. For example, they can notice when a colleague has noticed something, and that noticing can engender actions by various staff within the line control room (cf. Heath and Hindmarsh, 1997). It is the fixed line diagram, as a resource for interaction and collaboration, which makes the display a critical resource in the work of control room staff.

It is unlikely that a more conventional requirements analysis would be concerned with the relatively fine details of the participants' conduct, especially the ways in which staff co-ordinate their activities with each other, both visually and vocally. Yet, it is through these details that activities are accomplished. In the case at hand, we were able to convince London Underground that to replace the fixed line diagram with individual localised displays might well undermine the ways in which different personnel co-ordinate their activities with each other. In this and other cases, therefore, these more naturalistic and interaction-based studies can be relevant to the assessment of proposed technologies. A parallel example can be found in research on proposed systems for deal capture in trading rooms (Jirotka et al., 1993).

The original study has also formed the basis of two design projects. The first project was to consider the design of systems to support the modification of timetabled information and its real-time distribution to others, both those within the line control room, and others requiring relevant information outside. It will be recalled that almost all problems involve the rewriting of the timetable, or 'reformation', and it is critical that others, both within the line control room and elsewhere, gain information of changes as they emerge. At the present time, staff within the line control room rely upon an array of socially organised practice and procedures for rendering such changes visible and gleaning relevant information from others. However, those outside the line control room, such as crew managers, drivers and station staff, have to be informed of such changes, and within the control room itself it was noticed that, as the number of staff increased, the more implicit methods of distributing information became increasingly fragile, just as the number of personnel who require the information increased (cf. Heath and Luff 1992a).

Drawing from the observations and findings discussed earlier and elsewhere (Heath and Luff 1992a, 1996), the project suggested the development of a screen-based timetable which embodied the critical properties of the paper timetable. For example, the design provided for two pages to be viewed at a time, which would be sketched over using an electronic pen, thus allowing individual marks and indications whilst also being easily returned to its original form. Whilst preserving the character of the paper document, the electronic timetable would then communicate these changes to electronic timetables held by others, both within the line control room and elsewhere. The aim of the system, therefore, was not only to enhance the distribution of information within the line control room itself, but also to provide more reliable and yet unobtrusive ways of delivering relevant information to others outside the line control room. It was also recognised that, in the longer term, the system could be augmented to allow, for example, controllers to try candidate reformations and receive feedback of their knock-on consequences, or even to be recommended particular reformations.

Whilst not being able to proceed with the development of this particular system due to lack of funding, a related project has emerged involving London Underground, other transport organisations, system design and electrical engineering companies. The project derives once again from the original analysis and considers how, and in what ways, information and other resources, available within the control room, can be made available to other staff located outside.

One issue that has emerged from our study relates to the problems that staff, those based both on trains and in stations, have because of limited access to relevant events and information whilst on the move. For example, in stations, even though most staff have to be able to be mobile around the area, almost all information is fed into, and emerges from, the station operations room. The project is concerned, therefore, with the ways in which appropriate information could be made available to staff; particularly how they could gain and communicate relevant information concerning events and changes, including modifications to the timetable and running times of trains. In this light, the project is considering the potential of mobile multimedia devices to provide such capabilities.

Whilst the original observations and findings are forming the background to identifying the general need for, and shape of, the system, current video-based field research at stations and on trains is providing more specific findings concerning work and interaction between different mobile staff, and between mobile staff and staff based in control centres (cf. Luff and Heath, 1998).

The project raises a number of interesting issues, both for using video-based field studies for design, and providing support for collaboration amongst different personnel, with differing responsibilities, who are mobile. For example, while it may seem that certain personnel need particular types of information, the form in which they require that information, and the mechanisms through which it is best accessed, may not be clear cut. In many cases, it is necessary to support an individual's awareness of changes to the service, or events occurring elsewhere in the network, but critical not to disrupt the current activity in which he or she may be engaged. Similarly, it may be mistaken or pointless to provide all, or certain sorts of, functionality on a single device, particularly a mobile one. Not only would this make the system unnecessarily complex, it would be difficult to shape the use of the technology to the practical circumstances at hand. The project, therefore, is investigating how to tailor the functionality and, more interestingly perhaps, distribute this between the device and other artefacts within the local environment. Indeed, we suspect that enhanced support for collaboration amongst mobile personnel may well demand that we begin to take 'augmented reality' seriously and address the ways in which functionality can be embedded, and accessed, through everyday objects and artefacts. The project, therefore, is developing prototype systems which combine the use of mobile technologies with other fixed devices, like screens and monitors, which are located around the domain. These are being assessed with respect to the ordinary concerns of staff; particularly how they can be used within their everyday tasks and activities, and their interactions with other staff and passengers. An important issue for our approach, like others, is therefore how particular solutions evolve and are selected, and to what extent they preserve a resonance with the interactional organisation of the workplace activities under consideration.

8.3.2   *Supporting consultative practice*

The analysis of the use of both paper and screen-based records during the medical consultation also points to the ways in which video-based field studies of work and interaction may contribute to the design and development of new technologies. Although the original analyses of medical consultations were funded by the research councils and were not concerned with system design, these studies led to a close collaboration with system designers at Rank Xerox Research Centre in Cambridge who are concerned with developing novel forms of support for workplace activities. The medical consultation was a particularly demanding case to consider the potential of various kinds of technology to support real-time, co-present activities and interaction, the project involving the development of preliminary designs, assessment of potential solutions and the evaluation of particular prototype devices.

In part, the project was an exercise in delineating the ways in which video-based field studies could inform design and develop technology (cf. Heath and Luff 1992a; Luff 1992), and addressed two critical issues which arose from the original study. These were, firstly, that the ways in which relevant medical information is entered and retrieved from the system resonates with the ways in which the information is used by practitioners during the consultation. Secondly, that doctors should be able to use the system during the consultation, and in particular in the course of listening to and talking with, the patient.

The original study identified a number of problems with current technology and suggested ways in which these might be dealt with. The suggestions included the following:

(i)   The length of particular entries should be left to the doctor and not constrained by the system. It should be possible for doctors not only to provide discursive entries, but also to employ descriptive economics, even leaving out particular classes, when appropriate.

(ii) Diagnosis and treatment information should be presented together as a single entry and there should be no division between information concerning treatment for chronic and acute problems.

(iii) By presenting classes together it should be possible to omit classes of items within an entry, facilitating reading the entry as a whole.

(iv) It should be possible to scan or read an entry in relation to a series of entries and thereby formulate the career of particular illness(es). When made appropriate by the contents of related items, particular classes in an entry can be omitted.

(v)   The entries should be maintained in relation to a potential course of a treatment, i.e. in chronological order. It should be possible to easily read both a single entry, and a collection of entries, as a whole.

The analysis also raised a number of related issues of relevance to the design of a system, and, perhaps more importantly, the choice of hardware. Firstly, reading and writing should not be spatially separated, as is the case with a standard keyboard and monitor. Instead, text should be retrieved, entered and read in the same general location. Secondly, the technology should allow documents to be read at a glance and entries to be written with economic conciseness. Doctors need to be able to make a variety of marks and annotations on the document, such as quotation and exclamation marks, underlinings and marginal comments, and to enter information at various levels of completeness. Even the preservation of the writer's handwriting may assist the reader of the record. Thirdly, the technology should allow the records to be accessible whilst being used in relation to a variety of other activities, including diagnosis, the physical examination, discussion of issues with the patient and when prescribing treatment. Therefore, records may have to be read by the doctor when away from the desk, or when on the phone or talking to the patient. Some idea of the portability required can be gleaned from examining the use of the paper medical record cards. They can be propped up and viewed whilst the doctor is examining a patient, they can be lifted off the desk to be read at an angle, and the doctor can place a record on his knee either towards or away from the patient.

The requirements, and the analyses from which they were derived, were utilised to assess the potential of various technical options, whether they would provide, for example, appropriate capabilities for annotating records, presenting entries together and supporting record reading and writing in the midst of a consultation. These options included: advanced systems for scanning, printing and projecting images, for character, document and image recognition (e.g., Francik et al., 1991; Goldberg and Goodisman, 1981) and technologies that allowed for the mixed use of paper and electronic documents (Newman and Wellner, 1992; Wellner, 1992).

Mapping these and other devices against the requirements led us to a more straightforward solution, utilising a mobile technology, a notepad computer, which preserved the general format of the medical record card whilst augmenting this with various computational capabilities (cf. Weiser, 1991). Making use of the capabilities of a stylus as the input device also allowed for the production and recognisability of particular marks, including the ability to preserve some of the distinctiveness of handwriting. It is also possible to preserve some of the geographical features of the paper cards, for example the 'open area' for recording entries and the ability to locate one item close to another, independent of class or type. The principal focus of the technology, therefore, is not so much on maintaining a formally consistent document for various bureaucratic and

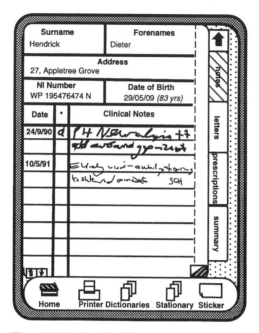

Figure 8.1 A sketch of the proposed system for supporting medical record keeping in consultations.

financial purposes, but rather on giving doctors greater textual flexibility so that they can tailor the documents with regard to diagnostic and prognostic practicalities. Diagnostic and treatment information could be presented together and chronological entries could be read together, allowing doctors, where appropriate, to write concise entries and elide classes of items within entries.

A small portable device, which co-locates writing, and reading would also enhance the doctor's ability to interweave the use of the system with the ongoing and contingent demands of the interaction with the patient. It also allows the record to be shown to, and discussed with, the patient. The ecological flexibility of the device also allows the doctor to take the same system to undertake home visits or visit patients in hospital, without having to transfer files from a bulky portable PC to the original workstation. Figure 8.1 is a sketch which was to developed for the design of the system.

Although the system would also include additional features for administering a series of consultations, for accessing related documents, like drugs guides and directories and for printing prescriptions, its design would principally be organised around record keeping. Indeed, at least at first, the appearance of the system would be based on the paper medical card, allowing for individual entries to be entered in chronological order and viewed together.

It is interesting to note that a number of the key issues, which arise in considering system design for general medical practice, arise in other working environments, especially those which involve document use during the interaction between professionals and their clients. Recent studies have revealed, in different ways, that designers have to be sensitive to how talk and the activities on the computer are interrelated (Gray et al., 1993; Whalen, 1994, 1995). It may also be that designers have to take account of the collaborative work of the participants when they are co-present. Whether the participants are located in the same place and, using conventional artefacts, are geographically dispersed and utilising novel technologies, or are merely just the reader and writer of a document, producing and making sense of what is on the document is achieved through tacit practices and common-sense reasoning about the entries.

To address these concerns requires a fundamental reconsideration of the design and development of technologies. For example, it is no longer sufficient for the 'user interface' to be considered in terms of the actions undertaken by an individual at a workstation. The ways in which items are displayed and information entered may have to be sensitive to the activities of others. These concerns require a rethinking of how screens are designed, the human–computer interaction techniques that allow for entry and presentation of information, and even the hardware through which these activities are accomplished. Such concerns led the researchers to investigate the affordances of devices differing in size and portability to support co-present activities in interaction and the demands these place on different kinds of interfaces. Indeed, the proposals for technologies to support medical record keeping were the background for a series of experiments which compared how such varied devices as fixed computer workstations, laptops and personal digital assistants were used within interactions (Dennis and Newman 1996); these experiments being part of a more general investigation into the 'affordances of paper' at the laboratory (e.g. Sellen and Harper 1997).

Despite the medical consultation being a specific domain with very particular demands, the detailed analysis within a setting can be the starting-point and a resource for a more general consideration of the requirements placed on technologies to support everyday, mundane activities.

8.3.3   Design and deployment of mobile technologies for mobile personnel

Until recently, systems to support collaborative work have provided facilities which enhance access between individuals who are based in fixed locations. Conventional systems have been based on the workstation, and even more radical approaches to support collaborative work, such as media spaces, have been developed for individuals to collaborate from particular fixed locations. It is increasingly recognised, however, that many individuals need to work with each other when mobile, and away from a fixed workstation or device. In different ways, the foregoing suggestions for technologies for London Underground and for the medical consultation have reflected such considerations. Moreover, in recent projects, we have been increasingly involved in various initiatives concerned with developing technologies to support collaboration between mobile personnel. These have included the design and assessment of particular systems for specific organisations, and more general investigations into novel mobile technologies and services. For example, in collaboration with the Automobile Association (AA), the largest vehicle recovery organisation in the United Kingdom, and the Department of Computer Studies at Loughborough University, we undertook some preliminary investigations into the needs of patrols. Field studies identified information and communication requirements which informed the development of a prototype system based on a notepad computer (Luff, 1997; Smyth et al., 1995). This system was assessed by patrols and management and helped the AA to develop a strategy for the introduction of mobile technologies.

In a very different way, we are currently involved in a large European project which is developing novel infrastructures for mobile telecommunications. This project, known as MEMO, brings together mobile telecommunications companies, device manufacturers and broadcasters to develop portable devices, networks and services that draw on two quite different, technological innovations: digital mobile phones (GSM) and digital radio (or Digital Audio Broadcasting, DAB). Through the MEMO infrastructure, these two different technical innovations can be brought together to enable individuals to access, through GSM, substantial data, broadcast through DAB: the infrastructure providing different ways of 'interacting' with broadcast material.

Such a novel technology raises a number of interesting issues, not only with regard to how it might be used and by whom, but with respect to its implications for 'information providers' such as radio stations and newspapers. To address these issues, we have undertaken a wide range of video-based field studies of potential 'user' organisations or personnel, including the construction industry (architects, site managers, construction companies), transport (both road and rail) and less specialist applications such as the general travelling public and the tourist. We have also undertaken studies of 'information providers', in particular those involved in news production, including radio (e.g. the BBC), newspapers (*Le Monde*), and on-line news services (such as Reuters). These studies have informed the specification of the requirements for mobile receivers for interactive DAB services (Luff et al., 1996) and identified a range of issues for information providers to enable them to exploit the opportunities which arise with these new novel infrastructures. The field studies have also informed the development of a more wide-ranging 'exploitation strategy' for both potential user and information provider organisations.

The development of a technology such as MEMO, which requires the integration of different standards and systems and the design of new devices and services, and demands collaboration between quite different organisations, takes a significant length of time. The critical technology it relies upon, DAB, is only now being deployed in Europe, and the standards and specifications which MEMO itself relies upon will take some time to agree. This is not unusual. Other generic technologies, such as media spaces and audio-visual infrastructures, demand considerable investment and, being based on technologies developed over the last thirty years, have yet to be deployed in more than a few advanced research laboratories. We can also see in specific domains, such as medical consultations, the London Underground and the AA, the development of new technologies inevitably facing an array of practical constraints before deployment. Given these constraints, and the fact that workplace studies have been used primarily in the design and development of advanced and innovative systems, it is hardly surprising that, as yet, they have not formed an integral part of many technologies now in place.

Taking more conventional systems, it is likely, in the short term, that workplace studies can inform the deployment and evaluation of new technology. For example, in a recent exercise we were asked to participate in the introduction of a mobile technology into a particular domain within the construction industry (Luff and Heath, 1998). In this case, the choice of the technology (a hand-held notepad computer), the personnel to be supported (foremen) and the activities to be supported (surrounding a form called the 'allocation sheet') had all been decided. We were asked to comment on, and to assist with, the introduction of the system onto the construction site.

It was envisaged that the system to be deployed would fulfil many of the functions currently covered by the paper allocation sheet, whilst also helping record information more quickly in a form that would make it more accessible to other, interested personnel. It was also believed that documenting data on a mobile system would allow foremen, when necessary, to discuss various details entered into the sheets with gang members and others out on site. Finally, it was also hoped that the system itself

CAIN McGRATH CIVIL ENGINEERING LIMITED — DAILY ALLOCATION SHEET

CONTRACT : A13 CONTRACT 2 SECTION: TEAM X DATE: 2-5-95 WEEK NUMBER:

DAY

LOCATION 6B

GANGER P. BLACK

ENGINEER GEORGE

WORKS NO.	NAME	TRADE	DESCRIPTION OF WORK AND GROSS HOURS: Cranking Starters Bars from piles for Cages Area 6B	Blocking ^ levelling Cages in AREA 6B	Walking there ^ Back to Wathem Creek as requested	Reinforcing Steel in South Wall Wathem Creek for Team 7		Prefabbing Cages in Area 6B	DEDUCT ANY NON PRODUCTIVE HOURS INCLUDED IN GROSS HOURS AGAINST THESE HEADINGS: NET HOURS	TIME TAKEN TO/ FROM WORKPLACE CLOCK	TIME TAKEN TO/ FROM CANTEENS / WORKPLACE	TIME TAKEN WAITING FOR / TO COLLECT MATERIALS	TIME STANDING AWAITING FOR PLANT	TIME STANDING DUE TO BROKEN DOWN PLANT	TIME STANDING DUE TO WEATHER CONDITIONS	AWAITING LINE/LEVE; ETC.	AWAITING INFORMATION FROM RE	GROSS HOURS
	P. BLACK	S/F	1	1	½	1		6	5½	10 MINS	20 MINS							10
	D. WHITE	S/F	;	;	½	;		5	8½	10 MINS	20 MINS							9
TOTAL LABOUR HOURS:			2	2	1	2		11										19

ORDER NUMBER	PLANT DESCRIPTION	HIRED FROM

Figure 8.2 An example allocation sheet, for a gang of steel fixers (S/F).

would provide a resource for foremen to become more proactive; to anticipate problems and difficulties and put solutions into place before trouble emerged.

The allocation sheet is a fairly conventional form that records what activities have been undertaken by which individuals, how long those activities have taken and any problems which have been found and managed (Figure 8.2).

The record is completed every day by those responsible for each 'gang' of manual workers out on site – the gangers – and is used by a range of personnel to monitor the progress of work, identify problems and co-ordinate activities. The document, therefore, is both a record of, and a resource in the organisation of, work. It is used and referred to by, amongst others, engineers, accountants, surveyors, clerks and managers. The paper allocation sheet is regarded as an outmoded artefact, and it is believed that new technologies can provide enhanced support for the documentation, evaluation and management of work on site. These ambitions informed the exercise undertaken by the system developers in the construction company to replace the paper sheets with an electronic system.

The system developers chose a Fujitsu 500 Stylistic notepad computer with which to replace the paper allocation sheet, and an interface was developed that replicated, as far as possible, the actions accomplished on the paper form. Communication from the device to the site hut was through a mobile phone via a modem.

Needless to say, there were difficulties associated with the introduction of the technology which derived, in part, from a misunderstanding concerning work and collaboration on sites. For example, an important part of a foreman's work does not consist simply of collecting the daily allocation sheets from gangers, but using this necessity to visit gangs at different parts of the site to 'monitor' the progress of work and to discern and discuss problems which may have arisen. The allocation sheets provide an occasion for talk; talk which is essential for the smooth operation of the site. With the introduction of the system, these occasions became preoccupied with entering the correct information into the system, and undermined the ability of the foreman and ganger to raise and discuss other matters. The difficulties became so severe that, within a short time, we recommended an alternative way of using the system, a solution which involved restructuring the division of labour and staffing, to help make the technology work.

In collaboration with the designers of the system and the members of the team on the construction site, we developed alternative ways of using the system. These involved changing the interface to the technology, the day-to-day procedures through which it was used and how it was deployed. In particular, it was agreed to continue using the paper sheets and employ someone else to enter and code the information from them. In this way, the foreman could remain mobile around the site, the gangers continued entering the information onto the paper sheets and data were available in an electronic form for a range of personnel in the site hut. The use of the computer system, even with the mobile phone connection, remained located in the hut. Fortunately, the use of prototyping and the involvement of staff helped facilitate a change in the aims of the project and the design of the system.

It is a shame that the ambitious aims of the proponents of the system did not quite match the way it was eventually used. But the individuals in the site hut did get the information, by and large, they required in an electronic form and the foreman was not overburdened with an additional and largely irrelevant task. Despite the identification of an individual who needed to be mobile, activities that appeared cumbersome and redundant, and a resource that seemed to require mobile support, the original focus of the exercise appears to have been chosen without paying enough attention to the nature of the activity that the system was intended to replace. This in itself did not require mobile support, or at least not in the form provided. Even the more radical aim of transforming the work of the foreman, encouraging him to be more involved in planning and more focused discussions about work on the site, was hampered rather than enhanced by the technology.

Although the introduction of the system may not have proceeded quite as intended, by undertaking field studies alongside the introduction of the system it was possible to shape the deployment of the technology. In particular, drawing on a more thorough understanding of the work of, and collaboration between, different personnel on the site, we could begin to identify the inadvertent consequences of the system, and the ways in which it facilitated or undermined the indigenous work practices of particular individuals. The field studies provided resources with which to reconsider how the technology should be used, when and by whom, and to recommend changes to the functionality of the system. For example, we were able to suggest particular alterations to the design of interface and to the system interaction to facilitate the individual who used it. Such suggestions derived not only from problems which could be noticed when the system was in use, but from observations of how work was organised on the site. These revealed that quite reasonable assumptions made by the designers, concerning the ordering of activities on the interface or even the identification of individual labourers, did not resonate with work accomplished on the site. We were therefore able to suggest redesigns of the system so that its operation better matched the ways items were 'read off' the sheets, better facilities to distinguish individuals and activities and additional capabilities for helping to check the information being entered into the electronic system.

In various ways, then, the field studies contributed to the deployment and design of the system. The contributions arose through the ways in which they reveal the 'seen but unnoticed' resources in and through which personnel accomplish, and co-ordinate, their activities with others. In the case at hand, it is interesting to note how field studies help illuminate the unanticipated significance of seemingly unimportant events.

In these examples, we have sketched only briefly how studies of work and interaction have informed design and deployment; they illustrate, perhaps, the very different ways in which the development of complex systems may draw from observations and findings generated through video-based field studies. These contributions differ in the part they play within the development process. So, for example, in MEMO we have been involved in the early stages of the design of a technology which contributes to the development of hardware as well as the specification of standards. In London Underground, and in the general practice, field studies have informed the assessment and evaluation of current systems, and are currently providing the building blocks for the development of more advanced and innovative technologies. In the construction site, we find an example of how field researchers may work in collaboration with system designers to ease the deployment of a new system. The character of these contributions to the development process also differs. In the case of general practice, for example, or current research with London

Underground, we have been responsible principally for the development of a requirements specification for a new system, whereas, in the case of media space or current projects on collaborative virtual environments, the contribution has been more concerned with delineating a number of specific issues that should form the foundation to the development of prototype systems. It would seem, therefore, that it is unlikely that 'ethnography' will provide a standard package for design, or necessarily contribute to a particular stage of the design process. As the examples discussed here suggest, the contribution of field studies to technology, like other 'methods', will, and should, derive from the practicalities and constraints of the particular project, and exploit the unique contribution that ethnography can make to our understanding of the organisation of work and collaboration.

8.4   Methods, cases and design

Video-based analyses of work and interaction, therefore, may generate findings which are relevant to the design and evaluation of new technologies, and in the coming years it is likely that an increasing number of projects will use various forms of ethnography to inform the development and even deployment of complex systems. Whilst it would be a mistake to consider the practical, rather than the academic, contribution of workplace studies as their principal contribution, there is a growing commitment amongst both researchers and engineers in seeking ways in which various forms of naturalistic research can inform design, development and deployment. As we have attempted to demonstrate, the growing interest in using workplace studies in design does not derive simply from the substantial cost that organisations incur when technologies go wrong, or fail to assist the activities that they are designed to support. Rather, the growing commitment to workplace studies derives from the recognition that naturalistic studies of work and interaction can generate a distinctive body of observations and findings concerning the accomplishment of organisational activities. In a sense, therefore, it is the analytic foci of naturalistic studies of work and organisations which have attracted the attention of computer scientists and engineers. Their concern with, and powerful demonstration of, the complex array of tacit 'seen but unnoticed' practices and procedures which underlie the accomplishment of even the more mundane workplace activities has begun to reveal a potentially critical domain for those concerned with technological support for practical organisational activities; a domain which determines the use of complex systems and their ability to support and resonate with the day-to-day demands of practical workplace actions. Moreover, the concern with the social, and the collaborative organisation of workplace activities, corresponds to the growing interest in, commitment to, and ability to develop, technologies which take co-operation seriously and support the ways in which individuals work together.

However, the relationship between workplace studies and design remains problematic, and there are still no unambiguous examples of ethnography, in its various guises, informing the design, development and successful deployment of a new technology. This is hardly surprising. It is early days, and, to a large extent, it is industrial researchers and those concerned with 'blue-sky' projects who have an interest in its application. Moreover, HCI has undertaken research on the use of technologies for more than fifteen years, and there is still some debate as to whether it has ever influenced the design of a successful system. All the same, researchers both in the UK and abroad are, in various ways, exploring how various forms of workplace studies might inform design and the sorts of methodological, theoretical and practical issues which arise when attempting to use naturalistic research to specify considerations and requirements for the development of complex systems. It is, perhaps, worth mentioning one or two issues and problems.

The conceptual framework(s) and classification(s) of observations which are used in various forms of naturalistic research are unlikely to correspond to interests of designers and the ways in which they require material to be presented in order to use findings to inform system design. Ethnographic observations require translation into a form which is suitable for design, in the way that more conventional requirements methods build procedures into the data analysis process which specifies observations in a form which it is argued is appropriate for engineers. For ethnography, however, with its emphasis on explicating the indigenous practices of participants themselves, it would seem somewhat perverse to introduce a proceduralised translation system which might well do damage to the socially and situationally sensitive descriptions on which qualitative analysis prides itself. The problem is further exacerbated by the very nature of ethnographic descriptions. They are 'thick descriptions' of human activity and practice, and are qualitative, and often designed to resist simple quantification of particular phenomena. In consequence, the conventional criteria that engineers and management might use to judge the validity of a body of findings, and discriminate the significance of different elements, are largely unavailable in conventional ethnographic descriptions. Moreover, in many forms of ethnography, the data consist of field notes of particular activities, and it may be unclear to the uninitiated how particular notes, themselves a product of the researchers' observations, can be used to legitimise particular conclusions. It is difficult to share such data with designers, and, coupled with no clear-cut criteria for identifying 'quality', they are unable to judge for themselves the validity and significance of particular observations and recommendations.

In this respect, video-based materials have certain advantages over more conventional 'qualitative' data. Not only do they provide researchers with the ability to share data and evaluate observations with regard to materials on which they are based, but they also provide designers with the opportunity of seeing for themselves the activities that they are attempting to support, and judging the 'adequacy' of the analytic observations and conclusions. It may also be argued that video-based materials provide designers with the opportunity of associating particular design decisions with particular data and analyses. In this way, earlier design decisions are 'traceable' and open to discussion at later parts of the development process. Video-based materials can also assist discussions between the ethnographers and designers. They provide a common set of materials with which to explore and discuss key issues, considerations, and designs, and to facilitate the process of translating ethnographic observations and analyses into a form which is fruitful for thinking about, and developing, complex systems. It should be said that, in the case of the examples discussed above, mobile medical records, the London Underground timetable and the media space, video materials of actual activities and interaction have provided a critical resource in our discussions with designers and our joint attempts to develop new and innovative technologies.

Other considerations also come into play. In our own experience, one rarely encounters an industrial project where the management and engineers do not have a very strong idea as to the appropriate solution before initiating the requirements analysis or design study. In many cases, the solution is not articulated, and part of the project becomes discovering the agenda which lies behind the commission of the study. Not surprisingly, most often, one discovers in the course of the requirements analysis that management are already committed to a particular technical solution, and believe they know the problems already, and that the sub-text is to reduce staffing levels and/or change working relations. The researcher can find a selective version of his or her analysis being used to justify decisions which are not legitimised by his or her findings, and thereby being an unwitting and unwilling participant in a wider organisational commitment to introduce a particular technology at whatever cost. But these are problems and dilemmas of working on more applied projects in general, and are not peculiar to undertaking workplace studies.

It has long been recognised that it is difficult, if not impossible, to proceduralise ethnographic research, and that to a large extent it has to be learnt through 'doing' and 'apprenticeship'. Whilst it may be feasible to provide general guidelines and analytic considerations, there is little advantage in attempting to solve the ethnographic-design problem by trying to specify a corrupt and simplified methodological framework. Rather, it would seem sensible to begin to develop guidelines and considerations for how we might relate various forms of ethnography to design in the light of particular cases and examples. There are, in fact, an increasing number of examples where workplace studies have informed the assessment, design and even deployment of a technology, and, as we accumulate these cases, we might be in a position to begin to identify some more general procedures, practices, issues and analytic considerations. These might consist, for example, of providing key concepts, specifying issues which arise across various workplaces, describing techniques for generating insights into indigenous practices and resources, and mechanisms for presenting and discussing findings with designers and engineers. In many ways, such guidelines simply would not be more suitable for, and more in the spirit of, ethnography, but would perhaps allow researchers to avoid the heavily stipulative and situationally insensitive procedures which have been promulgated in more conventional requirements methods.

8.5   Summary

The studies discussed here form part of a growing body of research concerned with work, interaction and technology. It may be unsurprising that innovations in information and communication systems have provided the background to the emergence of a range of empirical studies in the social and cognitive sciences; these technologies inviting a consideration of the human competencies and practices surrounding their use. More surprising, perhaps, is the way in which they have provided a vehicle for the emergence of a wide range of qualitative studies, in particular studies concerned with so-called details of social action and interaction in organisational settings. Undoubtedly, some will see the emergence of workplace studies, particularly those which focus on the practical and interactional accomplishment of specialised organisational activities, as evidence of the current influence, or worse, the corruption, of certain forms of sociological analysis. Nevertheless, it is interesting to observe how the substantive demands and developments, pose an array of methodological, conceptual and practical problems for those with an interest in the *in situ* accomplishment of practical action and interaction.

Informing the work discussed here is a range of practical concerns and problems. In part, the various studies were originally selected to allow us to address different sorts of new technology in different sorts of working environment. So, for example, with London Underground we were interested in the deployment and use of multimedia systems which combine various types of information and communications technologies, including devices for presenting video and audio, computer displays for dynamic and graphic material and more traditional types of documentation. With media space we had a concern with looking at how advanced telecommunication systems might support and transform human interaction and collaboration; the analysis providing a vehicle for considering how such technologies might be (re)configured to support practical conduct. Within general practice we had what we believed to be a straightforward example of the deployment of a very basic information system, and, with Reuters and Docklands, the problem of how such systems are 'transformed' so as to support the collaborative organisation of individual activities. Finally, an architectural practice provided a glimpse of how CAD systems were used to support the concerted accomplishment of practical design, and, in particular, the ways in which architects visualise and co-ordinate their activities with each other. In selecting these very different domains and technologies, we were interested in 'the work to make technologies work': in exploring the ways in which particular technologies in particular settings are used and oriented to by the participants themselves. In a general sense, therefore, the differing technologies and differing settings provided a substantive vehicle with which to address how particular tools and technologies feature in human practical activity. In this way, we hope to learn something of the life and character of these technologies and the work of which they are part.

A glimpse at the ways in which these various technologies are used within their respective settings has provided a little background to thinking about the design and the deployment of more advanced systems. In the first place, these and other workplace studies demonstrate in detail the complexity of even the most mundane organisational activity, and how seemingly individual actions are embedded in the real-time interaction of participants (those both within and outside the immediate environment). They also reveal how the various tools and artefacts that were hitherto believed to be a reflection of an outmoded and bygone age – paper notes, jottings, sketches, scribbles and the like – constitute critical resources in a broad range of organisational domains. Why such unsophisticated tools and artefacts remain an integral feature of workplace activities, despite the deployment of new technologies, cannot be treated as a curious example of 'cultural lag', but rather as an embodiment of a complex, and largely unexplicated, form of human practice which features in the accomplishment of mundane actions and activities. The studies also illustrate the resilience of people in organisations, and the ways in which they are able, despite the limitations and constraints of the technology, to accomplish whatever they have to accomplish, at least for the practical purposes at hand. Despite the propensity to blame problems arising from the use of technology on 'human error', designers rely upon the good will and complex abilities of individuals to make technologies work. As we have argued, developers and designers neglect the social organisation and the practical circumstances in which activities are accomplished at their peril.

In a large part, workplace studies are not principally concerned with the design or deployment of new technologies, and it is a mistake to judge their contribution solely with regard to their short-term practical implications. Rather, it is increasingly recognised that the contribution of workplace studies, especially those with their empirical and methodological foundations in ethnomethodology and conversation analysis, is to provide a vehicle with which to assemble a body of observations and findings that allow us to respecify some of the key concepts which have hitherto underpinned our understanding of work and organisational life. This respecification is accomplished from within, that is, with regard to the detailed naturalistic analysis of workplace activities, and delineates how particular organisational characteristics derive from, and are preserved in, the naturally occurring action and interaction of the participants. In taking practical action and human agency seriously, workplace studies allow us to rethink work, interaction and technology, and demonstrate how the organisational life and the characteristics it embodies are achieved in and through the practice and practical activity of its participants.

If, on the one hand, workplace studies allow us to embed organisational forms in the practical accomplishment of action and interaction, on the other, they provide a way of escaping the excessive individualism which permeates the study of human–computer interaction. In taking the fine details of work and technology seriously, workplace studies demonstrate, repeatedly, the socially organised character of system use. In the various studies presented here, for example, we find that in various ways the use of complex systems rests upon, and is inseparable from, mundane practice and action. Participants within the various settings rely upon a body of socially organised practices and procedures for reading what they read, for seeing what they see, for telling what they tell and for writing what they write; and they do this in real-time with regard to the contributions of their colleagues. The very intelligibility of the 'information' on which they rely, and their ability to accomplish their work using various tools and technologies, are founded upon their socially organised competencies. In considering the details of human–computer interaction, we hope to have shown how seemingly mundane and idiosyncratic conduct is not the mystical achievement of an information processing machine, but the product of culturally competent social beings in concert with each other.

One final remark: despite the talk, both lay and professional, concerning the glories of the information society, and the extraordinary changes engendered by the 'digital revolution', there remains little research on how ordinary working people have dealt with this upheaval. In part, the studies discussed here are concerned in a small way with attempting to redress this balance – to explore how an array of tools and technologies have been 'made at home' in various organisational settings and scenes (cf. Sacks 1992). It is reassuring to see how people work with technology, and to realise that, notwithstanding the impressive technical achievements of the digital revolution, these stand as little when placed alongside the richness and complexity of social action and interaction.

References

Ackerman, M. (1996). 'Merging Organizational Memory with Collaborative Help', in *Proceedings of CSCW '96,* Cambridge, MA, pp. 97–105.

Acroyd, S. (1992). 'Paradigms Lost: Paradise Regained', in *Rethinking Organization: New Directions in Organisation Theory and Analysis,* Reed, M. and Hughes, M. (eds.), London: Sage.

Agre, P. E. (1988). 'The Dynamic Structure of Everyday Life'. Unpublished Ph.D. Dissertation, AI Technical Report 1085. Department of Electrical Engineering and Computer Science, Massachusetts Institute of Technology, Cambridge, MA.

Aldridge, A. (1997). 'Engaging with Promotional Culture', *Sociology.* **31**: (3), 389–408.

Alty, J. L. and Johannsen, G. (1989). 'Knowledge Based Dialogue for Dynamic Systems', *Automatica.* **25**: 829–40.

Anderson, R. J. (1994). 'Representation and Requirements: The Value of Ethnography in System Design', *Human–Computer Interaction.* **9**: (2), 151–82.

Anderson, R., Hughes, J. and Sharrock, W. (1989). *Working for Profit.* Farnborough: Avebury.

Ankrah, A., Frohlich, D. M. and Gilbert, G. N. (1990). 'Two Ways to Fill a Bath, With and Without Knowing It', in *Proceedings of Interact '90 – Third IFIP Conference on Human–Computer Interaction,* Cambridge, pp. 73–8.

Argyle, M. and Dean, J. (1965). 'Eye-Contact, Distance and Affiliation', *Sociometry.* **28**: 289–304.

Atkinson, J. M. (1978). *Discovering Suicide: Studies of the Social Organisation of Sudden Death.* Basingstoke and London: Macmillan.

Atkinson, J. M. and Heritage, J. C. (1984). (eds.) *Structures of Social Action: Studies in Conversation Analysis.* Cambridge University Press.

Bakhtin, M. M. (1986). *Speech Genres and other Late Essays.* Austin, Texas: University of Texas Press.

Bannon, L. J., Bjorn-Andersen, N. and Due-Thomsen, B. (1988). 'Computer Support for Cooperative Work: An Appraisal and Critique', in *Information Technology for Organizational Systems: EURINFO '88,* Bullinger, H. J. (eds.), Brussels-Luxembourg: Elsevier.

Barnatt, C. (1995). *CyberBusiness: Mindsets for a Wired Age.* Chichester: Wiley.

(1997). *Challenging Reality: In Search of Future Organisation.* Chichester: Wiley.

Becker, H. S., Geer, B., Hughes, E. C. and Strauss, A. (1961). *Boys in White.* University of Chicago Press.

Bell, D. (1976). *The Coming of Post-Industrial Society: A Venture in Social Forecasting.* Harmondsworth: Penguin.

Bellotti, V. and Sellen, A. (1993). 'Design for Privacy in Ubiquitous Computing Environments', in *Proceedings of ECSCW '93,* Milan, Italy, pp. 77–92.

Benford, S. D., Bowers, J., Fahlén, L. E., Greenhalgh, C. M., Mairiani, J. and Rodden, T. R. (1995). 'Networked Virtual Reality and Co-operative Work', *Presence: Teleoperators and Virtual Environments.* 4: (4), 364–860.

Benford, S., Brown, C., Reynard, G. and Greenhalgh, C. (1996). 'Shared Spaces: Transportation, Artificiality, and Spatiality', in *Proceedings of CSCW '96,* Cambridge, MA, pp. 77–86.

Benford, S. and Fahlén, L. (1993). 'A Spatial Model of Interaction In Large Visual Environments', in *Proceedings of ECSCW 1993,* Milan, Italy, pp. 109–24.

Bentley, R. and Dourish, P. (1995). 'Medium vs Message: Supporting Collaboration through customisation', in *Proceedings of ECSCW '95,* Stockholm, Sweden, pp. 133–48.

Bentley, R., Horstmann, T., Sikkel, K. and Trevor, J. (1994). 'The BCSCW Shared Workplace System', in *Proceedings of ERCIM Workshop on CSCW and the Web,* Sankt Augustin, Germany.

Berg, M. (1997). *Rationalizing Medical Work: Decision Support Techniques and Medical Practice.* Cambridge MA: MIT Press.

Berlin, L. M. and Jeffries, R. (1992). 'Consultants amd Apprentices: Observations about Learning and Collaborative Problem Solving', in *Proceedings of CSCW '92,* Toronto, Canada, pp. 130–7.

Bignell, V. and Fortune, J. (1984). *Understanding System Failures.* Manchester University Press.

Bijker, W. E., Hughes, T. P. and Pinch, T. (1990). (eds.) *The Social Construction of Technological Systems.* Cambridge MA: MIT Press.

Birdwhistell, R. L. (1970). *Kinesics and Context: Essays on Body Motion Communication.* London: Allen Lane.

Bjerknes, G., Ehn, P. and Kyng, M. (1987). *Computers and Democracy.* Aldershot: Avebury.

Blumer, H. S. (1962). 'Society as Symbolic Interaction', in *Human Behaviour and Social Processes,* Rose, A. M. (ed.), pp. 179–92. London: Routledge Kegan Paul.

Bly, S. A. (1988). 'A Use of Drawing Surfaces in Different Collaborative Settings', in *Proceedings of CSCW '88,* Portland, Oregon, pp. 250–6.

Bly, S. A., Harrison, S. and Irwin, S. (1992). *Media Spaces: Bringing People Together in a Video, Audio and Computing Environment.* Draft (later published in CACM), Xerox PARC.

Bly, S. A. and Minneman, S. L. (1990). 'Commune: A Shared Drawing Surface', in *Proceedings of Conference on Office Information Systems (COIS '90), 25–27 April,* pp. 184–92.

Boden, D. (1994). *The Business of Talk: Organizations in Action.* Oxford and Cambridge, MA: Polity Press.

Boden, D. and Zimmerman, D. H. (1991). (eds.) *Talk and Social Structure: Studies in Ethnomethodology and Conversation Analysis.* Cambridge: Polity Press.

Bødker, S., Ehn, P., Kammersgaard, J., Kyng, M. and Sundblad, Y. (1987). 'A

UTOPIAN Experience: On Design of Powerful Computer-Based Tools for Skilled Graphic Workers', in *Computers and Democracy*, Ehn, P., Bjerknes, G. and Kyng, M. (eds.), pp. 251–78. Aldershot: Avebury.

Boehm, B. W. (1976). 'Software Engineering', *IEEE Transactions on Computers*. 25: (12), 1226–41.

Böhme, G. and Stehr, N. (1986). *The Knowledge Society*. Dordrecht: Kluwer.

Borning, A. and Travers, M. (1991). 'Two Approaches to Casual Interaction over Computer and Video Networks', in *Proceedings of CHI '91*, New Orleans, Louisiana, pp. 13–19.

Bowers, J. and Button, G. (1995). 'Workflow from Within and Without: Technology and Cooperative Work on the Print Industry Shop Floor', in *Proceedings of ECSCW '95*, Stockholm, Sweden, 10–14 September, pp. 51–66.

Bowers, J., Pycock, J. and O'Brien, J. (1995). 'Talk and Embodiment in Collaborative Writing Environments'. Submission to CHI '96, Department of Psychology, University of Manchester.

Brown, J. S. and Duguid, P. (1994). 'Borderline Issues: Social and Material Aspects of Design', *Human–Computer Interaction*. 9: (1), 3–36.

Bull, P. (1983). *Body Movement and Interpersonal Communication*. Chichester: John Wiley and Son.

Bush, V. (1945). 'As We May Think', *Atlantic Monthly*. 176: (1), 101–8.

Button, G. (1993). 'The Curious Case of the Disappearing Technology', in *Technology in Working Order*, Button, G. (ed.), pp. 10–28. London: Routledge.

Button, G. and King, V. (1992). 'Hanging Around is not the Point: Calling Ethnography to Account', in *Workshop on Ethnography and CSCW System Design, CSCW '94*, Toronto, Canada.

Button, G. and Sharrock, W. (1994). 'Occasioned Practices in the Work of Software Engineers', in *Requirements Engineering: Social and Technical Issues*, Jirotka, M. and Goguen, J. (eds.), pp. 217–40. London: Academic Press.

Card, S. K., Moran, T. P. and Newell, A. (1980). 'Computer Text-Editing: An Information Processing Analysis of a Routine Cognitive Skill', *Cognitive Psychology*. 12: 32–74.

(1983). *The Psychology of Human–Computer Interaction*. Hillsdale, NJ: Lawrence Erlbaum Associates.

Carroll, J. M. (1984). 'Minimalist Training'. *Datamation*. November 1.

(1990). 'Infinite Detail and Emulation in an Ontologically Minimized HCI', in *Proceedings of CHI '90*, Seattle, WA, pp. 321–7.

(1991). (ed.) *Designing Interaction: Psychology at the Human–Computer Interface*. Cambridge University Press.

Castells, M. (1996). *The Rise of the Network Society*. Oxford: Blackwell.

Cawsey, A. (1990). 'A Computational Model of Explanatory Discourse: Local Interactions in a Plan-Based Explanation', in *Computers and Conversation*, Luff, P., Gilbert, G. N. and Frohlich, D. M. (eds.), pp. 223–36. London and New York: Academic Press.

Collins, T. and Bicknell, D. (1997). *Crash: Ten Easy Ways to Avoid Computer Disaster*. London: Simon and Schuster.

Conein, B. and Jacopin, É. (1995). 'Situated Action and Cognition: Knowledge in the Place', Paper prepared for *International Colloquium on Workplace Studies*, King's College, London, October.

Corbin, J. M. and Strauss, A. (1993). 'The Articulation of Work through Interaction', *Sociological Quarterly*. **34**: (1), 71–83.

Coulmas, F. (1986). *Direct and Indirect Speech*. New York: Mouton de Gruyter.

Coulter, J. (1979). *The Social Construction of Mind: Studies in Ethnomethodology and Linguistic Philosophy*. London: Macmillan.

Cuff, D. (1992). *Architecture: The Story of Practice*. Cambridge, MA: MIT Press.

Darfel, R., Filippi, G., Grosjean, M., Heath, C., Joseph, I., Luff, P. and Thereau, J. (1993). (eds.) *Régulation du trafic et information de voyageurs au PCC de la ligne A du RER*. Paris: RATP.

Davis, F. (1963). *Passage Through Crisis*. Glencoe: Free Press.

Dennis, A. and Newman, W. (1996). 'Supporting Doctor–Patient Interaction: Using a Surrogate Application as a Basis for Evaluation'. *ACM SIGCHI '96 Conference, Companion Proceedings*, April 16–18, Vancouver, BC.

DiMaggio, P. J. and Powell, W. W. (1991). 'Introduction', in *The New Institutional in Organizational Analysis*, Powell, W. W. and DiMaggio, P. J. (eds.), pp. 1–38. Chicago and London: University of Chicago Press.

Dobson, J. E., Blyth, A. J. C., Chudge, J. and Strens, R. (1994). 'The ORDIT Approach to Organisational Requirements', in *Requirements Engineering: Social and Technical Issues*, Jirotka, M. and Goguen, J. (eds.), pp. 87–106. London: Academic Press.

Dordick, H. S. and Wang, G. (1993). *The Information Society. A Retrospective View*. Newbury Park: Sage.

Dourish, P. (1992). *Computational Reflection and CSCW Design*. Rank Xerox Cambridge EuroPARC.

Dourish, P., Adler, A., Bellotti, V. and Henderson, H. (1996). 'Your Place or Mine? Learning from Long-Term Use of Video Communication', *CSCW Journal*. **5**: (1), 33–62.

Drew, P. and Heritage, J. C. (1992). (eds.) *Talk at Work: Interaction in Institutional Settings*. Cambridge University Press.

Dreyfus, H. L. (1992 (1972)). *What Computers Still Can't Do: A Critique of Artificial Reason*. Cambridge, MA: MIT Press.

Durkheim, S. (1951/1897). *Suicide: A Study in Sociology*. Glencoe IL: The Free Press.

Ehn, P. (1988). *Work Oriented Design of Computer Artifacts*. Stockholm: Arbetslivscentrum.

Ekman, P. and Friessen, W. V. (1969). 'The Repertoires of Nonverbal Behaviour: Categories, Origins, Usage and Coding', *Semiotica*. **1**: 49–98.

Emmott, S. (1995). (eds.) *Information SuperHighways: Multimedia Users And Futures*. London and New York: Academic Press.

Espejo, R. (1980). *Information and Management: The Cybernetics of a Small Company*. Netherlands: North-Holland Publishing Company.

Evans, C. (1979). *The Mighty Micro: The Impact of the Micro-Chip Revolution*. Sevenoaks: Hodder and Stoughton.

Filippi, G. and Theureau, J. (1993). 'Analysing Cooperative Work in an Urban Traffic Control Room for the Design of a Coordination Support System', in *Proceedings of ECSCW '93*, Milan, Italy, pp. 171–86.

Finn, K. E., Sellen, A. J. and Wilbur, S. B. (1997). (eds.) *Video-Mediated Communication*. Mahwah, NJ: Lawrence Erlbaum Associates.

Fish, R. S., Kraut, R. E. and Chalfonte, B. L. (1990). 'The Videowindow System in Informal Communication', in *Proceedings of CSCW '90*, Los Angeles, CA, pp. 1–11.

Fisher, D. F., Munty, R. A. and Senders, J. W. (1981). *Eye Movements: Cognitive and Visual Perception*. Hillsdale, NJ: Lawrence Erlbaum Associates.

Flood, R. L. and Jackson, M. C. (1991). *Creative Problem Solving: Total Systems Intervention*. Chichester: Wiley.

Francik, E., Rudman, S. E., Cooper, D. and Levine, S. (1991). 'Putting Innovation to Work: Adoption Strategies for Multimedia Communication Systems', *Communications of the ACM*. 12: 55–63.

Frohlich, D. M. and Luff, P. (1989). 'Conversational Resources for Situated Action', in *Proceedings of CHI '89*, Austin, TX, pp. 253–8.

Galegher, J. and Kraut, R. E. (1990). 'Technology for Intellectual Teamwork: Perspectives on Research and Design', in *Intellectual Teamwork: The Social and Technological Foundations of Cooperative Work*, Kraut, R. E., Galegher, J. and Egido, C. (eds.), pp. 1–20. Hillsdale, NJ: Lawrence Erlbaum Associates.

Garfinkel, H. (1967). *Studies in Ethnomethodology*. Englewood Cliffs, NJ: Prentice-Hall.

Garfinkel, H. and Sacks, H. (1970). 'On Formal Structures of Practical Actions', in *Theoretical Sociology*, McKinney, J. C. and Tiryakian, E. A. (eds.), pp. 338–60. New York: Appleton-Century-Crofts.

Gaver, W. W. (1991a). 'Sound Support for Collaboration', in *Proceedings of ECSCW 1991*, Amsterdam, Netherlands, pp. 293–324.

(1991b). 'Technology Affordances', in *Proceedings of CHI '91*, New Orleans, LA, pp. 79–84.

Gaver, W. W., Moran, T., Maclean, A., Lovstrand, L., Dourish, P., Carter, K. A. and Buxton, W. (1992). 'Realizing a Video Environment: EuroPARC's RAVE System', in *Proceedings of CHI '92*, Monterey, CA, pp. 27–35.

Gaver, W. W., Sellen, A., Heath, C. C. and Luff, P. (1993). 'One is not Enough: Multiple Views in a Media Space', in *Proceedings of INTERCHI '93*, Amsterdam, Netherlands, pp. 335–41.

Gaver, W. W., Smets, G. and Overbeeke, K. (1995). 'A Virtual Window on Media Space', in *Proceedings of CHI '95*, pp. 257–64.

Geertz, C. (1973). *The Interpretation of Cultures*. New York: Basic Books.

Gladwin, T. (1964). 'Culture and Logical Process', in *Cultural Anthropology: Essays Presented to George Peter Murdock*, Goodenough, P. (ed.), pp. 265–83. New York: McGraw-Hill.

Goffman, E. (1961). *Asylums: Essays on the social Situation of Mental Patients and other Inmates*. Harmondsworth: Penguin.

(1974). *Frame Analysis: An Essay on the Organisation of Experience*. North Eastern University Press.

(1981). *Forms of Talk*. Oxford: Blackwell.

Goguen, J. A. and Linde, C. (1993). 'Techniques Requirements Elicitation', in *Proceedings of RE '93: IEEE International Symposium on Requirements Engineering*, San Diego, CA, 4–6 Jan. pp. 152–64.

(1994). 'Requirements Engineering as the Reconcilliation of Social and Technical Issues', in *Requirements Engineering: Social and Technical Issues*, Jirotka, M. and Goguen, J. (eds.), pp. 165–200. London: Academic Press.

Goldberg, D. and Goodisman, A. (1981). 'Stylus User Interfaces for Manipulating Text', in *Proceedings of Fourth ACM SIGGRAPH Symposium on User Interface Technology (UIST '91)*, pp. 127–35.

Goodwin, C. (1981). *Conversational Organisation: Interaction between Speakers and Hearers*. London: Academic Press.

Goodwin, C. and Goodwin, M. H. (1996). 'Seeing as a Situated Activity: Formulating Planes', in *Cognition and Communication at Work*, Engeström, Y. and Middleton, D. (eds.), pp. 61–95. Cambridge University Press.

Gray, W. D., John, B. D. and Atwood, M. E. (1993). 'Project Ernestine: Validating a GOMS Analysis for Predicting and Explaining Real-World Task Performances', *Human–Computer Interaction*. **8**: (3), 237–309.

Greatbatch, D., Heath, C. C., Luff, P. and Campion, P. (1995). 'Conversation Analysis: Human–Computer Interaction and the General Practice Consultation', in *Perspectives on HCI: Diverse Approaches*, Monk, A. and Gilbert, G. N. (eds.), pp. 199–222. London: Academic Press.

Greatbatch, D., Luff, P., Heath, C. C. and Campion, P. (1993). 'Interpersonal Communication and Human–Computer Interaction: An Examination of the Use of Computers in Medical Consultations', *Interacting With Computers*. **5**: (2), 193–216.

Greenberg, S., Hayne, S. and Rada, R. (1995). (eds.) *Groupware for Real-time Drawing: A Designer's Guide*. Maidenhead: McGraw-Hill.

Grint, K. and Woolgar, S. (1997). *The Machine at Work: Technology, Work and Organization*. Cambridge: Polity.

Grudin, J. (1988). 'Why CSCW Applications Fail: Problems in the Design and Evaluation of Organizational Interfaces', in *Proceedings of CSCW '88*, Portland, OR, pp. 85–93.

Grudin, J. and Palen, L. (1995). 'Why Groupware Succeeds: Discretion or Mandate?', in *Proceedings of ECSCW '95*, Stockholm, Sweden, pp. 263–78.

Gurwitsch, A. (1964). *The Field of Consciousness*. Jurgen University Press.

Harper, R. (1998). *Inside the IMF*. London: Academic Press.

Harper, R. and Carter, K. (1994). 'Keeping People Apart', *CSCW Journal*. **2**: (3), 199–207.

Harper, R., Hughes, J. and Shapiro, D. (1989). 'Harmonious Working and CSCW: Computer Technology and Air Traffic Control', in *Proceedings of ECSCW '89*, Amsterdam, Netherlands, pp. 73–86.

Hart, H. L. A. (1961). *The Concept of Law*. Oxford: Clarendon Press.

Heath, C. C. (1981). 'The Opening Sequence in Doctor/Patient Interaction', in *Medical Work: Realities and Routines*, Atkinson, P. and Heath, C. C. (eds.), pp. Farnborough: Gower.

(1982). *Talk and Recipiency: Sequential Organization in Speech and Body Movement*. Cambridge University Press.

(1986). *Body Movement and Speech in Medical Interaction*. Cambridge University Press.

(1992). 'The Delivery and Reception of Diagnosis in the General-Practice Consultation', in *Talk at Work; Interaction in Institutional Settings*, Drew, P. and Heritage, J. (eds.), pp. 235–67. Cambridge University Press.

(1997). 'The Analysis of Activities in Face to Face Interaction using Video', in *Qualitative Methods*, Silverman, D. (ed.), London: Sage.

Heath, C. C. and Hindmarsh, J. (1997) 'Les objets et leur environnement local. La production interactionnelle de réalités matérielles'. *Raison Pratiques. Cognition et Information en Société. Paris: Éditions de l'École des Hautes.* Études en Science Sociales, pp. 149–76.

Heath, C. C., Jirotka, M., Luff, P. and Hindmarsh, J. (1994–5). 'Unpacking Collaboration: the Interactional Organisation of Trading in a City Dealing Room', *CSCW.* **3**: (2), 147–65.

Heath, C. C. and Luff, P. (1991). 'Disembodied Conduct: Communication through Video in a Multi-Media Office Environment', in *Proceedings of CHI '91,* New Orleans, LA, pp. 99–103.

(1992a). 'Collaboration and Control: Crisis Management and Multimedia Technology in London Underground Line Control Rooms', *CSCW Journal.* **1**: (1–2), 69–94.

(1992b). *Design Workshops: Social Science and the Development of New Technologies.* Cambridge EuroPARC Technical Report, Rank Xerox EuroPARC.

(1992c). 'Media Space and Communicative Asymmetries: Preliminary Observations of Video Mediated Interaction', *Human–Computer Interaction.* **7**: 315–46.

(1996). 'Convergent Activities: Line Control and Passenger Information on London Underground', in *Cognition and Communication at Work*, Engeström, Y. and Middleton, D. (eds.), pp. 96–129. Cambridge University Press.

Heath, C. C., Luff, P. and Sellen, A. (1995). 'Reconsidering the Virtual Workplace: Flexible Support for Collaborative Activity', in *Proceedings of ECSCW '95,* Stockholm, Sweden, pp. 83–100.

Hensel, M. (1980). *Die Informationsgesellschaft: Neuere Ansätze zur Analyse eines Schlagwortes.* Munich: Fischer.

Heritage, J. C. (1984). *Garfinkel and Ethnomethodology.* Cambridge: Polity Press.

Heritage, J. C. and Atkinson, J. M. (1984). 'Introduction', in *Structures of Social Action: Studies in Conversation Analysis,* Atkinson, J. M. and Heritage, J. C. (eds.), pp. 1–15. Cambridge University Press.

Hiltz, S. R. and Turoff, M. (1978 (1993)). *The Network Nation: Human Communication via Computer.* Cambridge, MA: MIT Press.

Holbrook, H. (1990). 'A Scenario-Based Methodology for Conducting Requirements Elicitation', *ACM Software Engineering Notes.* **15**: (1).

Hughes, E. C. (1958). *Men and their Work.* Glencoe: Free Press.

(1971). *The Sociological Eye: Selected Papers On Institution and Race (Part I) and Self and the Study of Society (Part II).* Chicago: Aldine Atherton.

Hughes, J. A., Randall, D. R. and Shapiro, D. (1992). 'Faltering from Ethnography to Design', in *Proceedings of CSCW '92,* Toronto, Canada. pp. 115–22.

Hutchins, E. L. (1995). *Cognition in the Wild.* Cambridge MA: MIT Press.

Hutchins, E. L., Hollan, J. D. and Norman, D. A. (1986). 'Direct Manipulation Interfaces', in *User-Centered System Design,* Norman, D. A. and Draper, S. W. (eds.), pp. 87–124. Hillsdale NJ: Lawrence Erlbaum Associates.

Ichigawa, Y., Okada, K., Jeong, G., Tanaka, S. and Matsushita, Y. (1995). 'MAJIC Videoconferencing System: Experiments, Evaluation and Improvement', in *Proceedings of ECSCW '95,* Stockholm, Sweden. pp. 279–92.

Iser, W. (1985). *The Act of Reading*. London: Routledge.

Ishii, H. (1990). 'TeamWorkStation: Towards a Seamless Shared Workspace', in *Proceedings of CSCW '90*, Los Angeles, CA, pp. 13–26.

Ishii, H. and Arita, K. (1991). 'Clearface: Translucent Multiuser Interface for TeamWorkStation', in *Proceedings of ECSCW '91*, Amsterdam, Netherlands, pp. 163–74.

Ishii, H. and Kobayashi, M. (1992). 'Clearface: A Seamless Medium for Sharing Drawing and Conversation with Eye Contact', in *Proceedings of CHI 92*, Monterey, CA, pp. 525–32.

Jackson, M. (1995). *Software Requirements and Specifications: A Lexicon of Practice, Principles and Prejudices*. Wokingham and Reading, MA: Addison Wesley.

Jirotka, M. (forthcoming). *Documentary Data Types*. Centre for Requirements and Foundations Research Report. Oxford University.

Jirotka, M. and Goguen, J. (1994). (eds.) *Requirements Engineering: Social and Technical Issues*. London: Academic Press.

Jirotka, M., Luff, P. and Heath, C. (1993). 'Requirements for Technology in Complex Environments: Tasks and Interaction in a City Dealing Room', *SIGOIS Bulletin (Special Issue) Do Users get what They want? (DUG '93)*. 14: (2 (December)), 17–23.

Jones, M. (1990). 'Mac-thusiasm: Social Aspects of Microcomputer Use', in *Proceedings of Interact '90 – Third IFIP Conference on Human–Computer Interaction*, Cambridge. pp. 21–6.

Joseph, I. (1995). (ed.) *Métiers du public; les compétences de l'agent et l'espace des usagers*. Paris: Études du CNRS.

Keenoy, T., Oswick, C. and Grant, D. (1997). 'Organisational Discourse: Text and Context', *Organisation*. 4: 147–57.

Kendon, A. (1970). 'Movement Coordination in Social Interaction: Some Examples Described', *Acta Psychologica*, 32: 100–25.

(1990). *Conducting Interaction: Studies in the Behaviour of Social Interaction*. Cambridge University Press.

Kirwan, B. and Ainsworth, L. K. (1992). (eds.) *A Guide To Task Analysis*. London: Taylor and Francis.

Knoblauch, H. (1996). 'Arbeit als Interaktion. Informationsgesellschaft, Post-Fordismus und Kommunikationsarbeit', *Soziale Welt*. 3: 344–62.

(1997). 'Die kommunikative Konstruktion postmoderner Organisationen. Institutionen, Aktivitätssysteme und kontextuelles Handeln', *Österreichische Zeitschrift für Soziologie*. 2: 6–23.

Kolski, C. and Millot, P. (1991). 'A Rule-Based Approach to the Ergonomic "Static" Evaluation of Man–Machine Graphic Interface in Industrial Processes', *International Journal of Man–Machine Studies*. 35: 657–74.

Kreibich, R. (1986). *Die Wissenschaftsgesellschaft*. Frankfurt: Suhrkamp.

Kuutti, K. (1991). 'The Concept of Activity as a Basic Unit of Analysis for CSCW Research', in *Proceedings of ECSCW '91*, Amsterdam, Netherlands, pp. 235–48.

Landauer, T. K. (1995). *The Trouble with Computers: Usefulness, Usability and Productivity*. Cambridge, MA: MIT Press.

Lave, J. (1988). *Cognition in Practice*. Cambridge University Press.

Lévi-Strauss, C. (1962). *The Savage Mind*. London: Weidenfield and Nicolson.

Lind, M. (1988). 'System Concepts and the Design of Man–Machine Interfaces for Supervisory Control', in *Tasks, Errors and Mental Models*, Goodstein, L. P., Andersen, H. B. and Olsen, S. E. (eds.), pp. 269–77. London: Taylor and Francis.

Lodge, D. (1990). *After Bakhtin*. London: Routledge.

Loucopoulos, P. and Karakostas, V. (1995). *System Requirements Engineering*. Maidenhead: McGraw-Hill.

Luff, P. (1992). *Requirements for a System to Support Medical Consultations*. Working Paper, Rank Xerox Cambridge EuroPARC.

(1994). *The AA: Preliminary Notes on the Activities, Communication and Organisation of the Work of the Operations Centre and Mobile Workers*. WIT Report, University of Surrey.

(1997). 'Computers and Interaction: The Social Organisation of Human–Computer Interaction in the Workplace'. Ph.D. dissertation University of Surrey.

Luff, P. and Heath, C. C. (1993). 'System Use and Social Organisation: Observations on Human Computer Interaction in an Architectural Practice', in *Technology in Working Order*, Button, G. (ed.), pp. 184–210. London: Routledge.

(1998). 'Mobility in Collaboration', in *Proceedings of CSCW '98*, Seattle, WA.

Luff, P., Knoblauch, H. and Heath, C. C. (1996). 'Innovation or Integration: The Development of Interactive Broadcast Services', in *Proceedings of Mobile Communications Summit*, Granada, Spain, pp. 471–7.

Macaulay, L. (1994). 'Co-operative Requirements Capture: Control Room 2000', in *Requirements Engineering: Social and Technical Issues*, Jirotka, M. and Goguen, J. (eds.), pp. 67–86. London: Academic Press.

Mackay, W. (1990). 'Patterns of sharing Customizable Software', in *Proceedings of CSCW 90*, Los Angeles, CA, pp. 209–22.

Mackenzie, D. (1996). *Knowing Machines: Essays on Technical Change*. Cambridge, MA: MIT Press.

Mackenzie, D. and Wajcman, J. (1985). (eds.) *The Social Shaping of Technology: a Reader*. Milton Keynes: Open University Press.

Mantei, M., Baecker, R., Sellen, A., Buxton, W., Milligan, T. and Wellman, B. (1991). 'Experiences in the Use of a Media Space', in *Proceedings of CHI '91*, New Orleans, LA, pp. 203–8.

McCarthy, J. C., Miles, V. C. and Monk, A. F. (1991). 'An Experimental Study of Common Ground in Text-Based Communication', in *Proceedings of CHI'91*, New Orleans, LA, pp. 209–15.

McDermid, J. A. (1994). 'Requirements Analysis: Orthodoxy, Fundamentalism and Heresy', in *Requirements Engineering: Social and Technical Issues*, Jirotka, M. and Goguen, J. (eds.), pp. 17–40. London: Academic Press.

McLeod, R. W. and Sherwood-Jones, B. M. (1992). 'Simulation to Predict Operator Workload in a Command System', in *A Guide To Task Analysis*, Kirwan, B. and Ainsworth, L. K. (eds.), pp. 301–10. London: Taylor and Francis.

Mead, G. H. (1934). *Mind, Self and Society*. University of Chicago Press.

Miles, R. E. and Snow, C. C. (1986). 'Organisations: New Concepts for New Forms', *California Management Review*. **34**: (Summer), 53–72.

Rogers, Y. (1992). 'Ghosts in The Network: Distributed Troubleshooting in a Shared Working Environment', in *Proceedings of CSCW '92*, Toronto, Canada. pp. 346–55.

Roth, J. A. (1963). *Timetables: Structuring and the Passage of Time in Hospital Treatment and other Careers*. Indianopolis: Bobbs Merrill.

Sacks, H. (1964 (1992)). Lecture 4, Spring 1964, in *Lectures on Conversation: Volume I*, Schegloff, E. A. (ed.), pp. 26–31. Oxford: Blackwell.

(1972 (1992)). Lecture 3, Spring 1972, in *Lectures on Conversation: Volume II*, Schegloff, E. A. (ed.), pp. 542–553. Oxford: Blackwell.

(1992). *Lectures on Conversation: Volumes I and II*. Oxford: Blackwell.

Sacks, H., Schegloff, E. A. and Jefferson, G. (1974). 'A Simplest Systematics for the Organisation of Turn-Taking for Conversation', *Language*. 50: (4), 696–735.

Salomon, G. (1993). (eds.) *Distributed Cognitions: Psychological and Educational Considerations*. Cambridge University Press.

Schegloff, E. A. (1984). 'On Some Gestures' Relation to Talk', in *Structures Of Social Action: Studies In Conversation Analysis*, Atkinson, J. M. and Heritage, J. C. (eds.), pp. 266–96. Cambridge University Press.

Schegloff, E. A. and Sacks, H. (1973). 'Opening up Closings', *Semiotica*. 7: 289–327.

Schenkein, J. N. (1978). (ed.) *Studies in the Organisation of Conversational Interaction*. London and New York: Academic Press.

Schmidt, K. (forthcoming). 'The Critical Role of Workplace Studies in CSCW', in *Workplace Studies: Recovering Work Practice and Informing System Design*, Luff, P., Hindmarsh, J. and Heath, C. (eds.), Cambridge University Press.

Schmidt, K. and Bannon, L. (1991). 'Taking CSCW Seriously Supporting Articulation Work', *Computer Supported Cooperative Work*. 1: (1–2), 7–40.

Schneiderman, B. (1992). *Designing the User Interface: Effective Strategies for Effective Human–Computer Interaction (2nd Edition)*. Reading, MA: Addison-Wesley.

Schutz, A. (1962). *Collected Papers I: The Problem of Social Reality*. The Hague: Martinus Nijhoff.

(1970). *On Phenomenology and Social Relations: Selected Writings*. Chicago University Press.

Schwab, R. G., Hart-Landsberg, S., Reder, S. and Abel, M. (1992). 'Collaboration and Constraint: Middle School Teaching Teams', in *Proceedings of CSCW '92*, Toronto, Canada, pp. 241–56.

Scientific American (1880). 'The Future of the Telephone'. *Scientific American*.

Scrivener, S. A. R., Clark, S., Smyth, M., Harris, D. and Rockoff, T. (1992). 'Designing at a Distance: Experiments in Remote-Synchronous Design', in *Proceedings of OZCHI '92*, pp. 44–53.

Searle, J. R. (1980). Minds, Brains and Programs, *The Behavioural and Brain Sciences*. 3: (3).

Sellen, A. (1992). 'Speech Patterns in Video-Mediated Conversations', in *Proceedings of CHI '92*, Monterey, CA, pp. 49–59.

(1995). 'Remote Conversations: The Effects of Mediating Talk with Technology', *Human–Computer Interaction*. 10: (4), 404–44.

Sellen, A. and Harper, R. (1997). 'Paper as an Analytic Resource for the Design of

New Technologies'. *Proceedings of CHI'97*, Atlanta, GA, 22–27 March, pp. 319–26.

Sharples, M. (1993). (ed.) *Computer Supported Collaborative Writing*. London and Berlin: Springer Verlag.

Shortliffe, E. H. (1976). *Computer-Based Medical Consultations: MYCIN*. New York: American Elsevier.

Silverman, D. (1997). 'Studying Organizational Interaction: Ethnomethodology's Contribution to the "New Institutionalism"', *Administrative Theory and Praxis*. **19**: (2), 178–95.

Smith, R. B., O'Shea, T., O' Malley, C. and Taylor, J. S. (1989). 'Preliminary Experiments with a Distributed, Multi-media Problem Solving Environment', in *Proceedings of First European Conference on Computer Supported Cooperative Work*, London, pp. 19–35.

Smyth, M., Luff, P., Anderson, B. (1995). *Final Report on the Pilots*. Deliverable D9, MITS Project (R2094) Report.

Sommerville, I., Rodden, T., Sawyer, P., Bentley, R. and Twidale, M. (1993). 'Integrating Ethnography into Requirements Engineering', in *Proceedings of RE '93*, San Diego, CA.

Sproull, L. and Kiesler, S. (1991). *Connections: New Ways of Working in the Networked Organization*. Cambridge, MA: MIT Press.

Starkey, K. and Barnatt, C. (1997). 'Flexible Specialisation in the Reorganisation of Television Production in the UK'. *Technology Analysis and Strategic Management*. **9**: 271–286.

Still, A. and Costall, A. (1991). (eds.) *Against Cognivitism: Alternative Foundations for Cognitive Psychology*. London: Harvester Wheatsheaf.

Strauss, A., Schatzman, L., Bucher, R., Ehrlich, D. and Sabshin, M. (1964). *Psychiatric Ideologies and Institutions*. London: Free Press.

Strauss, A. L. (1987). *Qualitative Analysis for Social Scientists*. Cambridge University Press.

Strauss, A. L., Fayerhaugh, S., Suczek, B. and Weiner, C. (1985). *The Social Organisation of Medical Work*. London: University of Chicago Press.

Suchman, L. (1987). *Plans and Situated Actions*. Cambridge University Press.

(1993). 'Technologies of Accountability: On Lizards and Aeroplanes', in *Technology in Working Order*, Button, G. (ed.), pp. 113–26. London: Routledge.

Suchman, L. A. and Wynn, E. (1984). 'Procedures and Problems in the Office', *Office: Technology and People*. **2**: 133–54.

Sundström, G. (1991). 'Process Tracing and Decision Making: An Approach for Analysis of Human–Machine Interactions in Dynamic Environments', *International Journal of Man–Machine Studies*. **35**: 842–58.

Tang, J. C. (1990). *Findings from Observational Studies of Collaborative Work*. SSL Report, Xerox Palo Alto Research Center.

Tang, J. C. and Leifer, L. J. (1988). 'A Framework for Understanding the Workspace Activity of Design Teams', in *Proceedings of CSCW '88*, Portland, OR, pp. 244–9.

Tang, J. C. and Minneman, S. L. (1991a). 'VideoDraw: A Video Interface for Collaborative Drawing', *ACM Transactions on Information Systems*. **9**: (2), 170–84.

(1991b). 'VideoWhiteboard: Video Shadows to Support Remote Collaboration', in *Proceedings of CHI '91*, New Orleans, LA, pp. 315–22.

Tani, M., Yamaashi, K., Tanikoshi, K., Futakowa, M. and Tanifuji, S. (1992). 'Object-Oriented Video: Interaction with Real-World Objects Through Live Video', in *Proceedings of CHI 92*, Monterey, CA, pp. 593–8.

Taylor, S. (1954). *Good General Practice*. Oxford University Press.

Thereau, J. (1992). *Le Cours D'Action: analyses sémio-logique*. Berne: Peter Lang.

Todorov, T. (1990). *Genres in Discourse*. Cambridge University Press.

VAMP (1993). *VAMP Medical Manual*. London:VAMP Health.

Varela, F. J., Thompso, E. and Rosch, E. (1993). *The Embodied Mind: Cognitive Science and Human Experience*. Cambridge MA: MIT Press.

Vera, A. H. and Simon, H. A. (1993). 'Situated Action: A Symbolic Interpretation', *Cognitive Science*. **17**: (1), 7–48.

Vitruvius (1960). *The Ten Books of Architecture*. New York: Dover.

Vogel, D. R. and Nunamaker, J. F. (1990). 'Design and Assessment of a Group Decision Support System', in *Intellectual Teamwork: The Social and Technological Foundations of Cooperative Work*, Kraut, R. E., Galegher, J. and Egido, C. (eds.), pp. 511–28. Hillsdale, NJ: Lawrence Erlbaum Associates.

Volosinov, V. N. (1973). *Marxism and the Philosophy of Language*. Translated by Matejka, L. and I. R. Titunik. London: Seminar Press.

Vortac, O. U., Edwards, M. B. and Manning, C. A. (1994). 'Sequences of Actions for Individual and Teams of Air Traffic Controllers', *Human–Computer Interaction*. **9**: (3 & 4), 319–44.

Watts, J. C., Woods, D. D., Corban, J. M., Patterson, E. S., Kerr, R. L. and Hicks, L. C. (1996). 'Voice Loops as Cooperative Aids in Space Shuttle Mission Control', in *Proceedings of CSCW '96*, Cambridge, MA, pp. 48–56.

Webster, F. (1995). *Theories of the Information Society*. London: Routledge and Kegan Paul.

Weiser, M. (1991). 'The Computer for the 21st Century', *Scientific American*. September.

Wellner, P. (1992). *Interacting With Paper on the DigitalDesk*. Rank Xerox EuroPARC and University of Cambridge Computer Laboratory.

Wertsch, J. V. (1986). *Voices of the Mind: A Sociocultural Approach to Mediated Action*. London: Harvester Wheatsheaf.

(1991). *Voices of the Mind: A Sociocultural Approach to Mediated Action*. London: Harvester Wheatsheaf.

West, C. (1985). *Routine Complications: Tasks and Troubles in Medical Encounters*. Indiana University Press.

Whalen, J. (1994). *Making Standardization Visible*. Department of Sociology, University of Oregon.

(1995). 'A Technology of Order Production: Computer-Aided Dispatch in Public Safety Communications', in *Situated Order: Studies in the Social Organisation of Talk and Embodied Activities*, ten Have, P. and Psathas, G. (eds.), pp. 187–230. Washington: University Press of America.

Wieder, D. L. (1972). 'On Meaning by Rule', in *Understanding Everyday Life*, Douglas, J. D. (ed.), London: Routledge Kegan Paul.

(1974). 'Telling the Code', in *Ethnomethodology*, Turner, R. (ed.), pp. 144–71. London: Penguin.

Wiener, L. R. (1993). *Digital Woes: Why We Should Not Depend on Software.* Reading: MA: Addison Wesley.

Winograd, T. and Flores, F. (1986). *Understanding Computers and Cognition: A New Foundation For Design.* Norwood, NJ: Addison-Wesley.

Young, R., Howes, A. and Whittington, J. (1990). 'A Knowledge Analysis of Interactivity', in *Proceedings of Interact '90 – Third IFIP Conference on Human–Computer Interaction,* Cambridge, pp. 115–20.

Zimmerman, D. H. (1970). 'The Practicalities of Rule Use', in *Understanding Everyday Life,* Douglas, J. (ed.), Chicago: Aldine.

Index